Probation anc

Probation and Parole Departments must provide for the protection of society as well as the rehabilitation of the offending individual. *Probation and Parole: Current Issues* presents leading authorities offering various broad and specific aspects of the controversial topic along with the latest research. This handy source provides illustrative examples of current hot button issues and can be used as an excellent core or complement textbook for a probation and parole class. Issues discussed range broadly from mental health considerations to rehabilitation options.

The book provides wide multi-national perspectives of the issues, including research and comparisons on juvenile recidivism between the United States and Australia. This crucial work provides a detailed look at the research on individuals in the system, the programs for those citizens that are successful, and those methods that may be ineffective. A study is also presented with data on the positive impact of Assertive Community Treatment workers who provide mental health treatment in the community. The book is extensively referenced and includes several figures and tables to clearly present data.

This book is a useful resource for educators, students, and anyone in the probation and parole field. It was published as a special issue of the *Journal of Offender Rehabilitation.*

Dan Phillips is Associate Professor of Sociology and Criminal Justice at Lindsey Wilson College.

Probation and Parole

Current Issues

Edited by Dan Phillips

Routledge
Taylor & Francis Group
LONDON AND NEW YORK

First published 2009 by Routledge
2 Park Square, Milton Park, Abingdon, Oxon, OX14 4RN

Simultaneously published in the USA and Canada
by Routledge
270 Madison Avenue, New York, NY 10016

Routledge is an imprint of the Taylor & Francis Group, an informa business

Typeset in Times by Value Chain, India
Printed and bound in the United States of America on acid-free paper by IBT Global

British Library Cataloguing in Publication Data
A catalogue record for this book is available from the British Library

ISBN10: 0-7890-3784-X (hbk)
ISBN10: 0-7890-3785-8 (pbk)
ISBN13: 978-0-7890-3784-8 (hbk)
ISBN13: 978-0-7890-3785-5 (pbk)

CONTENTS

NOTES ON CONTRIBUTORS

Earl Angel is a Research Associate in the Center for Criminal Justice Education and Research in the Department of Correctional and Juvenile Justice Studies at Eastern Kentucky University, Richmond, Kentucky.

Brad Astbury is Research Fellow, Centre for Program Evaluation. Alice Hoy Building, The University of Melbourne, Victoria 3010 Australia.

Steven Banks is Research Associate Professor of Psychiatry at the University of Massachusetts Medical School, Worcester, Massachusetts.

William D. Burrell is Director of the Executive Master of Arts program at the Department of Criminal Justice, Temple University, Philadelphia, Pennsylvania.

Deeanna M. Button, is a graduate student at the University of Delaware, Newark, Delaware.

Kristin Davis is Assistant Research Director of Thresholds Psychosocial Rehabilitation Centers, Chicago, Illinois.

Cherie Dawson-Edwards is Assistant Professor of Correctional and Juvenile Justice at Kentucky State University, Richmond, Kentucky.

Matthew DeMichele is a Senior Research Associate at the American Probation and Parole Association, Council of State Governments. He is also a doctoral candidate in Sociology, University of Kentucky, Lexington, Kentucky.

Rebecca Denning is Manager, Criminal Justice Research, Department of Premier and Cabinet, Brisbane, Australia.

John Fallon is Program Manager of Reentry, "Returning Home Initiative," Corporation for Supportive Housing, Chicago, Illinois.

Robert S. Gable is Professor of Psychology Emeritus at Claremont Graduate University, Claremont, California.

Zachary Hamilton is Data Analyst at the Center for the Integration of Research & Practice (CIRP), National Development & Research Institutes, Inc. (NDRI), New York, New York.

Ross Homel is Director, Centre of Ethics, Law, Justice and Governance, Mt. Gravatt Campus, Griffith University, Nathan, Australia.

Dr. Kimora is Adjunct Assistant Professor at the John Jay College of Criminal Justice, New York, New York.

Diane Kincaid is Information Specialist/Public Relations Coordinator at the American Probation and Parole Association, Lexington, Kentucky.

Nathan C. Lowe is a part-time faculty member in the Department of Correctional and Juvenile Justice Studies at Eastern Kentucky University, Richmond, Kentucky. He also works for the Department of Juvenile Justice.

Karen McKendrick, is Project Director at the Center for the Integration of Research & Practice (CIRP), National Development & Research Institutes, Inc. (NDRI), New York, New York.

David C. May is Professor and Kentucky Center for School Safety Research Fellow, Eastern Kentucky University, Department of Safety, Security and Emergency Management.

Kevin I. Minor is Professor and Chair of the Department of Correctional and Juvenile Justice Studies at Eastern Kentucky University, Richmond, Kentucky.

Nathan T. Moore is a trooper with the Kentucky State Police.

Brian K. Payne is Professor of Criminal Justice and Chair, Department of Criminal Justice, Georgia State University, Atlanta, Georgia.

JoAnn Y. Sacks is Deputy Director of the Center for the Integration of Research & Practice (CIRP), National Development & Research Institutes, Inc. (NDRI), New York, New York.

Stanley Sacks is Director of the Center for the Integration of Research & Practice (CIRP), National Development & Research Institutes, Inc. (NDRI), New York, New York.

Marlies Schoeneberger is Project Director at the Center for the Integration of Research & Practice (CIRP), National Development & Research Institutes, Inc. (NDRI), Denver, Colorado.

Joanie Shoemaker is Assistant Director of Prisons at the Colorado Department of Corrections, Colorado Springs, Colorado.

Joseph Stommel is Chief of Rehabilitation Programs at the Colorado Department of Corrections, Colorado Springs, Colorado.

Alexandra Teachout is a Research Associate at the Thresholds Psychosocial Rehabilitation Centers, Chicago, Illinois.

Sue Vogel is a Consultant, based in Chicago, Illinois.

James B. Wells is Professor and Director of the Center for Criminal Justice Education and Research in the Department of Correctional and Juvenile Justice Studies at Eastern Kentucky University, Richmond, Kentucky.

Alisha Williams is a senior and McNair scholar at Eastern Kentucky University, Richmond, Kentucky. She is also a past recipient of the American Society of Criminology Minority Scholar Award.

Peter B. Wood is Professor and Department Head in the Department of Sociology, Anthropology, and Criminology at Eastern Michigan University.

PREFACE

At the end of 2005, there were 4.9 million people on probation or parole while there were 2.2 million people in jail or prison (BJS 2006a, BJS 2006b). This means that for every five people incarcerated on any given day, there were approximately 11 people under probation and parole. Probation and Parole Departments have as their task the protection of society and the rehabilitation of the individual. Community offender rehabilitation can take on several faces: mental health treatment; substance abuse treatment; self-help groups such as Alcoholics' Anonymous, Narcotics' Anonymous, anger management, and sex offender treatment; formal educational attainment; and various work skills training programs. Protecting the public can also come in various forms, most of them focused on surveillance of the individual: drug tests, electronic monitoring, home visits, work visits, and community registration for those who are sex offenders.

The authors of this special edition examine many aspects of probation and parole, general and specific. Dr. Kimora leads off the special edition by teasing out the "emerging paradigm in probation and parole." Kimora discusses treatment and surveillance, the need for research, and how best to use revocation. Dawson-Edwards reports on "enfranchising convicted felons." Some states make it easy for an ex-convict to restore their voting privileges while other states revoke them forever. Restoring voting rights is a form of rehabilitation in that it allows the ex-convict to see him/her self as a "regular" or "restored" person.

Astbury provides data from Australia concerning the "problems of implementing offender programs in the community." Astbury examines the many dimensions to program implementation. While selection of the proper program is necessary it is not sufficient; programs must be implemented in the correct way including allowing for flexibility. Well designed, rigid program will most likely fail as there are implemented at the local level. The piece authored by Moore, May, and Wood along with the piece authored by Williams and May explore attitudes toward alternative sanctions and prison. Moore, May, and Wood focus on the attitudes of offenders, judges, and officers while Williams and May examine offenders' attitudes. Each set of authors successfully reveals that not everyone views prison and alternatives the same way and that some offenders see prison as a more desirable placement than alternative sanctions.

Kincaid reveals an increasingly difficult issue in probation and parole: dealing with those who are undocumented. With all of the rhetoric about what to do with undocumented residents in the U.S., probation and parole offices nationwide are being expected to monitor people who have no legal right to reside in the United States. Burrell and Gable, and DeMichele, Payne, and Button examine the use of electronic monitoring in probation and parole. While the former article takes an historical approach to electronic monitoring the latter reveals "unanticipated consequence" of the practice with regard to sex offenders.

Lowe et al. provide readers with an understanding of the "decision to pursue revocation of intensive supervision." Some probation and parole offices may allow offenders more leeway before he/she is revoked while others may keep the offender on a short leash. Minor, Wells, and Angel look at gender differences in juvenile recidivism from residential placements. Similarly, Denning and Homel examine juvenile recidivism but use Australian data. The last two articles focus on mental health treatment among women, a fast-growing group among those under court supervision. Davis et al. focus on jail aftercare while Sacks et al. examine "prison therapeutic treatment" In the Davis et al. study, Assertive Community Treatment (ACT) workers provided mental health treatment in the community and were able to have some positive effects such as cutting down on the number of days spent in jail per year. Sacks et al. report on different mental health treatment models for women as those women move from the prison and live in the community for six months.

It was a pleasure to edit this edition as all authors involved were passionate about their work, provided manuscripts in a short period of time, and in a way that revealed their research skill and writing quality. The topics involved are of great import: the emerging probation and parole paradigm, ex-convict enfranchisement, program implementation specifics, attitudes toward prison versus alternative sanctions, supervision of undocumented immigrants, electronic supervision, revocation, juvenile recidivism, mental health care, and gender. With nearly 5 million

U.S. citizens on probation and parole, operating these programs in the best, most informed manner will pay dividends. Without the research contained in this volume and others like it, practitioners are more likely to use the methods from the past, whether or not they work.

Daniel W. Phillips III

REFERENCES

Bureau of Justice Statistics. (2006a). *Probation and Parole Statistics*. Washington, D.C. Bureau of Justice Statistics. Retrieved on April 28, 2007 from http://www.ojp.usdoj.gov/bjs/pandp.htm.

Bureau of Justice Statistics (2006b). *Prison Statistics*. Washington, D.C. Bureau of Justice Statistics. Retrieved on April 28, 2007 from http://www.ojp.usdoj.gov/bjs/prisons.htm.

FOREWORD

As a practitioner of Probation and Parole, I experience first hand, many of the issues plaguing the field of correctional probation supervision. There is an ongoing attempt by many states to correct, or manipulate, probation policies and supervision tactics to curb the high recidivism rates associated with community corrections in the United States. Many of these changes, including zero tolerance towards violations of conditions, evidence based practices, and criminal sentencing commissions to promote fairness in state sentencing are in effect throughout the United States. However, there are many more issues facing community corrections that are being addressed less and may be directly related to the overall high recidivism rates associated with probation and parole services. Among these issues are training practices employed by community corrections departments: "social work vs. law enforcement," offender and officer perceptions of intermediate sanctions, and the stigmatization of felony offenders. All of these issues are important and could lend some insight into the world of probation and parole.

A current trend that has been employed in the State of Florida in recent years is a "zero tolerance" towards probation violations by offenders. This tactic was adopted after a violent felony offender murdered several members of a local family and it was found that he was not in compliance with some of the conditions of his probation supervision. Following this incident there was large portion of the public that demanded answers concerning why this violent offender had been allowed to remain on the streets when he could have been incarcerated on probation violations. In addition to this, there was a lawsuit filed against the Florida Department of Corrections by surviving family members and shortly after the department adopted a "zero tolerance" policy regarding probation violations. In short, this means that any condition not complied with by the offender results in a warrant sent to the Court asking for the offender to be arrested and a violation hearing scheduled. As a result of this policy Probation Officers spend a large part of there day preparing violation reports and attending court hearings. As one would infer, this practice drastically reduces the amount of time an individual officer spends supervising offenders in the field. It also causes many problems for the offenders including monetary loss of wages, loss of employment due to incarceration, and an ever declining opinion of their supervision officer.

Training of probation officers differs in as many ways as there are states in the union. Each state has instituted it own training program based on the needs of the department and in compliance with the laws of that particular state. How an individual department trains it personnel reflect directly on the attitudes of the trainees. For example, if a department commits its new employees to a training regiment that is paramilitary, like a police academy, then the trainees may adopt a more law enforcement approach to their supervision duties. On the other hand, if training programs are regimented by the individual department the trainees may be molded according to the individual opinions and needs of that community or region. This may encompass a social work approach, law enforcement approach, or combination of both. Regardless of the individual outcome there is a gap that offenders must breach when it comes to interacting with different officers with different ideologies on how probation supervision should be administered. This could lead to confrontations between offenders and officers regarding the handling of the case.

There has been much talk about the stigmatization, or disenfranchisement, of felony offenders in corrections. The one issue that seems to surface in probation and parole more than any other are the difficulties felony offenders face in the employment arena. In some states it is required that the offender notify his employer of his felony conviction, which in my experience, adds to the challenge of the offender obtaining gainful employment and intensifies an already immense stress load. This stress can transfer to the supervising officer, as in many cases it is a condition of probation and parole, that the offender be gainfully employed and could cause a rift between the offender and the officer on how the case is being managed. Evidence based practices tries to address this issue on several levels.

Evidence based practices is being employed by several states, including the Virginia Department of Corrections. It includes the use of graduated sanctions, and in some cases, attempts to remove the stigma of "felony offender" by offering alternative names such as "client" or "subject." This attempt to remove the felony stigma and reinsert offenders back into the communities that they have victimized has long been a practice of community corrections in the United States and is a core mission of probation and parole authorities. For instance, if an offender is out of compliance with one or more of the conditions of his/her probation supervision, the supervising officer may instruct the individual to perform 100 hours of community service in the area where the crime was committed. This allows the offender to retain his freedom and return something back to the victimized community, and at the same time, it is a specific deterrent to try and bring the individual offender back into compliance. There is a direct effect on recidivism rates when evidence based practices are used, if the offender is not returned to court for a violation hearing his/her supervision will not be terminated and there is no increase in recidivism rates at that time.

The formation of Criminal Sentencing Commissions to promote fair and equitable sentencing dispositions across a state is a fairly new trend in the criminal justice arena. Criminal Sentencing Commissions attempt to balance the severity of sentences throughout a state so that Possession of a Controlled Drug is no more harshly punished in a metro area than in a rural area, for example. In Virginia, many factors are taken into consideration in forming an appropriate sentence for probation violators and those offered probation as an alternative sanction. These factors include prior record (juvenile and adult), number of prior probation violations, type of crime (person, property, drug), and if the person was under any form of supervision at the time of the offense (for new sentencing events). Although Judges may deviate from the sentencing guidelines, a judicial reason must be provided and the Sentencing Commission reviews all of these decisions. One of the side effects of Sentencing Commissions and Guidelines is that is removes Judicial discretion and does not allow for sentencing based on the needs of an individual community. For example, robbery may be a crime that plagues a metro area, whereas Prescription Drug Fraud may cause more problems in a rural area. The sentences for the crimes, according to Sentencing Guidelines, should have similar sanctions, but Judges and the public at large, may demand stiffer penalties for crimes that plague their individual communities and not care about crimes that do not affect them directly.

There are a plethora of issues and new trends to cope with them in Probation and Parole in the United States. Many of these are being implemented by Community Corrections Departments across the United

States to help curb the high recidivism rates associated with Community Supervision. However, much more research is needed to evaluate the effectiveness of these programs on both offenders and supervision officers.

Christopher Flory

The Emerging Paradigm in Probation and Parole in the United States

KIMORA

INTRODUCTION

There is an emerging paradigm in probation and parole in the United States. That new outlook encompasses a realization that these two forms of supervision of offenders must meet the challenges of an increasing number of parolees and probationers. There are now 7 million Americans incarcerated or on probation or parole, an increase of more than 280 percent since 1980 (The Sentencing Project, 2007). The number of people on parole and probation is astounding: 1,344,883 offenders are on probation in this country and 477,704 are on parole (Manza, 2004). Policy changes advocated by several leaders in the areas of probation and parole are examined.

THE EMERGING PARADIGM IN PROBATION

Recidivism continues to be the primary outcome measure for probation, as it is for all corrections programs. The American Probation and Parole Association (APPA), representing U.S. probation officers nationwide, argues that recidivism rates measure just one probation task while ignoring others. The APPA has urged its member agencies to collect data on other outcomes, such as the following: amount of restitution collected, number of offenders employed, amounts of fines and fees collected, hours of community service performed, number of treatment sessions attended, percentage of financial obligations collected, rate of enrollment in school, number of days of employment, educational attainment, and number of days drug free (Schmalleger & Smykla, p. 133, 2007).

Advocates of measures other than recidivism tell us that probation should be measured by what offenders do while they are in probation programs, not by what they do after they leave (Schmalleger & Smykla, p. 133, 2007).

To implement credible and effective probation programs, several steps appear necessary. Joan Petersilia, director of the UCI Center for Evidence-Based Corrections, a research and policy center funded by the California Department of Corrections and Rehabilitation, offers us five suggestions:

1. **Implement High-Quality Programs and Enforce Them.** Experienced probation officers tell us that besides using the techniques and strategies of coercion and threats of incarceration to induce offenders to comply with the conditions of probation supervision, we should not neglect to reward cooperative behavior and compliance. That is the practice in drug courts nationwide, for example. Reclassifying offenders, reducing their level of supervision (e.g., face-to-face contacts and drug testing), and advocating early termination are used to encourage offenders to comply and cooperate (Tonry, p. 149-200, 1997).

2. **Invest in Adequate Resources in Treatment *and* Surveillance.** When probationers receive *both* surveillance (e.g., unannounced contact and random drug tests) and treatment, recidivism can decline by one-third. (Institute for Court Management, 2001). Probation can become more effective by giving some offenders more intensive supervision and treatment and others less and by targeting the effort to offer precise services and meet objectives by using a standardized assessment of probationer risks and needs. This approach can help probation staffs determine more reliably which clients need intensive supervision, special services, or routine probation. When appropriate interventions (e.g., residential drug treatment, outpatient treatment, urine monitoring) are used with drug-involved clients, scarce treatment resources are utilized more effectively to reduce recidivism and relapse. However, treatment, surveillance, and classifying probationers to appropriate levels of supervision cost money. Adequate funding will be available only if the public believes that new supervision conditions are punitive as well as effective in reducing crime (Schmalleger & Smykla, 2007).
3. **Demonstrate That Probation Is Tough on Crime.** Policymakers say they send large numbers of persons to prison because the public wants to be tough on crime. But there is a groundswell of evidence that tough punishment may no longer equate with prison (Petersilia and Turner, 1993). Some offenders see probation as more punitive and restrictive than prison. For example, researchers in Texas and Oregon gave offenders the choice of serving a prison term or serving probation with mandatory drug testing, community service, employment, counseling and frequent visits with a probation officer. In Oregon, 25 percent of those eligible for probation chose prison. In Texas, many offenders described common prison terms as less punitive than even only three to five years on probation. Prison was more attractive than the pressures of close supervision. The public must be convinced that probation sanctions can be just as punitive as prison. Of course, the choice of probation or prison should be for the judge to make, not the offender (Schmalleger & Smykla, 2007).

4. **Target Drug Offenders.** Drug offenders are prime candidates for tough probation programs. Research has revealed that different risks and needs of traffickers, addicts, and low-level users (Fields, 1999). Even if drug offenders are coerced into treatment by the court, there is evidence that treatment can reduce both later drug use and later crimes. The largest study of drug treatment outcomes found that criminal justice clients stayed in treatment longer than clients without involvement in the justice system and had higher than average success rates (Gerstein & Harwood, 1990). Indeed, offenders in outpatient drug treatment programs have significantly lower rates of arrest and relapse if they stay in treatment for more than three months than if they drop out earlier (Tims & Ludford, 1984).

The new knowledge is resulting in different laws and punishment strategies for different kinds of drug offenders. Many Americans prefer prison sentences for drug traffickers but are willing to accept something other than prison for other drug offenders. Nationally, seventeen states have either reformed their drug laws or are considering it. In 1996, the people of Arizona led the way in drug reform by passing the Drug Medicalization, Prevention and Control Act. The centerpiece of the act is the diversion of persons convicted of possession or use of a controlled substance. The act requires drug offenders to be placed on probation and participate in appropriate drug treatment. In the second year of operation, 62 percent of probationers complied with treatment. Probation supervision and community treatment cost approximately $1.1 million. Based on prison costs of almost $53 per day, Arizona saved an estimated $6.7 million in incarceration. Four years later, 61 percent of California voters passed Proposition 36–the Substance Abuse and Crime Prevention Act. This act allows first- and second-time nonviolent drug offenders convicted of possession, use, or transportation of drugs substance abuse treatment instead of incarceration. As of February 2002, of the 4,329 defendants sentenced to drug treatment in Los Angeles County from July 1, 2001, to December 31, 2001, 69 percent were still receiving treatment. Judges and county officials say they are pleased with the program, and preliminary reports are that the program is working. Similar ballot initiatives are being considered across the country (Schmalleger & Smykla, 2007).

5. **Make Probation Research a Priority.** With so many people under probation supervision today, probation research should be a priority. The suggestion is to incorporate research on causes and effective interventions into local probation programs. Furthermore, local probation departments need to conduct research into their programs to see what works best in reducing recidivism (Schmalleger & Smykla, 2007). It would also be useful for probation research to asses the value of revoking probation for persons who commit technical violations (which are failures to fulfill the conditions of probation-attending counseling, paying restitution, contacting the probation officer) instead of committing new offenses. Judges need assurance that probationers will be held accountable for their behavior, and the public schools need assurance that probation sanctions are punitive. More research is needed on the relationship of technical violations to criminal behavior. For example, what types of conditions are imposed? How do those conditions manage offenders, encourage rehabilitation, and protect the community? What are the trends in the number of technical violators and the effect on jails and prisons? What innovative programs, policies, and statutes have emerged in other jurisdictions to deal with technical violators? (Schmalleger & Smykla, 2007).

THE EMERGING PARADIGM IN PAROLE AND PROBATION

The last three years have witnessed a number of state legislative developments focused on sentencing reform. The growth of reentry programs across the country has accelerated over recent years. This momentum indicates both an acknowledgment of the value of pre-release transitional planning, as well as the role that its absence in recent decades has played in contributing to high recidivism rates (King, 2007).

The following are policy changes that state lawmakers can enact to institute sound, evidence-based criminal justice policies that can better meet the goals of sentencing while also controlling unnecessary and expensive growth in the use of incarceration (King, 2007).

1. **Expand the Use of Drug Treatment as a Sentencing Option.** While there has been a virtual explosion in the use of drug courts since the early 1990s, in far too many jurisdictions available treatment resources fall short of the need among the defendant population. Drug courts and other diversion options have shown success in reducing drug use and drug-related crime, and can therefore produce long-term cost savings while reducing inappropriate incarceration.
2. **Expand Options to Reduce Probation and Parole Revocations.** Many jurisdictions across the country have adopted programs and policies to reduce the number of violators sent back to prison, while addressing public safety concerns. Beginning in the late 1980s, the Missouri Board of Probation and Parole established a range of supervision strategies for violators–including electronic monitoring, residential centers, and intensive supervision–that led to fewer returns to prison while also reducing the rearrest rate among people under supervision (Burke, 1997). Similarly, the probation department in Macomb County, Michigan implemented a risk assessment system that resulted in greater use of intermediate sanctions for lower risk offenders, resulting in significant reduction of violators returned to prison (Burke, 1997).
3. **Reconsider Policies Regarding Time Served in Prison.** Over the past fifteen years, the amount of time offenders serve in prison has been steadily increasing. This is the case not only for long-term sentences but for shorter prison terms as well. Research has demonstrated that increasing the length of prison terms produces little in the way of increased deterrence of crime or reduced recidivism, yet contributes significantly to higher costs of corrections. Policymakers should examine time served in prison to determine if the goals of sentencing can be achieved through shorter prison terms for selected offenders.
4. **Repeal Mandatory Minimum Sentencing.** A broad range of scholarship has demonstrated that mandatory sentencing produces no impact on crime, but results in unnecessarily lengthy and unjust prison terms in many cases. Judges who wish to incarcerate serious offenders for long prison terms can readily

do so under existing sentencing policy in every state. Mandatory sentencing only results in obligating judges to impose such terms on far less culpable offenders as well. The American Bar Association has recommended repeal of such policies, which would result in more rational sentencing practices.

5. **Reconsider Life and Long Term Sentences.** In states such as Louisiana and Michigan, parole boards have adopted policies of "life means life" for offenders who previously have been eligible for parole. Persons affected by these policies include those convicted of serious violent offenses, but also persons convicted of drug offenses. In all but the most serious cases, parole boards should be free to consider the use of parole for long-term prisoners who no longer present a threat to public safety. Similarly, policies such as "three strikes and you're out" in California have resulted in 8,000 persons serving 25 years to life, nearly half of whom have been convicted of a non-violent property or drug offense as their third strike.
6. **Review State Sentencing and Corrections Policies.** Policymakers are increasingly recognizing that the size and composition of state prison populations are a function of a variety of policy choices regarding sentencing, time served in prison, and parole supervision practices. Stabilization or reduction of prison populations will only be achieved through a comprehensive examination of contributing factors, whether conducted by a state sentencing commission or other body. Efforts to address these issues include a 2005 Connecticut bill that called upon the judiciary and Parole Board "to develop a plan to reduce by at least 20% the number of incarcerations due to technical violations" of probation and parole. Kansas established a bipartisan task force, the Criminal Justice Recodification, Rehabilitation, and Restoration Project, "to address growing problems within the Kansas criminal justice system regarding offenders," and California legislators have recently expressed interest in establishing a sentencing commission to examine the state's criminal code and recommend reforms (King, 2007).

THE EMERGING PARADIGM OF THE ROLE OF THE JUDICIARY IN PROBATION

As far as the court is concerned, probation officers should stress the following in their supervisory responsibilities:

1. The public wants probation to deliver public safety.
2. Probation can raise public safety and help probationers become law-abiding citizens.
3. Probation needs to enforce probation orders and help offenders.
4. The idea "get tough on probationers" doesn't need to lead to more imprisonment; in fact, it could lead to an increase in general deterrence (Champion, 2005).

Recommendations from judges to probation officers include the following admonitions:

1. Public safety comes first.
2. Probation officers should spend more time supervising offenders who pose the greatest risk to public safety.
3. Probation officers should be assigned to supervise specific geographical areas rather than being randomly assigned to offenders.
4. Permissive practices should be abandoned, and in their place a response that is certain and incorporates graduated sanctions to deal with technical violations.
5. Probation should encourage involvement of other agencies, organizations, and interest groups in offender treatment.
6. Program performance should be used as the measure for the allocation of resources (Champion, 2005).

THE REDEFINITION OF THE PURPOSES OF PAROLE REVOCATIONS

President Jeremy Travis, President of John Jay College of Criminal Justice, New York City, is a national leader on reentry. He advocates a redefinition of the purposes of parole revocations.

This review would determine, among other things, whether like cases are treated alike, racial minorities receive disparate treatment, and punishments are proportionate to offenses. Answers to these questions might lead to legislation or sentencing guidelines that would could create sentencing grids for parole violations, much like the grids used for front-end sentencing by judges in many jurisdictions (Travis, 2005).

Travis mentions that the current system of parole has created a "back-end" sentencing in America, a system that sends many parolees back to prison each year. He advocates calling for guidelines for parole revocations.

Before conducting such an analysis, however, state legislatures must address threshold questions of sentencing jurisprudence: What is the purpose of this form of sentencing? Is there a distinction between the purposes of front-end and back-end sentencing? Is there a difference between revoking liberty for committing a new crime and revoking liberty for failing to abide by other conditions of supervision? The answers to these questions can reveal a level of commitment to prisoner reintegration (Travis, 2005).

Some additional guidelines for parole revocation should also be established. Legislation reforming parole revocation policies should ensure that arrests for new crimes committed while under supervision are handled separately, with enhanced penalties. Statutory limits should be placed on the length of the new sentences that can be imposed for "technical" violations. Returning prisoners should be authorized to demonstrate, at regular intervals, that their reentry has been successful and they have avoided a return to crime and, therefore, should be released from supervision entirely. As with the reentry preparation credit proposed earlier, this requirement would create incentives for prosocial behavior and allow supervisory agencies to focus on individuals needing attention. Consistent with the devolution of supervision to the local level, this legislation should require that these sentences be served in local jails, not state prisons (Travis, 2005). Travis also advocates the creation of reentry courts by the states to oversee the reintegration process so that there are incentives for the parolees for prosocial behavior.

CONCLUSIONS

There is an emerging paradigm in probation and parole in the United States. That new realization encompasses a realization that these two forms of supervision of offenders must meet the challenges of an increasing number of parolees and probationers.

Recidivism continues to be the primary outcome measure for probation. The American Probation and Parole Association (APPA) argues that other factors be examined such as: amount of restitution collected, number of offenders employed, amounts of fines and fees collected, hours of community service performed, number of treatment sessions attended, percentages of financial obligations collected, rate of enrollment in school, number of days of employment, educational attainment, and number of days drug free.

It is recommended by this author that we examine Joan Petersilia's suggestions in order to implement credible and effective probation programs: (1) Implement high-quality programs and enforce them; (2) Invest in adequate resources in treatment *and* surveillance; (3) Demonstrate that probation is tough on crime; (4) Target drug offenders; and (5) Make probation research a priority.

The last three years have witnessed a number of state legislative developments focused on sentencing reform. The following are policy changes that state lawmakers can enact to institute sound, evidence-based criminal justice policies that can better meet the goals of sentencing: (1) Expand the use of drug treatment as a sentencing option; (2) Expand options to reduce probation and parole revocations; (3) Reconsider policies regarding time served in prisons; (4) Repeal mandatory minimum sentencing; (5) Reconsider life and long term sentences; and (6) Review state sentencing and corrections policies.

The emerging paradigm of the role of the judiciary in probation is summarized by Dean John Champion, Department of Applied, Behavioral Sciences and Criminal Justice, Texas A & M International University. Increasingly, the judiciary is moving toward greater collaboration with community agencies and organizations to deliver sentences that not only preserve public safety, but also tend to hold offenders accountable to their victims in restorative ways (Champion, 2008).

Finally, Travis calls the current parole system "a patchwork quilt of state-level experiments in sentencing reform." He advocates a redefinition of the purposes of parole revocations so that the criminal justice system can refocus on rehabilitation and the effective reintegration of parolees back into the community.

REFERENCES

Burke, P. B. (1997). *Policy-Driven Responses to Probation and Parole Violations*. National Institute of Justice.

Champion, D. J. (2008). *Probation, Parole, and Community Corrections*. Upper Saddle River, New Jersey: Pearson/Prentice Hall.

———. (2005). *Corrections in the United States: A Contemporary Perspective, 4e*. Upper Saddle River, NJ: Pearson/Prentice Hall.

Fields, C. B. (1999). *Controversial Issues in Corrections*. Boston: Allyn & Bacon.

Gerstein, D. R. & H. J. Harwood (1990). *Treating Drug Problems, vol. 1*. Washington, D. C: National Academy Press.

Institute for Court Management. (2001). *Private Probation in Georgia: A New Direction, Service and Vigilance*. Atlanta: Administrative Office of Courts.

King, R. S. (2007). *Changing Direction? State Sentencing Reforms, 2004-2206*. Washington, D.C: The Sentencing Project.

Manza, J. & Christopher Uggen. (2004). *Locked out: Felon Disenfranchisement and American Democracy*. Washington, D.C: Bureau of Justice Statistics.

Petersilia, J. & Susan Turner. (1993). *Evaluating Intensive Supervision Probation/Parole: Results of a Nationwide Experiment*. Washington, D.C: National Institute of Justice.

Schmalleger, F. & John Ortiz Smykla. (2007). *Corrections in the 21st Century*. Boston: McGraw Hill.

Tims, F. & J. Ludford. (1984). *Drug Abuse Treatment Evaluation: Strategies, Progress and Prospects*. Rockville, MD: National Institute on Drug Abuse.

Tonry, M. (1997). *Crime and Justice: A Review of Research*, vol. 22. Chicago: University of Chicago Press.

Travis, J. (2005). *But They all Come Back: Facing the Challenges of Prisoner Reentry*. Washington, D.C: The Urban Institute Press.

Enfranchising Convicted Felons: Current Research on Opinions Towards Felon Voting Rights

CHERIE DAWSON-EDWARDS

INTRODUCTION

Convicted felons remain the only directly disenfranchised population across the nation upheld by constitutional law (Johnson-Parris, 2003).

The history of the felon's severance from the democratic process dates beyond the conception of American society (Special Project, 1970; Thompson, 2002); however, the modern day interpretation and applicability of felon disenfranchisement laws is rooted in the post-Civil War America when the American electorate drastically changed due to the passage of the Reconstruction Amendments (13th, 14th, and 15th). Over 100 years later, remnants of these antiquated laws still exist. The Supreme Court has upheld states' rights to criminal disenfranchisement (*Richardson v. Ramirez*, 1974) and interpreted its relation to the 14th Amendment's protection from discriminatory intent (*Hunter v. Underwood*, 1985). An estimated four million Americans are currently disenfranchised by the laws of 48 states and the District of Columbia (Coyle, 2003; Manza, Brooks & Uggen, 2004; Uggen & Manza, 2002). This article will present a synopsis of current research on opinions towards felon disenfranchisement and the related topic of punishment preferences while offering suggestions for future research.

In early America, civil death was explicitly outlawed by Article I, Section 10 of the U.S. Constitution, which reads: "no state shall pass any bills of attainder . . ." Felon voting restrictions would seem to violate this prohibited civil death; however, the U.S. Supreme Court has made it clear that the "bills of attainder" clause refers to using disenfranchisement as a punishment (*Green v. Board of Elections*, 1967). In *Green v. Board of Elections* (1967), the bills of attainder clause was used to argue against the disenfranchisement of felons. *Green,* a convicted felon, disputed the New York State Constitution's felon voting prohibition on the grounds that it was a violation of Article I, Section 10 of the U.S. Constitution (Johnson-Parris, 2003). The Court held the clause constitutionally permissible because it provided a "non-penal exercise of power to regulate the franchise" (Johnson-Parris, 2003, p. 116).

The Green court's distinction of felon voting restrictions as "non-penal" complicates legal arguments against the practice. For if collaterally losing a fundamental citizenship right is regulatory and not punitive, it then becomes difficult to argue that public opinion supporting reform should directly impact public policy. An easier argument would be based on modern day cruel and unusual punishment determinations outlined by the U.S. Supreme Court's *Trop v. Dulles* (1958) decision. In *Trop*, the Court held that if a punitive purpose is apparent in the formulation of a law, then it is penal; however, when there is no obvious punitive purpose, the law should be deemed regulatory. As such, regulations are not subject to the same 8th Amendment "evolving standards of decency" scrutiny as punitive laws.

This standard was created by the *Trop* Court to appropriately address whether or not a punishment was in violation of the 8th Amendment. Since *Trop*, the U.S. Supreme Court has relied on "evolving standards of decency" to make numerous determinations of the temperature of society for certain punishment-related issues. The *Green* Court, though finding felon voting restrictions to be regulatory, hypothesized a decision made from a cruel and unusual punishment argument. They found that the standards of decency in 1967 would not support a decision to strike down felon voting restrictions.

> *The Green court's conclusion that 1967 America was not offended by the disenfranchisement of felons was a correct interpretation and application of Trop. The fact that 42 states disenfranchised those convicted of a crime in 1967 was overwhelming evidence that society did not consider felony disenfranchisement offensive. Rather, national opinion clearly endorsed such disenfranchisement.* (Thompson, 2002, p. 202)

This standard was recently revisited and defined in the monumental death penalty case *Roper v. Simmons* (2005), in which the Court found "objective evidence of a national consensus as expressed by legislative enactments or jury practices" (Death Penalty Information Center [DPIC]). These standards are assessed through a variety of mechanisms. In *Roper*, in addition to a national consensus rational, the majority used international confirmation to determine whether or not a particular punishment violated "evolving standards of decency" (*Roper v. Simmons, 2005*; DPIC).

Due to their original intent, collateral consequences, such as felon voting restrictions, are still held to be civil in nature, but increasing evidence shows that over time their results have become punitive. In contrast to *Green*, the U.S. Supreme Court has noted the punitive nature, not intent, of felon disenfranchisement laws. In *Richardson v. Ramirez* (1974), the Court found felon disenfranchisement laws to be "deeply rooted in this Nation's history and are a punitive device stemming from criminal law" (*Richardson v. Ramirez*, 1974; *Johnson v. Bush*, 2005, p. 36). This article is based on a similar hypothesized premise to the *Green* court argument–if felony disenfranchisement was legally considered a punishment in 2007, would evolving standards of decency support its continued use?

To answer this question this article will explore how punishments philosophies of the U.S. have changed in the last thirty years, then it will examine current opinion research that focuses on the re-enfranchisement or enfranchisement of convicted felons.

PUNISHMENT PHILOSOPHIES AND FELON DISENFRANCHISEMENT

For decades, the purpose of criminal punishment has been debated and studied. Favorable views toward the treatment of criminal offenders were dominant from the 1950s to 1970s, but shifted around the mid-1970s when the Martinson Report suggested that correctional treatment was ineffective (Flanagan & Caufield, 1994; Flanagan, 1996; Martinson, 1974, p. 25). In the late 1980s, public sentiment began to mirror the findings of the Martinson Report, which was reflected in the ABC News poll where 86% of the respondents opposed the claim: "If a person spends time in jail, chances are good he won't commit more crimes after he gets out of jail" (Flanagan, 1996, p. 76).

In the mid-1980s, rehabilitation returned as a sentencing policy preference. Unlike its previous dominance in the 1960s and 1970s, the 1980s rehabilitation ideas were coupled with more punitive ideas (Sundt, Cullen, Applegate & Turner, 1998). Much literature exists that indicates there was a combination of punishment preferences in the 1980s (Sundt et al., 1998).

The 1990s revealed yet another shift in the correctional philosophy of the American public. This shift is evident in the public policy changes of various states. First, some states begin enacting "three strikes and you're out" laws, which mandated sentences of life without the possibility of parole for individuals convicted of their third felony. Between 1993 and 1994, a variation of three strikes laws had been implemented in 15 states (Sundt et al., 1998; Turner, Sundt, Applegate & Cullen, 1995). Second, in the mid-1990s, Alabama and Arizona both introduced the chain gangs for individuals housed in a correctional facility (Cullen et al., 2000). The decision to reincarnate the chain gang is reflective of a perception that the public wants to punish offenders, since chain gangs are not proven to have any rehabilitative functions. Third, another result of the punitive 1990s was the reduction of "inmate amenities" such as the loss of federal funding for post secondary education and restricted access to computers, television and athletic equipment (Cullen, 1995).

Though the 1990s was obviously a decade of policies that revealed a punitive America, empirical evidence indicates that rehabilitative ideals remained a fixture of the public's goal for punishment and sentencing.

Tonry (1998) refers to the public's hybrid theory of corrections (p. 206), which he defines as an interconnection of "restributivist and utilitarian" justifications (Cullen et al., 2000).

As a result of changing public opinion toward treatment, Americans began to change their attitudes toward the necessity of correctional facilities and the rationale for imprisonment. Since then, attitudes as well as correctional philosophies have fluctuated. Currently, in the midst of the War on Drugs and rising prison populations, the concept of community corrections has emerged and led to increased alternatives to incarceration, such as electronic monitoring, "intermediate confinement facilities," and boot camps (Flanagan, 1996, p. 77).

The philosophical confusion on the purpose of punishment contributes to the felon voting debate in that the arguments for and against criminal disenfranchisement arguably have been rooted in a philosophy of punishment. Since felon disenfranchisement occurs as a collateral consequence once an individual has been convicted of a felony it arguably qualifies as an issue under the broader subject of punishment. Due to the gap in the literature directly related to felon disenfranchisement there is some utility in exploring how public punitiveness has previously been measured and the implications this may have on future research related to this topic.

According to Payne et al. (2004), there are two critical areas in correctional policy attitude studies–punishment and sentencing. Punishment attitude research explores "why" offenders should be punished (Payne et al., 2004). The central issue in studying opinions about punishment is whether the public believes the purpose of corrections is to punish or rehabilitate the offender. Sentencing attitude research examines "how" offenders should be punished (Payne et al., 2004). Research that examines attitudes towards sentencing is concerned with the type and severity of the criminal punishment.

Punishment and sentencing both have potential implications for this article. First, since felony disenfranchisement resembles criminal punishment, then it follows that answering why felons are disenfranchised is a valid question for the public. When criminal sanctions date back to over 200 years it seems appropriate for a civilized society to reevaluate and perhaps adjust to modernity. Second, due to the diversity among state felon voting prohibition laws it may be time to examine how disenfranchisement should be used in conjunction with criminal sentencing. Some states do not disenfranchise convicted felons, others partially disenfranchise, and still others have lifetime bans on felon voting absent an executive pardon (The Sentencing Project, 2005). If the American public still supports felon voting prohibitions as a collateral consequence, then it might serve a policy interest to recognize which type of disenfranchisement law is supported with particular emphasis on state specific attitudes since states dictate which citizens are granted the right to vote.

When it comes to contemporary American public opinion on correctional issues, Warr (1994, p. 52) proposed that "there is no single dominant ideology of punishment among the U.S. public." Furthermore, he found that when given the option, Americans tend to appeal to several punishment orientations (Warr, 1994). Cullen et al. (2000) purported that "people's understanding of sentencing severity and options is restricted and often distorted" (p. 3), which brings the validity of their opinions in question.

Past research depicts confusion amongst the public regarding why offenders should be punished. Though public opinion may be hypocritical and conflicting at times, the rationale for punishment is an important domain to examine in criminal justice research. The level of public punitiveness can play a determining role on the types of crime policy developed and ultimately implemented by legislators. This would suggest that recent legislative changes related to felon disenfranchisement reflect a public who may believe in the rehabilitative effects of criminal punishment.

Punishment schemes in the U.S. retain elements of all four dominant rationales–retribution, deterrence, incapacitation and rehabiliation. This diversity in opinions has been studied in a variety of different ways; still there is no authoritative assessment to guide policy makers. Instead, what exists is the ability for interested parties to "weave together various strands of information gathered from [the] diverse studies" and extract three inferences:

> 1. Citizens are accepting of specific policies that inflict penal harm on offenders (Clear, 1994);
> 2. Punitive views exist side by side with progressive views, and thus do not preclude support for policies aimed at improving the lives of offenders;
> 3. Individuals tend not to hold punitive views rigidly . . . they will moderate these views if given a compelling reason to do so (Cullen et al., 2000, p. 28).

These conflicting ideas become more obvious when considering various types of offenders. Oftentimes public opinion is fluid when it comes to certain situations (Cullen et al., 2000). Further evidence of a fluid punitive public is seen in its likelihood to prefer rehabilitation for youthful offenders (Cullen et al., 2000), nonviolent offenders (Sundt et al., 1998) and those already incarcerated (Cullen et al., 2000). In addition, there appears to be increasing public support for intermediate sanctions such as: restitution, community service, electronic monitoring, and intensive probation supervision (Cullen et al., 2000, p. 42).

The search for the literature reported above did not yield any examples of research that couples punitive attitudes with public opinion and felony disenfranchisement. The closest relationship that exists in the literature deals with measuring the tenacity of rehabilitation. This inference derives from the arguments for and against disenfranchisement. Typically, supporting philosophies of felon voting restrictions are based on similar rationales to the tough on crime stance (i.e., incapacitation, deterrence and retribution). Arguments against felon voting restrictions derive from treatment rationales (i.e., rehabilitation), which assert that once an offender has completed his/her sentence then he/she should be rehabilitated and free to live as a law abiding citizen.

Whether or not the public still supports felon voting prohibitions remains an unanswered question. The need for more of this type of research is evident by the many changes in state felon voting laws in recent years and research exposing the negative effects on certain communities. The missing piece to motivate change is overwhelming evidence of a shift in public opinion regarding felon voting rights.

Public Opinion and Felon Disenfranchisement

Public opinion research has become increasingly important as one of the mechanisms by which citizens can communicate with policymakers. Democratic theory assumes that "opinions of the public are to be translated into action" (Bardes & Oldendick, 2003, p. 3). In other words, in a representative democracy, theoretically, elected officials represent the ideals of their constituents and public opinion serves as a communication outlet for the citizens to voice their ideas to elected officials. It is then the responsibility of the elected official to transform those ideas into policy.

Due to the infancy in advocacy related to felony disenfranchisement laws, there is a dearth of criminal justice research regarding attitudes toward the topic. However, attitudinal research on other crime-related policies is more common. It has been argued that the occasional collection and assessment of criminal justice issues is useful for several reasons

(Hindelang, 1974). First, public opinion research provides a permanent documentation of the fluctuations in the public's attitude toward criminal justice issues (Hindelang, 1974; Flanagan, 1996). Second, the public sentiment serves the purpose of determining the "public's mood and priorities for criminal justice reform" (Flanagan, 1996; Hindelang, 1974). Other notable researchers have suggested that public attitudes can influence governmental actions in response to arising crime issues (Flanagan, 1993; Key, 1961). Though research has shown that the public's knowledge of criminal justice is deficient, this deficiency does not curb their "diverse, multi-dimensional, and complex" attitudes (Gerber & Engelhardt, 1996).

GENERAL PUBLIC OPINION AND FELONY DISENFRANCHISEMENT

In the first "comprehensive assessment" of attitudes toward felony disenfranchisement, the Pinaire, Heumann, and Bilotta (2003) study sought to explore attitudes toward felony disenfranchisement from a civil liberties perspective. The authors presumed that Americans generally accepted "justice" and "rights" while maintaining that the criminal justice system should guard both (Pinaire et al., 2003). They also predicted that the public would believe that rights are accompanied by rules that should be followed (Pinaire et al., 2003). If one breaks the rules, then one must face the appropriate punishment. However, they questioned whether or not the public would support collateral consequences of conviction, such as felony disenfranchisement (Pinaire et al., 2003).

The Pinaire et al. study used a cross sectional, exploratory research design (Pinaire et al., 2003). Their goal was to lay a framework for subsequent research on felony disenfranchisement. The authors also expected to find some supportive attitudes toward felony disenfranchisement due to the fact that 48 states continue to disenfranchise felons (Pinaire et al., 2003). Stratified random sampling was used to yield a sample size of 503 (Pinaire et al., 2003). The survey questions were grouped into the following categories:

- Purpose of the criminal justice system
- Public attitudes about offender treatment
- Public support and rationale for felony disenfranchisement

The research findings somewhat supported the researchers' assumptions about the public's opinion (Pinaire et al., 2003). They concluded that the predominant public opinion was somewhere in between supporting and opposing felony disenfranchisement (Pinaire et al., 2003). Overwhelmingly, Americans did not strongly agree with policies that never limit a felon's right to vote, while at the same time being unsupportive of permanent felony disenfranchisement. They found that 81.7% of the respondents rejected permanent disenfranchisement of convicted felons (Pinaire et al., 2003).

There were some important findings between attitudes toward fairness of their respondents and several independent variables: race/ethnicity, party affiliation, and education. African-Americans, Hispanics and those who indicated a level of education at "some high school" were less likely to consider the system "generally fair" (Pinaire et al., 2003). African-Americans were more inclined than whites to believe the criminal justice system was unfair (Pinaire et al., 2003). As it relates to respondents' opinions on the goal of the criminal justice system correlated with race and party affiliation, African-Americans absolutely opposed permanently restricting felon voting rights (Pinaire et al., 2003). They also felt that rehabilitation was the priority of the criminal justice system. Republicans felt punishment was the goal of the system, while Democrats favored rehabilitation (Pinaire et al., 2003).

Though the research contributed to an area of study that has been largely neglected, the authors suggested that future research should be more focused on individual states that continue to permanently ban all convicted felons. They hope that individual state-wide studies will be conducted in order to examine how attitudes are affected by the state's "political culture, history, and tendencies" (Pinaire et al., 2003, p. 1549). Additionally, they wish to compare public opinion of residents with the public policy of the state (Pinaire et al., 2003).

The 2002 Manza, Brooks and Uggen study shared similar goals with the abovementioned research. However, rather than question respondents directly regarding their opinions of felony disenfranchisement, Manza et al. (2002) used two types of attitudinal measures to assess how the public felt about enfranchisement, rather than disenfranchisement. The study sought to examine the following research questions:

- Do Americans support the enfranchisement of individuals convicted of a crime?
- Does the level of support vary depending upon the level of supervision or the specific nature of the crime?

Conducted in July 2002, the study used a stratified, random sample of 1,000 adult U.S. residents and had a response rate of approximately 29.3 to 38.7 percent (Manza et al., 2004). The questionnaire design consisted of a "battery of wording experiments" intended to assess "attitudes toward crime, punishment and the civil liberties of criminals and ex-offenders" (p. 278). The wording experiments also served as an avenue for the researchers "to examine how specific references to target groups and other framing processes used by competing elites or other opinion leaders may affect public opinion concerning enfranchisement" (Kinder, 1998; Manza et al., 2004, p. 278).

The questionnaire was designed around the two attitudinal measures from the research questions. A total of three categories of questions were used: Dimension 1, Dimension 2, and Civil Liberties. Dimension 1 items were used to observe respondents attitudes based on the status of the offender in question (Manza et al., 2004). Dimension 2 items dealt with attitudes toward ex-felons and differed by the type of crime committed by the ex-felon in question (Manza et al., 2004). The Civil Liberties component of the study consisted of a baseline civil liberties variable, which contained First Amendment content that was totally unrelated to felony disenfranchisement (Manza et al., 2004).

Overall, the study produced support for enfranchising convicted felons. However, support wavered for giving incarcerated individuals the right to vote. No demographic variables were correlated with the public attitudes and only descriptive statistics were reported. Manza et al. (2003) found that the most favorable enfranchisement responses were toward probationers and parolees. Respondent opinions were not necessarily impacted by a convicted felon's previous incarceration. However, their opinions did appear to be related to current incarceration offenders. Only 31% of respondents favored enfranchisement for prisoners. Eighty percent of the respondents supported the enfranchisement of a general ex-felon (Manza et al., 2004). The majority of respondents favored enfranchisement for white collar (63%) and violent (66%) ex-felons, but only 52% supported voting rights for sex offense ex-felons (Manza et al., 2004).

The assessment of civil liberties ideas yielded overwhelming support with 82% favoring a right to basic civil freedoms (Manza et al., 2004). Eighty-five percent favored allowing an ex-felon the First Amendment rights to free speech and freedom of religion (Manza et al., 2004). However, the support slightly diminished when respondents were asked to consider the freedom of speech of an ex-felon convicted of drug trafficking (72%) and an advocate for the legalization of drugs (72%) (Manza et al., 2004).

In sum, the Manza et al. study produced innovative information regarding public support for felon voting rights. Their findings also support previous research (Pinaire et al.), which showed that the public may be more inclined to protect civil liberties over the dominant perception of support for punitiveness.

A third related study served as a follow-up to Pinaire et al.'s (2003) previous research on attitudes toward felony disenfranchisement. In this study, Heuman, Pinaire and Clark (2005) utilized focus group research to assess public opinions toward collateral consequences of convictions. The study possessed a broader focus but included questions directly pertaining to felony disenfranchisement. The authors' previous survey research experience contributed to the idea for this focus group methodology because they felt it would allow more "interaction and deliberation" between the study participants (Heuman et al., 2005). Utilizing a snowball sampling method, the researchers recruited participants who would then recruit others, which resulted in four focus groups–two with Rutgers University staff members and two with Rutgers University students (Heuman et al., 2005).

From the data gathered, the researchers noticed several insights. First, participants declined expressing all inclusive "lock'em up" approach to criminal justice (Heuman et al., 2005). Instead, they preferred forming opinions on the basis of details of the "proposed situation, the alleged crime and mitigated circumstances" (Heuman et al., 2005, p. 31). As a result, their toughness or softness toward offenders was contingent on the details of the case. Second, the participants displayed disdain for felon voting prohibitions. Most of them preferred a utilitarian punishment so felon disenfranchisement made little practical sense. In other words, they did not see the utility, or the greater good, imposed on society by restricting felon voting rights (Heuman et al., 2005). Though the majority of participants were in favor of felon enfranchisement, there were some dissenters, but even they argued that disenfranchisement should be distributed only to certain offenders (Heuman et al., 2005). Finally, the last relevant discovery from this research was the awareness level of the participants. It was apparent to the researchers that most participants had little prior information regarding collateral consequences (Heuman et al., 2005). They were unaware that felons lost the right to vote upon conviction and were unable to grasp the reasoning behind collateral consequences in general (Heuman et al., 2005).

FELON OPINIONS TOWARD FELONY DISENFRANCHISEMENT

In another study, Uggen and Manza (2002) focused on felon political attitudes providing another method for gauging attitudes toward felony disenfranchisement. This study included information on "political attitudes, preferences, engagements, and voting behavior" of convicted criminals (p. 3). Two primary data sources were utilized, but the results from the qualitative research on convicted criminals are reported here. Uggen and Manza conducted semi-structured interviews with 33 Minnesota inmates of varying correctional statuses. The interviews were conducted at "two [Minnesota] correctional facilities and one community corrections office" (p. 12). The demographic information for the respondents was not specifically reported. However, Uggen and Manza described the respondents' race and gender as "varied" and their age range between 20-54 years.

The key research question related to the topic of felon voting rights was worded as follows:

> How does losing the right to vote affect their ideas about being part of a community?

Respondents' attitudes reflected their connection between enfranchisement and offender reentry. One female inmate explained disenfranchisement as "salt in her wounds" (p. 17), in that the policy serves as a reminder that even though released into free society, the ex-offender will not regain full citizenship (Uggen & Manza, 2002). The citizenship argument was furthered by responses that conveyed the opinion that nonvoters are not citizens because they have no voice (Uggen & Manza, 2002).

Overall, Uggen and Manza (2002) learned that felon political attitudes widely vary though they are often treated as a "homogenous mass" (p. 29). Also, the felons felt that disenfranchisement laws should be constricted to not include criminal conduct that was unrelated to voting. The participants also question felony disenfranchisement as a "collateral consequence" to their criminal punishment (Uggen & Manza, 2002).

Another variation of a qualitative study on felon voting opinions was conducted by Steinmetz (2003), who chose to speak with those who were directly impacted by felony disenfranchisement laws. She explained that the research served two purposes. First, she sought to establish a rationale for the disproportionate social class and racial effects of felony disenfranchisement (Steinmetz, 2003). Second, she attempted to examine the beliefs of convicted felons toward their disenfranchised status and the coping mechanisms they used in dealing with their inability to participate as a full U.S. citizen (Steinmetz, 2003).

Her sample derived from inmates from the Baltimore Pre-Release Unit for Women (BPRU-W) where she conducted voluntary, face-to-face interviews with thirteen inmates (Steinmetz, 2003). Similar to other studies regarding felony disenfranchisement, Steinmetz assessed voting behavior and the level of knowledge participants possessed toward felon voting laws, as well as their opinions regarding felon disenfranchisement in Maryland (Steinmetz, 2003). Approximately seventy-seven percent (n = 10) of participants reported being registered voters before they were arrested (Steinmetz, 2003). Eight participants indicated they had voted before their imprisonment (Steinmetz, 2003).

The study participants were also asked to share their views on the purpose and rationale of the correctional system. Several participants reportedly mentioned the paradox between the rehabilitative correctional philosophy and felony disenfranchisement laws (Steinmetz, 2003). They apparently recognized and resented the contradiction as well as doubted the effectiveness of rehabilitation (Steinmetz, 2003).

Most of the participants were initially unaware of Maryland's distinction between violent and nonviolent offenders and the number of offenses committed by an individual. When they were subsequently questioned about their attitudes regarding whether or not convicted felons should be able to vote, twelve participants responded favorably to automatic re-enfranchisement once an individual is no longer incarcerated and while on probation and parole (Steinmetz, 2003).

Opinions toward an incarcerated offender's voting rights received mixed responses. Economic citizenship was a recurring issue in responses related to enfranchising incarcerated individuals (Steinmetz, 2003). Steinmentz (2003) reports that as a pre-release facility, BPRU-W requires all inmates to be gainfully employed. Though some are employed at the facility, others work off-site and actually pay rent and taxes (Steinmetz, 2003). Economic citizenship appears to be such an issue because the women believe individuals who work and pay taxes, regardless of their incarceration, should be allowed to vote. Steinmetz (2003) found that female felons appear to be concerned about voting and related political issues. All of the women considered voting a significant issue. She found that the inmates' restricted freedoms and related dependence on the government contributed to their appreciation in having a voice in this society (Steinmetz, 2003).

In a more recent study on attitudes toward felony disenfranchisement, Cardinale (2004) conducted 50 in-depth, face-to-face interviews with homeless, male, convicted felons. Unlike previous research, Cardinale (2004) sought to address several issues related to disenfranchised felons. His interviews consisted of questions about political participation (including pre- and post-conviction voting and registration information), political behavior (including lobbying and protesting), and political alienation (Cardinale, 2004).

Cardinale's study represents a divergent approach to other studies and attempts to explore the practical ramifications of felony disenfranchisement. In order to gauge attitudes about their status as a disenfranchised felon, Cardinale asked "What was your reaction when you first learned you had lost the right to vote? Did you have feelings about it?" (Cardinale, 2004, p. 7). This question produced a variety of thoughts concerning citizenship, alienation and distrust, and anger and apathy (Cardinale, 2004). The question was asked as a component of the in-depth interview; therefore, Cardinale's findings were not presented in a complete quantitative format, but instead mostly qualitative. Thirty-four respondents reported a negative impact felt after losing their right to vote (Cardinale, 2004).

Disenfranchisement reportedly caused some respondents to feel like "a fraction of a citizen" (Cardinale, 2004, p. 7). Cardinale suggested that this information should be used to direct comprehension of "how disenfranchisement influences people's views of themselves and the legitimacy of politics in general" (Cardinale, 2004, p. 7). Detachment from the political process, specifically voting, appears to be linked to resentment toward the whole voting process.

Similar to Cardinale's study, Wahler (2006) conducted 40 interviews with felony parolees in an urban area in Kentucky. The study respondents were recruited by flyers that were posted in community agencies heavily utilized by parolees (Wahler, 2006). Participants were asked about their opinions regarding losing the right to vote, knowledge of the state's restoration of civil rights process, and perceptions of their ability to complete the restoration application process (Wahler, 2006).

The study sample was predominantly male (n = 30), with a high school education or less (n = 30), who had committed a nonviolent offense (n = 33) (Wahler, 2006). The sample comprised a mixture of Caucasian (n = 18) and African-American (n = 19) participants (Wahler, 2006). Approximately 43 percent did not report any pre-incarceration voting behavior, though approximately 38 percent reported voting multiple times prior to their incarceration (Wahler, 2006).

This study represents the first study of its kind in the Commonwealth of Kentucky. The results revealed that permanent disenfranchisement in Kentucky isolates a considerable number of people who would vote if permitted (Wahler, 2006). Overwhelmingly, the participants also displayed misinformation or lack of information regarding the restoration of civil rights process in Kentucky (Wahler, 2006). One participant stated, "You know, to me it seems like they want to penalize you for the rest of your life for a mistake that you've made" (p. 11) (Wahler, 2006).

Wahler (2006) concluded that a change is needed in Kentucky. With the amount of misinformation reported, she suggests that more public education on the current restoration process is necessary (Wahler, 2006). She also suggests a constitutional amendment changing the disenfranchisement policy or at the minimum, an executive change that makes the process less cumbersome (Wahler, 2006).

The review of the current literature above reveals that the methodology, sampling techniques and study participants vary widely when measuring opinions towards felon disenfranchisement. Survey research (Pinaire et al., 2003; Manza et al., 2004), focus groups (Heuman et al., 2005) and interviewing (Cardinale, 2004; Steinmetz, 2003; Wahler, 2006) have all been used to examine the felon voting opinions of certain members of the U.S. population. In addition, the sampling techniques have included random sampling of the adults across the country (Pinaire et al., 2003; Manza et al., 2004), as well as snowball (Heuman) and convenience samples (Cardinale, 2004; Steinmetz, 2003; Wahler, 2006) of ex-felons (Cardinale, 2004), inmates (Steinmetz, 2003), parolees (Wahler, 2006), the general public (Pinaire et al., 2002; Uggen & Manza) and college students and faculty (Heuman et al., 2005).

It appears that regardless of the methodology, sampling technique, sample size or composition, these members of the American public believe that convicted felons depending on their correctional status or offense should be eligible to vote. This holds true especially for non-incarcerated probationers, parolees and ex-felons. This evidence is important because throughout legal history, the Court has found that national consensus changes over time on a variety of constitutional issues, such as equal protection (*Plessy v. Ferguson,* 1896*; Brown v. Board of Education,* 1954) or privacy (*Bowers v. Hardwick*, 1986*; Lawrence v. Texas*, 2003). It is apparent through recent changes to state felon voting provisions that the national consensus has come to support rehabilitation and subsequently granting the franchise certain felons. Legislative changes across the country coupled with public opinion research like the above-mentioned would lead us to believe that felon voting prohibitions may no longer be acceptable in our society.

REFERENCES

Bardes, B. A., & Oldendick, R. W. (2003). *Public Opinion: Measuring the American Mind.* (2nd ed.). Wadsworth: Belmont, CA.

Cardinale, M. (2004). *Triple Decker Disenfranchisement: First Person Accounts of Losing the Right to Vote Among Poor, Homeless Americans with a Felony Conviction.* The Sentencing Project. Available online at: www.sentencingproject.org.

Clear, T. (1994). *Harm in American Penology: Offenders, Victims, and Their Communities.* Albany, N.Y.: SUNY Press.

Coyle, M. (2003). State-based advocacy on felony disenfranchisement. Available online at: http://www.sentencingproject.org/pdfs/5083.pdf

Cullen, F. T. (1995). Assessing the penal harm movement. *Journal of Research in Crime & Delinquency, 32*, 338-358.

Cullen, F. T., Fisher, B. S., & Applegate, B. K. (2000). Public opinion about punishment and corrections. In M. Tonry (Ed.). *Crime and Justice A Review of Research* Vol. 27. University of Chicago Press.

Death Penalty Information Center [DPIC]. Roper v. Simmons Resource Page. Available online at http://www.deathpenaltyinfo.org/article.php?scid=38&did=885. Last retrieved: January 17, 2005

Flanagan, T. J. (1993). Twenty years of public opinion on crime and criminal justice, 1973-93. Paper presented at the Annual Meeting of the American Society of Criminology, Chicago.

Flanagan, T. J. (1996). Reform or Punish: Americans' View of the Correctional System. In T. J. Flanagan & D. M. Longmire (Eds.), *Americans View Crime and Justice: A National Public Opinion Survey*. Thousand Oaks, CA: Sage.

Flanagan, T. J., & Caufield, S. L. (1984). Public opinion and prison policy: A review. *Prison Journal,* 64, 39-59.

Gerber, J., & Engelhardt, S. (1996). Just and Painful: Attitudes toward sentencing criminals. In T. J. Flanagan & D. M. Longmire (Eds.), *Americans View Crime and Justice: A National Public Opinion Survey*. Thousand Oaks, CA: Sage.

Green v. Board of Elections, 380 F. 2d 445 (2nd Cir. 1967).

Heuman, M., Pinaire, B. K., & Clark, T. (2005). Beyond the Sentence: Public Perceptions of Collateral Consequences for Felony Offenders. *Criminal Law Bulletin,* 41(1), 24-46.

Hindelang, M. J. (1974). Public opinion regarding crime, criminal justice, and related topics. *Journal of Research in Crime and Delinquency*, 11, 101-116.

Hunter v. Underwood, 471 U.S. 222 (1985).

Johnson v. Bush, 405 F.3d 1214, (2005)

Johnson-Parris, A. S. (2003). Felon disenfranchisement: The unconscionable social contract breached. *Virginia Law Review, 89,* 109.

Key, V. O. (1961). *Public Opinion and American Democracy.* New York: Knopf.

Kinder, D. (1998). Communication and opinion. *Anuual Review of Political Science*, 1, 167-187.

Manza, J., Brooks, C., & Uggen, C. (2004). Public attitudes toward felon disenfranchisement in the United States. *Public Opinion Quarterly*, 68(2), 275-286.

Martinson, R. (1974). What works? Questions and answers about prison reform. *Public Interest*, 35, 22-54.

Payne, B. K., Gainey, R. R., Triplett, R., & Danner, M. J. E. (2004). What drives punitive beliefs? Demographic characteristics and justifications for sentencing. *Journal of Criminal Justice*, 32, 195-206.

Pinaire, B., Heuman, M., & Bilotta, L. (2003). Barred from the vote: Public attitudes toward the disenfranchisement of felons. *Fordham Urban Law Journal*, 30, 1519.

Richardson v. Ramirez, 418 U.S. 24 (1974).

Roper v. Simmons, 125 S. Ct. 1183 (2005).

Special Project. (1970). Collateral Consequences of a Criminal Conviction. *Vanderbilt Law Review, 23*, p. 929.

Steinmetz, E. K. (2003). Access denied: The construction of criminality and the consequences of felon disenfranchisement. (Masters thesis, American University, 2003), *Master Abstracts International*, 42, 432.

Sundt, J. L., Cullen, F. T., Applegate, B. K., & Turner, M. G. (1998). The tenacity of the rehabilitative ideal revisited: Have attitudes toward rehabilitation changed? *Criminal Justice & Behavior*, 25, 426-442.

The Sentencing Project. (November, 2005). Felony Disenfranchisement Laws in the United States. Available online at: http://www.sentencingproject.org/pdfs/1046.pdf.

Thompson, M. E. (2002). Don't do the crime if you ever intend to vote again: Challenging disenfranchisement of ex-felons as cruel and unusual punishment. *Seton Hall Law Review, 33*, 167.

Trop v. Dulles, 356 U. S. 86; 78 S. Ct. 590; 2 L. Ed. 2d 630; (1958)

Turner, M. G., Sundt, J. L., Applegate, B. K., & Cullen, F. T. (1995). Three strikes and you're out: A national assessment. *Federal Probation*, 59(3), 16-35.

Uggen, C., & Manza, J. (2002). Lost Voices: The Civic and Political Views of Disenfranchised Felons. P. 165-204. In D. M. Dattilo, D. Weiman, & Western, B. (Eds.), *Imprisoning America: The Social Effects of Mass Incarceration*. New York: Russell Sage Foundation.

Wahler, E. (2006). Losing the right to vote: Perceptions of permanent disenfranchisement and the civil rights restoration application process in the state of Kentucky. The Sentencing Project. Available [online] at: http://www.sentencingproject.org/pdfs/ky-losingtherighttovote.pdf.

Warr, M. (1994). Public perceptions and reactions to violent offending and victimization. In A. J. Reiss, Jr., & J. A. Roth (Eds.), *Understanding and Preventing violence: Consequences and Control* (Vol. 4). Washington, DC: National Academy Press.

Problems of Implementing Offender Programs in the Community

BRAD ASTBURY

INTRODUCTION

Over the past 50 years the focus of correctional policy and practice has oscillated between punishment and rehabilitation. Throughout the 1950s and 60s there was considerable optimism about the effectiveness of correctional treatment in generating positive behavioral change. However, following an influential (although arguably misinterpreted) review of over 200 studies of offender treatment programs in the United States, Martinson (1974) concluded that: "With few and isolated exceptions, the rehabilitative efforts described so far have had no appreciable effect on recidivism" (p. 25). Funding for rehabilitative initiatives was dramatically reduced and policy makers emphasized deterrence and sanctions as a means of crime control.

Since that time, the philosophy of correctional policy has again changed to reflect a renewed emphasis on rehabilitation. A large and growing body of research has emerged to challenge the hegemony of "nothing works." Comprehensive meta-analyses and other reviews of criminal justice interventions suggest that some things do work. They argue that effective programs, that is, those that reduce re-offending, share a number of common features. These features are typically referred to as the 'what works' principles.

At present there appears to be broad agreement in the international "what works" literature regarding the features or principles of effective correctional interventions (Andrews et al., 1990; Andrews & Bonta, 1998; Gendreau, 1996; Lipsey, 1992, MacKenzie, 2000; McGuire, 2002; Motiuk & Serin, 2001). These include:

- *Risk classification*–treatment services should be matched to the risk level of the offender. High risk cases should receive intensive programming while low risk cases benefit most from minimal intervention and services.
- *Target criminogenic needs (dynamic risk factors)*–focus on dynamic risk factors that contribute directly to offending and can be changed through treatment (e.g., anti-social attitudes, drug dependency and criminal associates) rather than non-criminogenic needs or static risk factors (e.g., age, low self-esteem, and anxiety).
- *Responsivity*–match treatment style and mode to the personality and learning styles of individual offenders. Typically, programs should employ a participatory approach and be sensitive to diversity.
- *Treatment modality*–base the intervention on a psychological theory of human behavior that is skills and problem-solving oriented and draws upon cognitive-behavior and social learning methods. Target a number of criminogenic needs (multi-modal) in an intensive manner.
- *Community-based services*–programs that are delivered in the community rather than residential settings are more effective because new skills learned can be immediately applied in real world

situations. Institutional programs can also be effective if they emphasize supportive community reintegration.

- *Program integrity*–programs should be properly managed and delivered by trained personnel in accordance with stated aims and objectives that do not change over time. Effective programs should continually monitor implementation (process) and rigorously evaluate impacts (outcome).

These principles have been widely promoted in the Canada, the United Kingdom, America, New Zealand and Australia as "best practice" in offender assessment and treatment, and are now familiar to most correctional managers. Meta-analytic research suggests that when these principles are incorporated into correctional programming, reductions in recidivism range from 10% to 50%, with an average reduction of 26% to 30% (Andrews & Bonta, 1998; Gendreau, 1996).

GETTING "WHAT WORKS" TO "WORK": THE CHALLENGE OF IMPLEMENTATION

Implementation of the "what works" agenda has been challenging for correctional authorities. For example, findings from evaluations of recent large scale criminal justice reforms, such as the Home Office Crime Reduction Program in England and Wales, indicate that problems during implementation of new correctional programs and services significantly influence treatment outcomes (Furniss & Nutley, 2000; Mair, 2004; Merrington & Stanley, 2000; Raynor, 2004). Similar experiences have been reported in Canada and the United States (Bernfeld, Farrington & Leschied, 2001; Bourgon & Armstrong, 2005; Farabee et al., 1999; Ferguson, 2002; Petersilia, 1990). These studies suggest that basing correctional programs on good research and theories is not enough. Programs can fail because of poor implementation just as easily as they can from poor theory.

Unfortunately, limited guidance exists for those who wish to "narrow the gap between what we desire from our rehabilitation programs and what we actually deliver" (Bernfeld, Farrington & Leschied, 2001, p. xix). Gendreau, Goggin and Smith (2001) argue that while much has been written about offender assessment and treatment there has been very little research into factors relating to the successful implementation of correctional programs:

> It is ironic that the fundamental component in the delivery of effective offender treatment services, that of program implementation, has traditionally received the least attention. Only a dozen or so studies exist in the correctional literature which address this topic, in contrast to at least a thousand studies on offender assessment and treatment. (p. 247)

The way in which programs are delivered clearly does matter, and as such is it important to consider program integrity/implementation issues in corrections as a field of study in its own right (Lowenkamp, Latessa & Smith, 2006). An important task, therefore, is to get inside the 'black box' of correctional programming and identify the practical challenges that agencies are likely to confront as they attempt to transfer research knowledge about "what works" into daily practice.

THE STUDY CONTEXT

Like many countries around the world, Australia is experiencing a prison boom. Figures from the Australian Bureau of Statistics (2006) indicate that in the past 10 years, the size of the prison population has increased by 42%, from 18,193 in 1996 to 25,790 in 2006. This rise has exceeded the 15% growth in the Australian adult population, resulting in the adult imprisonment rate increasing from 132 to 163 prisoners per 100,000 adult population in the same period.

A direct result of increases in the size of the prisoner population is the costs associated with its maintenance. In the State of Victoria a review by the Auditor-General (2003) observed that:

> During the period, 1994 to 2003, Victoria experienced significant growth in prisoner numbers. At 10 October, 2003, there were 3,796 prisoners compared with 2 522 at 30 June, 1994–an increase of 50.5 per cent. In the absence of policy and program interventions, Corrections Victoria predicts continuing strong growth in prisoner numbers to around 4,220 prisoners by June, 2006. At an average annual cost of $66 530 per prisoner per year, continued growth in prisoner numbers has significant funding implications for government. (p. 17)

Confronted with the economically unsustainable situation of sending more and more offenders to prison, it is perhaps not surprising that

Australian jurisdictions have learnt from overseas experience that it is not possible to "build your way" out of a prison crowding crisis (Clear & Byrne, 1992). This financial imperative on governments coupled with renewed optimism about the effectiveness of rehabilitation has helped drive an expansion in the size and range of community-based sentencing options in Australia.

In Australia, correctional systems are the responsibility of separate states and territories. Australia is a federation comprising six States and two mainland Territories. This means that there is some variation in the operation of prisons and non-custodial sanctions across jurisdictions. Corrections Victoria, located in the State of Victoria, is one of many correctional agencies across Australia that is attempting to take the current findings of correctional research and implement them into daily practice (Birgden & McLachlan, 2002). Corrections Victoria manages more than 50 community correctional services locations and is also responsible for the management of the state's 11 public prisons as well as overseeing the contracts of two privately operated prisons. At any given time around 8,000 offenders are being supervised in the community.

This article draws on data that was collected as part of a larger evaluation of the implementation and impact of recent reforms to Victorian community correctional services. This four-year reform strategy (2001 to 2005) was designed to reduce some of the pressure on the adult prison system by enhancing the legitimacy of community-based sentences. It was envisaged that the introduction of an evidence-based platform of offending behavior programs and the provision of targeted pre- and post-release support for prisoners would strengthen the capacity of community corrections to manage offenders, and in the longer term reduce recidivism (Corrections Budget Briefing, 2001).

A multi-method evaluation design was developed to address questions about the process of effectiveness of the strategy. Major aspects of the methodology included: a review of policy documents, literature and existing secondary data on the Victorian correctional system; an econometric event-study analysis of average rates of change in prison receptions and community orders; site visits to randomly selected community correctional locations across Victoria; individual and group interviews with over 100 community correctional staff and 30 head office and senior management staff; interviews with a small sample of offenders; and interviews with sentencing and parole authorities.

These activities generated detailed information about problems encountered while attempting to introduce changes to organizational policy and practice in line with evidence from research into "what works" in offender management and treatment.

A MULTI-LEVEL PERSPECTIVE OF BARRIERS TO SUCCESSFUL IMPLEMENTATION

Research into human services organisations and models of service delivery suggest that is useful to think about implementation at four different levels: client, program, organization, and society. Implementation variables associated with each of these levels interact in a reciprocal and dynamic way (Bernfeld, Blase and Fixsen, 1990). Drawing on data from the study described above, this section identifies a number of challenges to the successful implementation of correctional interventions and discusses these from a multi-level perspective. The findings presented below should not be viewed as an exhaustive list, but rather as an example of the particular obstacles that are likely to operate at different levels within the implementation structure of correctional agencies.

Client Level: The Role of Offender Characteristics and Motivation to Change

The characteristics of offenders and their willingness to participate in treatment and supervision were reported to be one of the most important aspects of successful implementation. Offenders are generally not given a choice about whether or not they wish to attend programs or supervision sessions. That is, they are involuntary clients. In practice this means that although offenders may adhere to legal requirements of court orders by attending supervision sessions, fulfilling community work requirements and completing programs they may not be actively engaging. In effect "they are just a occupying a seat" or worse still disrupting a program by affecting the ability of others to participate.

Correctional staff were conscious that programs will only "work" if participants choose to make them work. That is, program attendance and completion did not guarantee that changes in offender knowledge, attitudes and behavior would necessarily follow. As one officer commented, paraphrasing an old saying, "you can lead a horse to water, but it will not necessarily take a drink."

To address these barriers, staff drew on techniques of motivational interviewing and their knowledge of the responsivity principle, which suggests that treatment programs and services should be matched to the individual personality and learning style of offenders. Demographic factors such as age, gender, race and ethnicity also influenced how different offenders responded to different types of treatment.

While assessment procedures were introduced to ensure that offenders were matched to programs and services appropriate for their level of risk, need and circumstances, a significant challenge in practice was the lack of tailored offending behavior programs designed to meet the diverse needs of the offender population. This is now being addressed as part of the next stage of reforms.

Finally, legislative requirements were seen to have been another barrier to effective program delivery. This is because of the way in which legislation can influence selection and referral to programs. Staff explained that determinations about offender participation in programs are typically made by sentencing officials prior to an offender entering corrective services. These earlier decisions sometimes conflicted with psychological assessments that occur after sentencing. However, because judicial orders are legally binding either an amendment needs to be sought, which takes time, or the offender must comply with the conditions of their order and attend the program.

Program Level: The Importance of Effective Staff Practice and Management of Recruitment, Training, Supervision and Turnover

Staffing issues were frequently associated with the successful implementation of programs. In particular, it was noted that there are certain characteristics of staff working in correctional environments that increase the likelihood that theoretically sound programs will be implemented well. These included: appropriate educational qualifications and academic credentials; sufficient skills and experience in working with offenders; professional values such as empathy, tolerance, integrity, flexibility, and a "firm but fair" approach; and good listening and communication skills. Offenders emphasized during interviews that effective staff practice involves being "patient," "friendly," "open," "dedicated" and "supportive." There was a strong and constant message from offenders that it is essential to feel that staff genuinely "care about them." This was further described as "going the extra yard," "not simply monitoring/policing activities," advocating on their behalf and encouraging change by helping to find their own solutions to their problems. Some examples which exemplified a caring attitude were in taking the offender out for a coffee, driving them to an important appointment such as a counseling session or job interview and making time to visit them at home or during community work.

This suggests that recruiting the right staff is critical. A key component of the reform process was the "bulk" employment of additional staff, including psychologists with qualifications and expertise in working with offenders. Prior to these reforms, the community correctional system in Victoria did not have "in-house" psychological services. Difficulties were encountered in trying to identify psychologists that understood and accepted the principles of effective correctional programming and thus were willing to conduct group programs based on cognitive-behavioral and social learning theories rather than focus exclusively on individual therapy. There were also some initial tensions and confusion about the role of psychologists that arose from professional differences in approaches to offender treatment.

The importance of staff training and supervision was also mentioned in relation to effective program delivery. Extensive formal training was provided to new staff prior to commencing work. The introduction of new programs and policies also required the provision of further relevant training to existing staff through workshops, conferences and structured training programs. However, due to a range of competing organizational demands there were often interruptions in the availability of training and along with escalating case loads this affected the ability of senior staff to adequately supervise new employees.

Staff turnover was also strongly linked to effective correctional program implementation. This factor appears to be important for various reasons. High rates of staff turnover can, among other things, lead to problems with continuity of care in the management of offenders. Offenders reported that ideally it was best to have one worker for the duration of their order –someone with whom they could develop rapport and a "trusting" relationship. Many offenders expressed frustration at having to "tell their [personal] story over and over again" to new workers. High rates of turnover can also result in a loss of expertise. Professional judgment is a key feature of offender rehabilitation and it was argued that evidence-based programs are unlikely to be successful without a stable, experienced and well-trained workforce:

> You can have the best programs in the world, you can have fantastic legislation, fantastic policies and procedures, but if you've got staff who are disillusioned, who are being paid badly, who are not trained and who are under so much pressure that they leave here then you've shot yourself in the foot.

Organizational Level: The Need for a Supportive Culture, Effective Change Management and Adaptation to Local Conditions

Correctional agencies attempting to implement major changes in the philosophy of offender management and treatment need to take account of existing organizational cultures and routines. Shifting the status quo from a 'nothing works' mentality to a rehabilitative focus was seen to be relatively unproblematic. Key figures within the organization acted as champions of the vision. There was also a pre-existing commitment to the value of rehabilitation among the majority of the community correctional workforce who had become frustrated with the surveillance/monitoring style of supervision. The organization was "ready to embrace the 'what works' approach."

Time and resource constraints coupled with structural changes within the broader organizational context, however, caused many problems for staff and managers who felt that there was "too much change too quickly." The introduction of new programs and services to the community correctional system was undertaken rapidly due to pressure to spend allocated budgets in the first year of reforms. The reform effort also occurred during a time of significant modification to management and governance arrangements. Previously the operational and strategic arms of the corrections system functioned relatively independently of each other. The consolidation of the system–although seen as a positive step in breaking down "a silo mentality" between strategic services, prisons and community corrections–impacted greatly on implementation by creating confusion about planning responsibilities and allocation of resources.

Another set of implementation problems flowed from the decision to replace an existing offender information database with a new system. The new database was designed to improve the quality and range of information, as well integrate corrections, police and court data. However, continual technical problems burdened staff with extra demands on their time and severely impacted on staff morale. At several stages throughout reform efforts, community correctional staff were involved in protracted industrial disputes with management about workloads and pay levels. This caused significant disruption and delays to the roll-out of major initiatives.

A centralized approach was employed to ensure that programs were rolled out quickly and met predetermined government targets for numbers and completion rates. This approach was also seen to be necessary because of concerns about program integrity and program drift. This style of management had the affect of alienating large sections of the workforce who perceived a need for local autonomy and discretion so that programs could be attuned to local circumstances and responsive to the needs of particular offenders.

Societal Level: Community Attitudes, the Media and Political Climate

Community attitudes towards punishment and a political environment that promotes a law and order response to crime, poses a significant barrier to the implementation of rehabilitative approaches to offender management and treatment. According to White and Tomkins (2003) "much of what occurs within community corrections is influenced by the general political climate" (p. 2).

In our interviews staff reported that the general public knew very little about the role and function of community corrections. Together with negative media reporting of crime they felt that this helped to fuel a perception that community-based sentences were a "soft option." These views presented challenges for the development and implementation of community-based offender rehabilitation programs. Staff highlighted, for example, how negative media coverage and a sustained political campaign presented a threat to a new home detention scheme by feeding a perception that the program presented a risk to community safety. After the program was introduced, sentencing and parole authorities were seen to be initially hesitant about placing offenders on home detention. This created a concern that if cost-effectiveness was used as the sole criteria for success then offender numbers might not be adequate to justify the existence of the program.

DISCUSSION

Drawing on personal experience and the technology transfer literature, Gendreau, Goggin and Smith (1999, 2001) have developed a list of factors to guide successful implementation of offender programs. They organize these into four general categories:

- *Organizational factors:* The organization has a history of adopting new initiatives, is efficient in putting in place new initiatives and is decentralized and flexible enough to deal with issues in a timely and non-confrontational fashion. The organization should also keep staff turnover levels low, offer adequate training in offender assessment and treatment and have links with appropriate educational institutions.

- *Program factors:* The need for the program is based on empirical evidence and stakeholders agree that the program is timely, relevant and matches the risk/needs of the offender population. The program should be based on credible scientific evidence, have realistic goals, be cost-effective, and funded by the host organization. The program should not be introduced during a period where the organization is struggling with other problems/conflicts and implementation should proceed incrementally.
- *Change agent factors:* The person who is primarily responsible for initiating the program should have detailed knowledge of the organization and its staff and support from both senior leaders and line staff. They should employ techniques such as motivational interviewing, reciprocity, authority, reinforcement, problem-solving and advocacy to bring about change and persist until effective change is evident and can be sustained. The change agent should also have a history of successful program implementation, professional credibility and an orientation and values should be congruent with the organization's vision and goals.
- *Staffing factors:* Staff should have the technical/professional knowledge and skills to implement the program and believe that they can do it effectively. They should be given an opportunity to participate directly in designing the new program, understand the theoretical basis of the program and have access to the change agent. Effective delivery of the program also requires staff to have sufficient time and adequate resources as well as feedback mechanisms.

Gendreau et al.'s set of implementation factors provide a valuable "checklist" which can provide guidance to those involved in seeking to implement correctional policy. For instance, when used in the form an "evaluability assessment" (Matthews, Hubbard & Latessa, 2001). Applying the list to findings from this study it can be seen that all four categories are relevant. Items that appear particularly valid include:

- Organizational item #7: Staff turnover at all levels has been less than 25 per cent during the previous 2 years
- Program item #9: The program is being initiated during a period when the host agency is free of other major problems/conflicts.

- Staff item #3: The staff have the technical/professional skill to implement the program. They have taken applied courses on the assessment and treatment of offenders.
- Staff item #6: In order to run the program efficiently, the staff are: (a) given the necessary time, (b) given adequate resources, and (c) provided with feedback mechanisms (e.g., focus groups and workshops).

This study found that micro-level client factors (e.g., offender characteristics and motivation/readiness to change) as well as macro level social and political factors (e.g., community attitudes to punishment and sentencing practices) are also related to successful implementation of community-based offender rehabilitation programs and services. These do not appear to be present in Gendreau et al.'s implementation guidelines.

Another concern with the guidelines is their apparent resemblance to "top-down" models for successful implementation that have been spelled out by political science theorists such as Lewis Gunn (1978), Christopher Hood (1976) and Paul Sabatier and Daniel Mazmanian (1979). The top-down approach to implementation is based on a theoretical construct of "perfect administration" whose focus is on controlling the conditions necessary to administer a policy or program. It presents a normative prescription of what ought to be, rather than what is.

Because of the way they are presented, Gendreau et al.'s specifications have the potential to be confused as another "ideal" representation of implementation that assumes too much and does not suggest what to do when implementation occurs in less than perfect circumstances. This, unfortunately, is the norm rather than the exception for most, if not all, correctional authorities. Harris and Smith (1996), writing on community corrections from an implementation perspective, seem to agree:

> Missing from the lists of attributes of successful implementation is information about *how* they are generated under conditions in which they are not already in place and how innovators manage when one or more of these conditions cannot be met. (p. 195, emphasis in original)

It is worthwhile then to also consider the implementation process in corrections from an alternative, bottom-up perspective. The major theorists here include Michael Lipsky (1980), Susan Barrett and Colin Fudge

(1981) and Benny Hjern (1982). The bottom-up approach is action-oriented and recognizes the difficulties of bringing under control the conditions for perfect implementation. Hill (1997) explains this well:

> The reality, therefore, is not of imperfect control, but of action as a continuous process of interactions with a changing and changeable policy, a complex interaction structure, an outside world which must interfere with implementation because government action impinges on it, and implementing actors who are inherently difficult to control. (p. 139)

Evidence-based offending behavior programs tend to be highly "scripted" and due to concerns about program integrity, correctional agencies have emphasized the need for control over the fidelity of implementation. Adherence to program design, often through "program manuals," is strictly enforced and negative sanctions are often imposed on staff who fail to carry out activities as they were specified in the design. In these circumstances emphasizing the need for local discretion and adaptation of programs might seem contrary to good programming.

However, divergence from program design can lead to improved implementation. According to Harris and Smith (1996, p. 197), "although there is much talk about replicated program models, each new program site is different . . . thus producing a need for differences in the program itself." This raises the possibility of seeing implementation less in terms of a top-down process and more in terms of other, more participatory images. Some of the images suggested by Lane (1987, as cited in Hill) are:

- Implementation as evolution,
- Implementation as learning,
- Implementation as coalition, and
- Implementation as responsibility and trust.

The challenge for correctional authorities seeking to implement programs based on "what works" principles seems to be in managing the delicate balance between strict adherence to program design and constructive adaptation to the organizational context in which the program is being implemented.

An early study by Musheno, Palumbo, Maynard-Moody and Levine (1989) is significant in this regard because it identifies local organizational conditions necessary to support change within different community correctional settings. Their research highlights the importance of a participatory management style that empowers staff and allows wide access to decision-making. The findings support the argument that programs can be adapted to suit local conditions without violating fundamental principles of effective offender rehabilitation through a process of "transformative rationality" which seeks to balance the tensions between top-down and bottom-up approaches to implementation.

SUMMARY AND CONCLUSIONS

Drawing on results from an evaluation of the implementation and impact of community correctional reforms in Australia, this article has illustrated that adoption of the principles of effective correctional intervention is not a simple task, but one that requires an understanding of the complexities of successful program implementation and organizational change management.

Despite advancements in the identification of effective correctional programs little is known about the conditions under which these programs work best. A number of researchers have expressed concern about the lack of attention to implementation issues within correctional programming. It has been argued that there is little practical guidance in the international correctional literature and "these shortcomings pose problems for organizations that wish to implement research findings and engage in effective correctional services" (Ferguson, 2002, p. 476).

The findings presented in this article remind us that community-based offender rehabilitation programs and services rarely look the same on paper as they do in the real world. A diverse range of barriers to implementation operate and interact at various levels: client, program, organization and society. Some barriers are foreseeable and easily controlled through a top-down management style, but many emerge during the process of implementation itself. Therefore, successful implementation requires correctional agencies to maintain some degree of flexibility to local adaptation–without necessarily compromising integrity–so that changes can be made in light of decisions and practices that evolve at the complex interface between program design and program delivery.

REFERENCES

Andrews, D. A., & Bonta, J. (1998). *The Psychology of Criminal Conduct (2nd Edition)*, Cincinnati: Anderson.

Andrews, D. A., Zinger, I., Hoge, R. D., Bonta, J., Gendreau, P., & Cullen, F. T. (1990). Does correctional treatment work? A clinically relevant and psychologically informed meta-analysis, *Criminology, 28*(3), 369-404.

Auditor General. (2003). *Addressing the Needs of Victorian Prisoners.* Report No. 52, Victoria: Auditor General.

Australian Bureau of Statistics. (2006). *Prisoners in Australia, Catalogue No. 4517.0*, Canberra: Australian Bureau of Statistics.

Barrett, S., & Fudge, C. (eds.) (1981). *Policy and Action.* London: Methuen.

Bernfeld, G. A., Blase, K. A., & Fixsen, D. L. (1990). Towards a unified perspective on human service delivery systems: applications of the teaching-family model. In R. J. McMahon & R. De V. Peters (eds.), *Behaviour Disorders of Adolescents: Research, Intervention and Policy in Clinical and School Settings.* New York: Plenum.

Bernfeld, G. A., Farrington, D. P., & Leschied, A. W. (eds.) (2001). *Offender Rehabilitation in Practice: Implementing and Evaluating Effective Programs.* Chichester, UK: John Wiley.

Birgden, A., & McLachlan, C. (2002, revised 2004). *Reducing Re-Offending Framework: Setting the Scene, Paper No. 1*: Melbourne: Department of Justice, Corrections Victoria.

Bourgon, G., & Armstrong, B. (2005). Transferring the principles of effective treatment into a "real world" prison setting, *Criminal Justice and Behaviour, 32*(3), 3-25.

Clear, T. R., & Byrne, J. M. (1992). The future of intermediate sanctions: questions to consider. In J. M. Byrne, A. J. Lurigio, & J. Petersilia (eds.) *Smart Sentencing: The Emergence of Intermediate Sanctions*, California: Sage Publications.

Corrections Budget Briefing. (2001). *$334.5 million to overhaul Victoria's Corrections System*, 15th May, Victoria: Minister for Corrections, State Budget.

Farabee, D., Prendergast, M., Bartier, J., Wexler, H., Knight, K., & Douglan Anglin, M. (1999). Barriers to implementing effective correctional drug treatment programs, *The Prison Journal, 79*(2), 150-162.

Ferguson, J. L. (2002). Putting the "what works" research into practice: an organisational perspective, *Criminal Justice and Behavior, 29*(4), 472-492.

Furniss, J., & Nutley, S. (2000). Implementing what works with offenders–the effective practice initiative, *Public Money and Management, 20*(4), 23-28.

Gendreau, P. (1996). Offender rehabilitation: what we know and what needs to be done, *Criminal Justice and Behavior, 23*, 144-161.

Gendreau, P., Goggin, C., & Smith, P. (1999). The forgotten issue in effective correctional treatment: program implementation, *International Journal of Offender and Comparative Criminology, 43*(2), 180-187.

Gendreau, P., Goggin, C., & Smith, P. (2001). Implementation guidelines for correctional programs in the "real world." In G. A. Bernfeld, D. P. Farrington, & A. W. Leschied (eds.) *Offender Rehabilitation in Practice: Implementing and Evaluating Effective Programs*, New York: John Wiley & Sons.

Gunn, L. (1978). Why is implementation so difficult? *Management Services in Government, 33*, 169-176.

Harris, P. & Smith, S. (1996). Developing community corrections: an implementation perspective. In A. T. Harland (ed.) *Choosing Correctional Options That Work: Defining the Demand and Evaluating the Supply*, California: Sage Publications.

Hill, M. (1997). *The Policy Process in the Modern State.* Harvester-Wheatsheaf, UK: Prentice Hall.

Hjern, B. (1982). Implementation research: the link gone missing, *Journal of Public Policy, 2*, 301-308.

Hood, C. (1976). *The Limits of Administration.* London: John Wiley.

Lipsey, M. (1992). Juvenile delinquency treatment: a meta-analytic inquiry into the variability of effects. In T. Cook, H. Cooper, D. S. Cordray, H. Hartmann, L. V. Hedges, R. L. Light, T. A. Louis & F. Mosteller (eds.) *Meta-Analysis for Explanation: A Case Book*, New York: Russell Sage.

Lipsky, M. (1980). Street Level Bureaucracy. New York: Russell Sage.

Lowenkamp, C. T., Latessa, E. J., & Smith, P. (2006). Does correctional program quality really matter? The impact of adhering to the principles of effective intervention, *Criminology & Public Policy*, *5*(3), 575–594.

MacKenzie, D. L. (2000). Evidence-based corrections: identifying what works, *Crime and Delinquency, 46*(4), 457-471.

Mair, C. (ed.) (2004). *What Matters in Probation.* Cullompton, UK: Willan.

Martinson, R. (1974). What works? Questions and answers about prison reform, *The Public Interest, 10*, 22-52.

Matthews, B., Hubbard, D. J., & Latessa, E. (2001). Making the next step: using evaluability assessment to improve correctional programming, *The Prison Journal, 81*(4), 454-472.

McGuire, J. (ed) (2002). *Offender Rehabilitation and Treatment: Effective Programs and Policies to Reduce Reoffending*, Chichester, UK: John Wiley & Sons.

Merrington, S., & Stanley, S. (2000). Doubts about the What Works initiative, *Probation Journal, 47*(4), 272-275.

Motiuk, L. L., & Serin, R. C. (eds.) (2001). *Compendium, 2000 on Effective Correctional Programming*, Volume One, Canada: Correctional Service Canada.

Musheno, M. C., Palumbo, D. J. Maynard-Moody, S., & Levine, J. P. (1989). Community corrections as an organisational innovation: what works and why, *Journal of Research in Crime and Delinquency, 26*(2), 136-167.

Petersilia, J. (1990). Conditions that permit intensive supervision programs to survive, *Crime and Delinquency, 36*, 126-145.

Sabatier, P., & Mazmanian, D. (1979). The conditions of effective implementation: a guide to accomplishing policy objectives, *Policy Analysis, 5*, 481-504.

White, R., & Tomkins, K. (2003). *Issues in Community Corrections,* Briefing Paper No 2, University of Tasmania: Criminology Research Unit.

Offenders, Judges, and Officers Rate the Relative Severity of Alternative Sanctions Compared to Prison

NATHAN T. MOORE
DAVID C. MAY
PETER B. WOOD

INTRODUCTION

In the dynamic world of corrections, alternative sanctions have become a widely used and viable option for judges and offenders. With the dramatic growth in the justice system over the past 30 years and the introduction of a range of new non-custodial sanctions, the study of their punitiveness compared to prison would seem a logical target for research. However, there has been only limited study of this issue (May, Wood, Mooney, & Minor, 2005). The scant literature on this topic has focused on the concept of severity and how alternative sanctions have changed the options by which our criminals can be punished, as well as their place germane to custodial sanctions (Crouch, 1993; Petersilia, 1990; Petersilia & Deschenes, 1994a, 1994b; Spelman, 1995; Wood & Grasmick, 1999).

With the implementation of alternative sanctions, interest arose regarding these sanctions' place in a "punishment continuum" (Petersilia, 1990; Von Hirsch, Wasik, & Greene, 1992). General assumptions placed probation and prison at the ends of the continuum, and alternative sanctions were presumed to fall somewhere in between. Offender perceptions of intermediate sanctions were first assessed in relation to prison in order to substantiate the belief that such measures were less onerous as custodial sentences (Crouch, 1993; Petersilia, 1990). However, it became clear that more in-depth analyses would be needed, and researchers began to study not only how these sanctions compared to prison but also how such punishment equivalencies varied by gender, race, and other offender characteristics (Morris and Tonry, 1990; Petersilia, 1994a, 1994b; Spelman, 1995; Wood & Grasmick, 1999; Wood & May, 2003). Such research has greatly enhanced the body of knowledge surrounding offender perceptions of punishment and the factors that influence these perceptions (May et al., 2005; Wood & Grasmick, 1999; Wood & May, 2003).

As the current body of knowledge continues to expand, however, one important population has been overlooked. Having a direct hand in whether (and what types of) alternative sanctions are imposed on offenders, it would seem that judges' perceptions and attitudes towards these punishments would be important to know. As the use of alternatives is somewhat dependent on judges' opinions of the severity of these sanctions, assessing their views of alternative sanctions is pivotal in taking the necessary steps toward the development of a more informed continuum of sanctions. Accordingly, this study contributes to such a development by exploring judges', offenders', and officers' perceptions of the relative severity of alternative sanctions compared to prison by examining punishment exchange rates generated by each group.

ASSESSING THE RELATIVE SEVERITY OF CRIMINAL JUSTICE SANCTIONS

In regard to measures by which we punish our offenders, the general public has traditionally perceived probation and imprisonment as marking the opposing ends of society's penalty continuum, with imprisonment viewed as the most punitive sanction short of death (von Hirsch, 1990; Wood & May, 2003). Misdemeanors and minor felonies might be assigned non-custodial sanctions, while more harmful and serious crimes would be punished through varying lengths of incarceration. Validating a continuum of sanctions, however, has been no easy task.

When legislators and policy makers develop alternative sanctions and make pivotal decisions concerning their implementation, they do not base such decisions on experiential data, but instead rely on personal assumptions and public opinion (Morris & Tonry, 1990). Nevertheless, the assumption that probation and prison are located at opposite ends of the continuum has been challenged of late, as recent work has sought to better understand how offenders perceive and experience a range of criminal justice sanctions (Crouch, 1993; Petersilia & Deschenes, 1994a, 1994b; Spelman, 1995).

Petersilia (1990) argued that a disjunction between offender perceptions of punishment severity and public perceptions of punishment severity is likely because (1) offenders typically do not live by the same norms and ideas as the public, as evidenced by the law-breaking actions that lead to their offender label and (2) offenders typically come from lower socioeconomic strata, meaning their standards for living will be significantly lower than the general population, especially when compared to those in the position of adopting and implementing criminal policies. Later, citing aspects such as the reduction in the harmful stigmatization, a less isolative environment, and less deleterious effects on future employment, Petersilia argued that prison itself may be losing its onerous effect on those incarcerated. Research has since supported that argument (see Flory, May, Minor, & Wood, 2006, for review).

The earliest literature exploring perceptions of alternative sanctions and their place in the punishment continuum focused mainly on the offenders' perceptions of prison and how these new programs coalesced with such views (Crouch, 1993; Petersilia, 1990; Petersilia & Deschenes,

1994a, 1994b; Spelman, 1995). Crouch (1993) followed Petersilia's original work with a similar study that examined the preferences of varying lengths of probation and prison among 1,027 male convicted felons in the Texas correctional system. Offenders were given 11 pairs of durations of either probation or prison and asked which one they would prefer if given the choice. In 5 of the 11 situational comparisons, between 25 and 66 percent of the offenders acknowledged a preference for prison over probation. Crouch (1993) also found that older respondents were more likely to prefer prison over alternative sanctions than their younger counterparts and married respondents were willing to serve less time in prison than their unmarried counterparts. His most significant finding, however, was that African Americans had a much stronger preference for prison than did whites.

Subsequently, Petersilia and Deschenes (1994a, 1994b) sampled 48 offenders who, according to statutes of the Minnesota Legislation, would be prime candidates for intermediate sanctions. After collecting basic demographic and background data, the authors solicited offender perceptions of intermediate sanctions through magnitude estimation (where a participant is presented with an average length of punishment [e.g., one year in prison] worth an equivalent of 100 points and then asked to rank other sanctions in terms of their total number of points) and a basic rank ordering of 15 popular sanctions. In rank ordering sanctions, offenders were given 15 alternative sanctions and asked to order them from least severe to most severe. Petersilia and Deschenes (1994a, 1994b) determined certain alternative sanctions were perceived as equally or more severe than shorter terms in prison, though five years in prison was rated the most severe penalty by far. Spelman's (1995) study of 128 Texas male offenders regarding the severity of 26 felony punishments also used magnitude estimation as a means of ranking offenders' perceptions of punishment. Spelman determined that the most severe sanctions were three and five years of prison while a $100 fine was perceived the least onerous and several intermediate sanctions were ranked to be at least as punitive as prison. Like Crouch, Spelman found that older and African American participants preferred a shorter prison term to intensive supervision.

Using Exchange Rates to Measure Relative Severity

In an attempt to address the methodological limitations with magnitude estimation which relied heavily on the "numeracy of respondents" among a population that is noted for being poorly educated (Spelman,

1995, p. 112), Wood and his colleagues developed the "exchange rate" method whereby researchers simply asked offenders to indicate the duration of an alternative sanction they would serve to avoid specific amounts of actual time in prison (May et al., 2005; Wood & Grasmick, 1999; Wood & May, 2003). This method allowed respondents to draw on their own personal experiences to generate a punishment equivalency, and required minimal mathematical aptitude to determine an accurate response (Wood & Grasmick, 1999). Furthermore, this technique not only allows for a comparison of alternatives with prison but also allows one to consider how the various sanctions relate to one another in severity.

Wood and his colleagues have utilized exchange rates to examine perceptions of alternative sanctions among a wide variety of groups, including prisoners (Wood & Grasmick, 1999), probationers and parolees (Wood & May, 2001; May, Minor, Wood, & Mooney, 2004; May et al., 2005; Williams, May, & Wood, 2006), and probation and parole officers (Flory et al., 2006). These studies have determined that, in general: (1) both boot camp and jail are viewed as more onerous than prison; (2) Blacks are more willing to go to prison than Whites; (3) offenders with previous prison experience are more willing to go to prison than offenders without prison experience; (4) males are more willing to go to prison than females; and (5) older offenders were also less likely to agree to serve in alternative sanctions, particularly over a long period of time, than their younger counterparts. Wood and his colleagues have suggested that these preferences for prison are explained by a number of factors, including: (1) failure to complete an alternative sanction results in revocation to prison; (2) offenders view alternative sanctions as difficult to complete; and (3) officers overseeing alternative sanctions may mistreat participants. As a consequence, offenders evaluate participation in alternatives as a sort of "gamble," choosing the option that they are most comfortable with, which often results in the selection of prison over an alternative.

Exchange Rates Among Criminal Justice Practitioners

As knowledge regarding offenders' perceptions of the severity of sanctions evolves, a logical progression is to extend the same questions to practitioner populations (i.e., supervising officers and judges). Flory et al. (2006) compared the exchange rates of 612 probationers and parolees with exchange rates generated by 208 of their supervising officers. Of the nine sanctions included in the instrument, Flory et al. (2006) found significant differences between offenders and officers in six alternatives. The most notable difference was in the officers' mean predicted exchange rate for probation, which was nearly double the mean rate presented by offenders. Though this was the greatest discrepancy, the same pattern was found among exchange rates for county jail, electronic monitoring, day reporting, and intermittent incarceration. The only sanction where the mean rate for offenders was higher than the officers was for community service, as offenders claimed they would serve more than twice the number of hours given by the officers. One explanation for this included shame, as officers may find community service more demeaning and embarrassing due to their possible exposure to community disapproval, something that may have little to no effect on offenders. In general, officers overestimate offenders' perceptions of the severity of prison.

One population with a direct hand in the implementing of alternative sanctions is judges. A small number of studies have examined, both directly and indirectly, judges' attitudes and perceptions of alternatives. Finn (1984) examined judges' responses to prison overcrowding and determined that most judges cited that overcrowding was associated with the lack of money needed to support the expanded services related to probation and parole, as well as the building and maintaining of the required alternative facilities. Judges also acknowledged the pressure from strong public sentiment to lock away criminals. Cole, Mahoney, Thornton and Hanson (1988) explored judges' application and attitudes toward the use of fines and determined that judges were willing to use fines for more severe offenses. Lurigio (1987) examined the attitudes of judges and attorneys from Cook County Illinois concerning the use and implementation of intensive probation supervision (IPS). In that study, a number of judges were reluctant to use IPS and none of the judges reported that sentenced offenders chose prison instead of IPS (perhaps because of its relative infancy in that jurisdiction). Wooldredge and Gordon (1997) used a random sample of 181 chief trial court judges to determine characteristics of the judiciary that would predict a greater use of alternatives as well as judges' willingness to use such sanctions. They determined that judges presiding in courts with less structured sentencing policies and longer minimum sentences were more likely to be amenable to using intermediate sanctions. The same was true for both smaller courts as well as courts with higher rates of plea bargaining. Judges also cited more structured sentencing policies as limiting their sentencing discretion and their ability to use alternative sanctions in lieu of prison (Wooldredge & Gordon, 1997).

Despite the previous studies that examine attitudes toward and use of alternative sanctions among judges, no studies have examined judges' perceptions of the relative severity of alternative sanctions when compared to prison. Because judges have direct input in decisions about what punishments offenders receive, their perceptions of the severity of punishments and, ultimately, the punishment continuum are important. Furthermore, it seems useful to compare judges' perceptions of alternative sanctions with those of offenders under community supervision, as well as their supervising officers. Doing so can not only expand the body of work surrounding the perceptions of alternative sanctions, but also provide evidence that could lead to more accurate sentences resulting in offenders experiencing the consequences intended by our judicial system.

Von Hirsch, Wasik, and Greene (1992) note that, "The time has come to apply a coherent penal rationale to the development of, and choice among, punishments in the community" (p. 370). In this study, we aid in this process by exploring judges' perceptions of alternative sanctions to reveal the opinions and viewpoints of a population that, up to this time, has been unobserved but has perhaps the most direct hand in the assignment of intermediate punishments. Furthermore, as a substantial body of knowledge exists that documents perceptions among offenders (Petersilia, 1994a, 1994b; Spelman, 1995; Wood & Grasmick, 1999; Wood & May, 2003), viable comparisons can be made between these two groups. Despite gains that have been made, "more work is needed to create a meaningful continuum of sanction severity and punishment equivalency" (Wood & Grasmick, 1999, p. 45). As this work is performed, studies may eventually shift from exploratory assessments to research with more direct policy implications. The present study will contribute a significant piece of the continuum puzzle that researchers have been constructing over the past decade.

RESEARCH DESIGN

Sample

The data utilized in this study originate from three different sources. Responses from judges were collected via surveys during the fall of 2004 from all the county judges that were currently serving in the state of Kentucky and had presided over a circuit court (or were currently in that role). Of the 132 active judges in the state, 96 presided in a circuit court and 36 in a family court. A list of the names and addresses of all the sitting judges in the state was solicited from the Administrative Office of the Courts and consequently served as the target sample. Responses from probation/parole officers and probationers and parolees were obtained from May and Wood who have described their data collection elsewhere (Flory et al., 2006 and May et al., 2005, respectively).

The instrument used to collect the data from the three groups under study here was a questionnaire adapted directly from the one utilized by Wood and Grasmick (1999) and Wood and May (2003) and has been described elsewhere (May et al., 2005; Flory et al., 2006). This survey was originally constructed after extensive consultation of incarcerated prisoners in Oklahoma. After creating the instrument, Wood and Grasmick then pretested it on 25 inmates asking them to pay close attention to its wording and structure. Revisions were then later made based on these findings as the instrument was then distributed to a larger sample.

Dependent Variable–Judges' Exchange Rates

The final section consisted of questions pertaining to 9 alternative sanctions including county jail, boot camp, electronic monitoring, regular probation, community service, day reporting, intermittent incarceration, placement in a halfway house, and day fines. Included with each sanction was a short but detailed description depicting the exact ramifications of that sanction in order to ensure that each respondent was considering the same penalty (see Appendix A). After each description, respondents were then asked to consider 12 actual months of medium-security imprisonment and to indicate the exact number of months of the particular sanction they personally would be willing to endure to avoid serving the 12 months of prison time. In doing this, the data will allow for the comparison of alternative sanctions to prison while also providing an indirect means of ranking such alternatives in terms of perceived punitiveness. Despite slight changes made to the wording of several of the demographic questions among each group, the structure and overall makeup of the instrument was maintained due to the acceptable reliability demonstrated in all previous studies where the instrument was used (Flory et al., 2006; May et al., 2005; Wood & May, 2003; Wood & Grasmick, 1999).

Procedures for Data Collection

Given that the procedures used to collect data from probationers, parolees, and their supervising officers have been described elsewhere (see May et al., 2005 and Flory et al., 2006), we will limit the discussion of the data collection for this study to the data from the judicial respondents. Permission to administer the questionnaires to judges was first solicited from the Kentucky Administrative Office of the Court (AOC). Once granted, the surveys were distributed at a state conference where nearly all of the 132 active county judges were expected to attend in the Fall of 2004. Despite our insistence that we be involved in the questionnaire administration at the conference, the distribution and collection of the surveys was delegated to an AOC representative that worked in conjunction with the research team. As such, the exact time, method, and manner the instruments were distributed could not be controlled or monitored. Nevertheless, we were able to compile the contents of the packet to be distributed and, in addition to the questionnaire, we included a cover page introducing the study, provided contact information in case of any problems or questions, and insured the respondents of its anonymous nature.

After the completed surveys were returned from the conference, follow-up packets were sent approximately 30 days later to every judge whose name and address was provided by the court administrator contact. The packet contained an introduction letter, the survey, and a pre-stamped return envelope. Given that we were no longer able to insure anonymity, the cover letter provided details of the research, declared the confidential basis with which data were to be collected, provided contact information in the case of any problems or questions, and instructed the judge to discard the questionnaire if they had completed it at the conference in the previous month. Packages containing follow-up letters and copies of the questionnaire were mailed approximately two weeks after the initial mailing; a similar packet was mailed for the third time approximately one month after the initial mailing.[1]

FINDINGS

Results presented in Table 1 reflect the general demographics of the respondents (N = 72). As expected, the majority of responding judges were middle-aged, white males who presided in big city suburbs. They generally received between 18 and 20 years of education, which roughly equates to earning a Master's or Juris Doctorate degree. Surprisingly, nearly two-thirds of respondents had been a judge either no longer than 5 years or between 13 and 20 years. Concerning respondents' practices and experiences in the courtroom, the majority of adjudicators conducted less than 20 trials per year and most indicated that over 85

TABLE 1: Judicial Sample Descriptive Statistics

Variable	Percentage
Age	
45 years old and younger	13.5%
46-60 years old	69.4%
61 years old and older	17.1%
Gender	
Male	84.3%
Female	15.7%
Race	
African American/Black	2.9%
Caucasian/White	97.1%
Setting where judge presides	
Country/Nonfarm	12.7%
Town of less than 50,000	14.1%
Big City Suburb	38.0%
Farm	12.7%
Town of 50,000-250,000	4.2%
City of more than 250,000	18.3%
Years of Education	
17 years or less	4.3%
18-20 years	85.6%
21 years or more	10.0%
Judicial Experience	
5 years or less	34.3%
6-12 years	18.3%
13-20 years	31.3%
21 years or more	15.7%

TABLE 1 (continued)

Variable	Percentage
Number of trials conducted each year	
10 trials or less	35.4%
11-20 trials	47.1%
21-30 trials	13.3%
30 trials or more	4.5%
Number of offenders sentenced to prison per year	
50 offenders or less	18.1%
51-125 offenders	40.9%
126-250 offenders	33.3%
251 offenders or more	7.5%
Percentage of cases that result in plea agreement	
50% or lower	3%
51%-85%	26.9%
85% or higher	70.2%
Percentage of those eligible for noncustodial sanctions that are sentenced to prison	
0%-10%	21.6%
11%-30%	30.8%
31%-60%	27.7%
61%-99%	20%
Percentage of offenders who refuse to serve an alternative sanction and opt for prison	
0%-2%	62.1%
3%-6%	21.2%
7%-15%	15.1%
16%-25%	1.5%

percent of cases resulted in plea agreements. While the bulk of respondents admitted incarcerating between 51 and 250 offenders each year, it was interesting to see such a wide and equal distribution of responses when asked the rate of incarceration concerning offenders who were eligible for noncustodial sanctions. Over half of the respondents reported incarcerating between 0 and 30 percent of alternative sanction eligible prisoners while their remaining counterparts designated prison terms to between 31 and 99 percent of those offenders who qualified for alternative sanctions. Results also indicated that a small number of judges did in fact have experience with offenders refusing to participate in alternatives and rather opting for a prison sentence. In fact, over one third of judicial respondents reported witnessing between 3 and 25 percent of offenders opting for incarceration in lieu of an alternative punishment.

Given that (1) no research compares exchange rates of judges with those of any other group and (2) we had access to data regarding exchange rates from offenders (probationers and parolees) and their supervising officers in Kentucky (May et al., 2005; Flory et al., 2006), we then compared the mean exchange rates of judges with offenders and officers. Results presented in Table 2 show that the exchange rates offered by offenders are concentrated in a much narrower range of duration than those generated by judges and officers. Exchange rates vary from 5.54 months to 23.56 months for offenders, but for judges the range is from 6.19 to 39.59 and for officers it is 6.05 to 44.23 months. The results presented in Table 2 further reflect that offenders routinely rate alternatives as more punitive than do judges or officers–with the exception of community service. Offenders will serve an average of 1,817 hours of community service, judges would serve 1,440, and officers would serve only 700.50 hours to avoid 12 months of prison. Offenders clearly view probation as much more severe as do either judges or officers because they will serve about half of the duration of probation as judges and officers. For every other sanction, however, offenders generate lower exchange rates than do either judges or officers–meaning that offenders will serve less of a given alternative to avoid 12 months of imprisonment and view alternatives as more severe than do judges or officers. Relatedly, offenders appear more willing to serve time in prison than judges or officers when compared to alternatives. Note that the least severe sanction in all three groups is regular probation, though judges and officers would do nearly twice the amount of probation to avoid imprisonment than would offenders.

A crude severity ranking of sanctions based on exchange rates provided in Table 2 is depicted in Table 3. Prison is given a score of 12.00 because all other sanctions are in reference to one year of imprisonment. Aside from variation in the range of exchange rates and the fact that judges and offices will do more of an alternative to avoid prison compared to offenders, offenders' and judges' rankings of the severity of criminal justice sanctions are remarkably similar, while officers' rankings diverge in some specific instances. Offenders rank halfway house as more severe than judges, while judges rank community service as more severe than

TABLE 2: Comparison of Mean Exchange Rates Among Offenders, Judges, and Officers

	Offenders (1)			Judges (2)			Officers (3)		
Alt. Sanction	**N**	**Mean**	**St.D.**	**N**	**Mean**	**St.D.**	**N**	**Mean**	**St.D.**
County Jail	587	5.54[2,3]	4.81	65	7.38[1]	3.71	206	8.12[1]	5.79
Boot Camp	574	6.07	5.54	67	6.19	3.72	206	6.05	4.02
Electronic Monitoring	584	13.95[3]	11.82	68	16.25	7.94	206	17.57[1]	12.15
Probation	584	23.56[2,3]	16.54	66	39.59[1]	24.95	206	44.23[1]	25.61
Comm. Service	583	1817.29[3]	1747.34	62	1440.00[3]	2145.44	199	700.50[1,2]	1013.82
Day Reporting	582	17.01[2,3]	14.96	63	32.83[1,3]	25.21	206	22.62[1,2]	20.24
Int. Incarceration	585	14.60	12.34	62	17.58	10.60	206	16.88	13.21
Halfway House	583	14.42[2]	11.96	64	18.47[1]	12.96	206	15.62	10.48
Day Fines	573	12.22[2]	12.80	57	15.62[1,3]	24.39	205	13.48[2]	18.83

[1] Signifies that this group is significantly different ($p < .05$–Tukey HSD test) than Group 1 (ANOVA)
[2] Signifies that this group is significantly different ($p < .05$–Tukey HSD test) than Group 2 (ANOVA)
[3] Signifies that this group is significantly different ($p < .05$–Tukey HSD test) than Group 3 (ANOVA)

TABLE 3: Comparison of Sanction Severity Rankings Among Offenders, Judges, and Officers Based on Exchange Rates in Table 2*

Severity Ranking	Offenders	Judges	Officers
Most Severe	County Jail	Boot Camp	Boot Camp
	Boot Camp	County Jail	County Jail
	Prison	Prison	Community Service
	Day Fines	Day Fines	Prison
	Electronic Monitoring	Electronic Monitoring	Day Fines
	Halfway House	Intermittent Incar.	Halfway House
	Intermittent Incar.	Community Service	Intermittent Incar.
	Day Reporting	Halfway House	Electronic Monitoring
	Community Service	Day Reporting	Day Reporting
Least Severe	Regular Probation	Regular Probation	Regular Probation

*With regard to community service, we assigned respondents 20 hours per week, at four weeks per month based on the total hours of community service for each group in Table 2. Few offenders perform that much community service per week, and our calculation of months of community service may serve to inflate the punitiveness of community service.

offenders. Offenders may not like the close supervision, the curfews, and the ban on visitors associated with halfway house. Judges (and officers), on the other hand, may rank community service as more severe due to aforementioned concerns about shame and embarrassment in the community. Surprisingly, officers rank community service as even more severe than imprisonment (3rd in the severity ranking compared to 7th among judges and 9th among offenders), and their ranking of electronic monitoring is much lower in the severity ranking (8th) than that of offenders and judges (5th). Officers clearly view community service as punitive, but view electronic monitoring as less severe than either judges or offenders.

CONCLUSION

In this study, we combined data collected from judges in Kentucky with data from other studies that we have conducted to compare exchange rates of judges with probationers, parolees, and probation/parole officers from Kentucky, extending the extant body of research on offender exchange rates (e.g., Flory et al., 2006; May & Wood, 2004; May et al., 2005; Wood & Grasmick, 1999; Wood & May, 2003). The results from this study suggest that, with limited exceptions, exchange rates offered by judges more closely resembled exchange rates provided by the officer sample than those of the offenders. With the exception of community service, judges would serve longer amounts of alternative sanctions to avoid prison than offenders themselves stated they would do. Furthermore, for county jail, regular probation, day reporting, halfway house, and day fines, there were statistically significant differences in the exchange rates among the two groups. In each of these cases, the exchange rates of the judges were *higher* than those of offenders, indicating that judges felt prison was a more stringent sanction (when compared to these alternative sanctions) than did the offenders.

Nevertheless, the findings reported here also reveal that judges, while offering higher exchange rates than offenders, differ slightly from officers in their exchange rates as well. Judges offered significantly lower exchange rates than probation and parole officers for community service and significantly higher exchange rates than officers for day reporting and day fines. Additionally, though the differences were not statistically significant, judges would serve lower amounts of probation and electronic monitoring and higher amounts of intermittent incarceration and halfway house to avoid prison. Interestingly, the mean exchange rates for jail were almost identical among each of the three groups. Consequently, the results from this research suggest five important conclusions with implications for policy.

First, the results from this research reveal that neither judges, officers, nor offenders view prison as the harshest punishment. In fact, if there is one universal finding across the three groups, it is the consensus among the groups that 12 months in medium-security prison is roughly equivalent to six months in boot camp. We have now replicated this finding in three states (Oklahoma, Indiana, and Kentucky) among four types of respondents (judges, probation/parole officers, probationers/parolees, and prisoners). As such, both the clients and practitioners in the criminal justice system agree that boot camp (no matter where that camp is located) is approximately twice as punitive as medium security prison.

Secondly, in comparison to offenders and judges, officers would serve far less time in community service to avoid prison. The implications of this finding are twofold. First, as we have suggested elsewhere (Flory et al., 2006), offenders (and now judges) may be basing their perceptions on how much they would be "willing" to serve to avoid prison while officers may be basing their perceptions on how much community service offenders on their caseload have "actually completed" to avoid prison. Second, on the one hand, judges and offenders evidently feel that community service is less hassle than what officers feel it would be for offenders. Judges evidently do not share the same shame/embarrassment or community disapproval that officers may feel while performing community service. Officers appear to view community service as a far more punitive sanction than the judges responsible for sentencing offenders to community service and the offenders sentenced to community service. On the other hand, it could be that this discrepancy is due to the intimate familiarity that officers have with the delivery of community service; in fact, the application of community service may be far more onerous than either offenders or judges know. No matter what the cause, this difference could have dramatic implications for community service as a condition of probation or parole. Future research should explore this topic in greater detail to determine why community service is perceived as such a severe sanction by officers but not judges and offenders.

A third important implication of this finding is that when community/local sanctions (electronic monitoring, halfway house, day reporting, and day fines) are compared with imprisonment, judges feel these sanctions are far less punitive than the offenders that they will sentence to those sanctions. This has major implications for sentencing strategies that are often based on the assumption that revocation followed by imprisonment is the ultimate punitive sanction as a means of enforcing compliance with conditions. The present findings, nevertheless, contradict that assumption and suggest that the "hammer" of incarceration for technical violations of community supervision is not near as heavy for the offenders receiving the sanctions as it is for the judges delivering them. Indeed, the findings presented here suggest that judges would do as well, or perhaps better, to rely on threats of electronic monitoring, day reporting, boot camp, or jail to enforce compliance. According to our data presented here and elsewhere, revocation and subsequent imprisonment are not as punitive to offenders as to officers or judges and supervision strategies that take this into account might assist in reducing the extent to which probation/parole revocations presently contribute to prison crowding.

Fourth, in results presented elsewhere, Moore (2007) determined that exchange rates for day reporting, halfway house, and day fine were best explained in a context whereby a number of factors combine to influence decision-making processes among the judges under study here. When considering each of these sanctions individually, however, all are fairly restrictive but still allow a participant to be somewhat bonded to society. Judges may be acutely aware that sentences are most effective when offenders can maintain with the community or family while serving out sentences. As such, despite the noticeable flexibility these particular punishments include, which allows for offenders to maintain their connections to the community, they are still somewhat restrictive.

This assumption may also explain the higher exchange rates offered by judges for day fines, day reporting, and, to a lesser extent, halfway house when compared to offenders and officers. These particular sanctions may be extremely appealing to judges in that they can serve a dual purpose by having "restrictive flexibility" that can satisfy the public outcry for punishment while also allowing individuals to maintain the established bond they have with the family or community. This initial attraction may bring about a more positive overall view of such sanctions, which, inevitably, converts into higher exchange rates.

Finally, though the initial tendency might be to simply dichotomize the three populations explored herein (i.e., offenders, officers, and judges) into either offending or non-offending groups, it is important that judges be viewed as a separate group due to the tendencies revealed in the data comparison. Like offenders, judges were found to have significantly different mean exchange rates than officers for three alternative sanctions (community service, day reporting, and day fines). Interestingly, each differing rate shared the trend of provided judicial exchange rates being higher than those offered by the probation and parole officers. As such, the data collected here would primarily suggest that, of the three groups explored, judges find prison the most punitive. However, an alternative explanation may be that judges may underestimate the punitive nature of the alternative sanctions, an act that would still explain the higher rates offered by the judicial population and be in accordance with the hedonistic calculus. This underestimation of sorts would be less likely to occur in either the offender or officer population due to their direct experience of either undergoing or enforcing each sanction. However, when comparing all three populations, the data suggest that more direct experience with the justice system tends to be associated with lower offered exchange rates to avoid a one-year prison sentence.

The research reviewed here is not without limitations. There was little variation by gender or race in the judge sample, two of the strongest predictors of preference for prison over alternative sanctions among offenders. This finding matches that of Flory et al. (2006) who determined few differences among the officers by race and gender as well. As such, research such as this should be conducted with larger, more diverse samples from other regions to insure that the findings presented here are not an artifact of the sample used. Secondly, research regarding perceived exchange rates needs to be extended to legislators and other criminal justice officials to determine how their exchange rates compare with those groups under study here. To develop a continuum of sanctions that is more effective at controlling recidivism, and more just in delivering punishments, input from all the aforementioned groups needs to be considered.

Within the limitations of these data, however, the results presented here allow for the exploration of the perceptions of the continuum of punishment among judges, offenders, and officers. Judges play an integral role in the sentencing process, and a better understanding of their perceptions of the punishments they impose should inform the development and implementation of a continuum of sanctions that more accurately embodies principles of desert and proportionate punishment in our criminal justice system. Nevertheless, this effort should not stop here. Efforts to examine perceptions of the punitiveness of prison should be extended to legislators, parole board members, and other influential figures in the realms of corrections and sentencing policy. These efforts should eventually allow researchers to do a better job in designing equitable punishments where some offenders serve their time in the community, rather than in the costly "alternative to alternatives," prison.

NOTE

1. The third mailing was sent only to judges who were indicated to be presiding over a circuit court because several family court judges returned incomplete questionnaires during the first two mailings where they claimed their experience and specialized niche in the justice system had little connection with decisions to impose alternative sanctions on offenders. Based on this evidence, we also assumed (but have no way of knowing with absolute certainty) that any family court judge who attended the fall conference likewise declined to participate in this study for the same reasons. As such, it is likely that all respondents were circuit court judges. Nevertheless, we feel a conservative response rate should be based on the total of 132 active judges, not solely those who presided over a circuit court.

REFERENCES

Cole, G. F., Mahoney, B. F., Thornton, M., & Hanson, R. A. (1988). The use of fines by trial court judges. *Judicature, 71* (6), 325-333.

Crouch, B. M. (1993). Is incarceration really worse than prison? Analysis of offenders' preferences for prison over probation. *Justice Quarterly, 10* (1), 67-88.

Finn, P. (1984). Judicial responses to prison overcrowding. *Judicature*, *67* (7), 318-325.

Flory, C. M., May, D. C., Minor, K. I., & Wood, P. B. (2006). A comparison of punishment exchange rates between offenders under supervision and their supervising officers in Kentucky. *Journal of Criminal Justice, 34* (1), 39-50.

Lurigio, A. J. (1987). The perceptions and attitudes of judges and attorneys toward intensive probation supervision. *Federal Probation, 51* (1), 16-24.

May, D. C., Minor, K. I., Wood, P. B., & Mooney, J. L. (2004). Kentucky probationers' and parolees' perceptions of the severity of prison versus county jail and probation. *Kentucky Justice and Safety Research Bulletin: Justice and Safety Research Center, 6* (4), 1-9.

May, D. C., Wood, P.B., Mooney, J. L., & Minor, K. I. (2005). Predicting offender- generated exchange rates: Implications for a theory of sentence severity. *Crime and Delinquency, 51* (3), 373-399.

Moore, N. T. (2007). *Continuing the reassessment of the punishment continuum: Judicial perceptions of the severity of alternative sanctions.* Unpublished Master's Thesis submitted to Eastern Kentucky University, Richmond, Kentucky.

Morris, N., & Tonry, M. (1990). *Between prison and probation.* New York: Oxford University Press.

Petersilia, J. (1990). When probation becomes more dreaded than prison. *Federal Probation, 54* (1), 23-28.

Petersilia, J., & Deschenes, E. P. (1994a). Perceptions of punishment: Inmates and staff rank the severity of prison versus intermediate sanctions. *Prison Journal, 74* (3), 306-329.

Petersilia, J., & Deschenes, E. P. (1994b). Perceptions of punishment: Inmates and staff rank the severity of prison versus intermediate sanctions. *Federal Probation, 58* (1), 3-8.

Spelman, W. (1995). The severity of intermediate sanctions. *Journal of Research in Crime and Delinquency, 32* (2), 107-135.

Von Hirsch, A. (1990). The ethics of community-based sanctions. *Crime and Delinquency, 36* (1), 162-173.

Von Hirsch, A., Wasik, M., & Greene, J. (1992). Scaling community punishments. In A. Von Hirsch & A. Ashworth, *Principled Sentencing* (pp. 368-388). Boston: Northeastern University Press.

Warr, M. (1989). What is the perceived seriousness of crimes? *Criminology, 27* (4), 795-821.

Williams, A., May, D. C., & Wood, P. B. (2006). The lesser of two evils? A qualitative study of offenders' preferences for prison compared to alternatives. Unpublished paper presented at the annual meetings of the Southern Criminal Justice Association, Charleston, South Carolina.

Wood, P. B., & Grasmick, H. G. (1999). Toward the development of punishment equivalencies: Male and female inmates rate the severity of alternative sanctions compared to prison. *Justice Quarterly, 16* (1), 19-50.

Wood, P. B., & May, D. C. (2003). Racial differences in perceptions of the severity of sanctions: A comparison of prison with alternatives. *Justice Quarterly, 20* (3), 605-631.

Wooldredge, J., & Gordon, J. (1997). Predicting the use of alternatives to incarceration. *Journal of Quantitative Criminology, 13* (2), 121-142.

APPENDIX A

(1) **County Jail**. If you are sent to a county jail, you may spend less time there than you would in prison. However, living conditions are more restrictive in a jail than they generally are in a large prison. Unless assigned to work, you may spend more time in your housing unit, and there are not as many opportunities for sports, school, etc. Jail time is generally viewed as more boring and more restrictive than prison time.

(2) **Boot Camp.** Boot camp is for a shorter time than you would have been sent to prison. But boot camp can be more unpleasant in many ways than living in prison. Boot camp is like basic training in the army. You live with about a hundred other people in one big room. There is regular drill instruction like in the military and you are pushed physically and psychologically to perform beyond your capabilities. You experience loss of sleep. You are required to become physically active and fit. You are constantly supervised by drill instructors that watch you closely. You are generally required to participate in an education program. Virtually all your time and activities are controlled. You are subject to random urinalysis tests and can be sent back to prison if you fail to obey the rules.

(3) **Electronic Monitoring**. On electronic monitoring, you live at home, but your freedom is greatly reduced. You wear an electronic device on your ankle. If you get more than 200 feet from the base unit, the device sends an alarm to a computer. Then an officer who is supervising you knows that you are not where you are supposed to be. On electronic monitoring you are being followed by the computer 24 hours a day. There are strict curfews and rules about when you must stay in your house. If you break these rules, you can be sent to prison. You are subject to random urinalysis tests and can be sent back to prison if you fail to obey the rules.

(4) **Regular Probation**. On probation, you do not spend time in prison, but the amount of time on probation usually lasts much longer than whatever prison sentence you might have gotten. You must see your probation officer at least once a month, but it can be every week if ordered. You must get permission from that probation officer to travel or to move. Your probation officer can require that you stay away from certain people. Your home or car can be searched at any time without a search warrant. If you do not follow the rules you can be sent to prison. You are also subject to random urinalysis tests.

(5) **Community Service**. When you are sentenced to community service, you live at home and can have a job. However, you must work some time without pay to make up for the crime for which you were convicted. You work for a government agency or some local non-profit organization, and you do not have any choice about where or what the job is. The judge decides the number of days and hours you must work. If you fail to work the required days and hours, you can be sent back to prison. You are also subject to random urinalysis testing.

(6) **Day Reporting**. If you are sentenced to day reporting, you can stay home at night, but you must check in at a parole office every day. During the day you must have a job *or* you must go to some center in the community and be involved in activities all day. These activities might include working for no pay in the community, looking for a job, counseling, job training, and education programs. At the end of the day you get to go home. You may be *required* to work, and if you do you must check in *every day* during non-work hours. Failure to abide by the rules can result in you going back to prison. You are also subject to random urinalysis testing.

(7) **Intermittent Incarceration.** With this punishment, you must spend weekends or evenings in the county jail, which typically is much more unpleasant than prison. But, since you are not in prison, you can have a job and be involved with your family and community

when you are not spending time in jail. However, failure to report to jail, or failure to pass a random urinalysis test can result in you returning to prison.

(8) Halfway House. A halfway house is a place where several people convicted of crimes live. There is no strict security like there is in prison, but there are firm rules that you must follow. Halfway houses have rehabilitative programs, and if your behavior improves you are treated better and given more freedom. Break the rules and you can be placed back in prison. As always, you are subject to random urinalysis and searches, and constant observation. You are not allowed to have visitors.

(9) Day Fine. A day fine is based on the amount of money you make each day. You are allowed to subtract some money for your rent, transportation, food, utilities, etc., but whatever is left over you have to pay as a day fine. For example, if you had $20 left each day after expenses, your day fine would be $20 for every day the judge says you have to pay. If the judge gives you a day fine of 90 days, and your day fine rate is $20, you would have to pay a total of $1,800. Failure to pay your fines can result in you being sent back to prison.

The Lesser of Two Evils? A Qualitative Study of Offenders' Preferences for Prison Compared to Alternatives

ALISHA WILLIAMS
DAVID C. MAY
PETER B. WOOD

INTRODUCTION

Despite misgivings about the necessity and effectiveness of mass imprisonment among penologists, the public, and criminal justice practitioners, corrections policy still leans "ever nearer to human warehousing and containment based on risk assessment rather than offending" (Reuss, 2003:429). Yet, an abundance of literature supports the idea that intermediate sanctions are potentially more promising (and possibly more practical) alternatives than incarceration and/or probation for meeting the needs of the offender, community, and correctional system (see Flory, May, Minor, & Wood, 2006, for review).

The use of electronic monitoring, community service, and supervised probation (among others) has grown rapidly over the past three decades to the point where 60% of all convicted criminals are serving community sentences in the United States (May, Wood, Mooney, & Minor, 2005). Such sentencing methods are expected to continue to be widely used due to the sheer volume of criminal actions and prison overcrowding that continues to exist (Flory et al., 2006). Nevertheless, it is plausible to expect that the routine use of intermediate sanctions in the future could increase, particularly if policymakers perceived that these sanctions could punish as severely as prison and are cheaper than prison (Petersilia & Deschenes, 1994; Spelman, 1995). This is a particularly viable option as alternatives to prison were initiated under the supposition that short-term imprisonment is detrimental and should be avoided when possible (Killias, Aebi, & Ribeaud, 2000).

Missing in much of the debate over the value of intermediate punishments and where they belong in a continuum of criminal justice sanctions, however, is an appreciation for how criminal offenders actually experience and rank them. Virtually all descriptions of criminal justice sanctions portray a continuum of severity with probation at one end and imprisonment at the other (Petersen & Palumbo, 1997; Morris & Tonry, 1990; Von Hirsch & Ashworth, 1992; NIJ, 1995; NIJ, 1993). But the development of a sanction continuum–and an associated severity ranking–has been the responsibility of legislators and criminal justice policy-makers that depend primarily on guesswork by persons with no direct knowledge of what it is like to serve various sanctions (Morris & Tonry, 1990). Under these circumstances, the conventional belief that correctional punishment is bounded by probation at one extreme and imprisonment at the other deserves to be questioned. The issue centers on the question of whose opinion is used to determine which sanctions are more severe than others, and whether convicted offenders calculate the same costs and benefits in the same fashion as policy-makers.

Despite a significant increase in research in this area of late (see Flory et al., 2006, for review), these examinations have been primarily quantitative analyses where offender-generated exchange rates are calculated to compare the amount of time respondents would serve in community-based sanctions to avoid specified durations of imprisonment. While these works provide insight into correlates of preference for prison over community supervision, no qualitative analyses that supplement quantitative findings to help understand the thought processes of convicted offenders are presently available. In this article, we use qualitative data from a sample of approximately 600 offenders currently under probation and parole supervision to explain why those who been incarcerated in prison are less willing to serve community sanctions than their counterparts, and more willing to serve prison.

LITERATURE REVIEW

Offenders Perceptions of Prison Compared to Alternatives

Under the presumption that incarceration is the most severe punishment, criminal justice officials often base their sentencing decisions regarding whether custodial or non-custodial sentences should be rendered, and (if custodial) how much to administer on the belief that prison is the most severe punishment an offender can receive (May et al., 2005). However, previous studies have revealed that some offenders opt for a prison term rather than an intermediate sanction. Furthermore, some offenders deem prison as a deterrent while others do not (Flory et al., 2006) and feel that "... prison is a holding tank ... and little or no attempt is made to rehabilitate ..." (Reuss, 2003, p. 427).

Those who support the use of incarceration for reasons associated with deterrence or incapacitation often suggest that the punishing nature of prison will deter individuals from crime. In recent years, however, a number of research efforts have begun to suggest that prison may not be considered to be the most stringent punishment an offender can receive (Wood, 2006). This perception is shared by incarcerated offenders (Spelman, 1995; Wood & Grasmick, 1999; Wood, May, & Grasmick, 2005; May & Wood, 2005), those under community supervision (Wood & May, 2003; May et al., 2005), and criminal justice professionals (Flory et al., 2006). Furthermore, these opinions of the severity of prison appear to differ based on demographic and correctional experience indicators. In a review of research conducted by the RAND Corporation, Petersilia (1990) noted that nearly one third of nonviolent offenders given the option of participating in Intensive Supervision Probation (ISP) chose prison instead. They felt that working everyday, submitting to random urinalysis, and having their privacy invaded were more punitive than a prison term. Many also stated that they would likely be caught violating conditions and revoked back to prison. Similarly, Wood and Grasmick (1999) found that 29.8% of male inmates refused to participate in any duration of ISP to avoid four months of imprisonment–nearly the same refusal rate noted by Petersilia, and over 20% chose a year of imprisonment over any duration of ISP. For these offenders, ISP seems to be viewed as more punitive than imprisonment.

Wood and Grasmick found that the three most important reasons why inmates would choose prison were: (1) "If you fail to complete the alternative sanction, you end up back in prison" (57.7% very important), (2) "Parole and program officers are too hard on the program participants, they try to catch them and send them back to prison" (46.8% very important), and (3) "Inmates are abused by parole and probation officers who oversee the programs" (40.5% very important). The common sentiment among inmates was that they would rather serve out their term and be released rather than invest significant time in an alternative sanction involving potentially abusive program officers and a high likelihood of failure and revocation. For many inmates, particularly those with prior experience serving time in prison, a prison term is preferred to the uncertainty of completing an alternative sanction (Wood & Grasmick, 1999).

Inmates in Spelman's (1995) study observed that: "Probation [ISP] has too many conditions. If you can't meet them, you end up in jail anyway. I'd rather just do the time and pay off my debt to society that way." "On probation, you're on a short leash. If you cross over the line, they give you more time." "The longer it lasts, the more chances you have to mess up. If you break [probation conditions], you'll do longer than a year in jail." (Spelman, 1995:126). What research does exist suggests that alternatives are perceived by many offenders as a significant "gamble" and inmates' assessment of this gamble influences many of them to rate alternative sanctions as more punitive than prison. This is manifested in two ways. Either offenders would choose prison over any duration of an alternative, or they would not serve as much of an alternative as they would prison (Wood & May, 2003; May et al., 2005). Particularly for offenders with prior imprisonment experience, prison may be "the lesser of two evils."

Prison Experience and Preferences for Prison Over Alternatives

Offenders with more prison experience are less willing to serve alternative sanctions and more likely to prefer to serve prison instead (May et al., 2005; Wood, 2006). This contradicts the idea of the traditional probation to prison severity continuum. If prison were perceived by inmates as significantly more punitive than alternatives, then persons with more prison experience should be more willing to serve alternative sanctions–and to serve longer durations of them–to avoid imprisonment. However, this is not the case. Offenders who have acquired knowledge and experience about living in prison appear less fearful of prison than those without such experience. For them, prison is less of an unknown, and for some it may be seen as easier than an alternative sanction–particularly if they perceive the alternative as involving an unacceptable degree of supervision, mistreatment, and/or a high likelihood of revocation. Particularly among inmates with experience serving time, imprisonment becomes familiar, while the outcome of involvement in alternatives is less certain and less attractive. In contrast, persons without prior experience in prison may be more fearful of it, and will opt to do the alternative–and a longer duration of it–in order to avoid prison. Again, this brings into question the deterrent value of imprisonment, since those who have served prison are more likely to choose it when given the choice between prison and an alternative sanction (May et al., 2005). While this may seem strange to those not familiar with serving time, it has been noted that most offenders would rather serve a longer prison term, for example, than a short jail sentence (Fleisher, 1995). Fleisher cites an offender who says he would rather do three or four years at the State Penitentiary before doing one year in the county jail, because "It be too hard to have a good time up in that ol' jail. Now, in prison, that's different." Fleisher goes on to note, "Prison isn't a risk that worries street hustlers. Things such as limited freedom, loss of privacy, violence, and variant sexual activity, which might frighten lawful citizens, don't frighten them" (1995:164).

Case Studies and Offender Publications on the Prison Experience

To our knowledge, no qualitative research exists that reflects offenders' perceptions of the relative punitiveness of correctional sanctions. Morash and Schram (2002) note it is difficult to conduct research in prisons because officials are reluctant to reveal often offensive conditions of institutions and negative effects of imprisonment on inmates, and due to the fear of lawsuits. Nevertheless, some published work draws on interviews with inmates to gain an understanding of life in prison, and a number of incarcerated offenders have written books describing life in prison and how they perceive and experience its effects, whether rehabilitative or dehumanizing.

Hassine (2004) is a prison inmate serving life without parole, and states, ". . . the American prison experience includes a slow, steady regression toward the threshold of madness" (p. 136). Santos (2004) has served over 15 years in prison and gives the correctional system high marks for achieving mass incapacitation of offenders. At the same time, he notes that "If rehabilitation remains a goal of the prison system . . . then administrators are failing miserably" (2004:217). Camhi (1989) sought the perspectives of California inmates on imprisonment. While some respondents were optimistic, others were far less enthusiastic about the rehabilitative proponents of incarceration. For example, one inmate retorted that prison is a "far cry from rehabilitation" (p. 103) and teaches people to perfect their criminal craft and makes them even more malicious. In contrast, a first-time offender stated that prison made him appreciate the value of life and freedom, and made him a more sensible, concentrated, and disciplined individual (Camhi, 1989). However, most inmates spoke about the lack of programming to help them prepare for reintegration into society, the violence, and inhumane treatment and conditions in prisons (e.g., inadequate medical care, poor meals, and victimization) (Camhi, 1989). Given that this programming is often more easily available in community settings, sentences to probation or parole in lieu of prison could be beneficial in this regard.

Santos (2004) notes that after five years or so of imprisonment, prisoners grow accustomed to it, and after spending most of his adult life in prison, it has become a way of life and he doesn't feel like he's being punished at all. As time progressed, it has become ". . . much more difficult for me to reconcile my time behind these fences with the crimes I committed during the Reagan presidency" (2004:216). After five years or so, inmates adjust to incarceration, and "life becomes normal and predictable, although within a restricted, harsh, and sometimes inhumane closed society" (2004:216). Santos likens imprisonment to exile, a context in which one learns to live with his/her environment.

Though ample work exists that documents offenders' adjustments to prison life and the experience of living in prison, these accounts are anecdotal and idiosyncratic at best, and to date there are no studies that provide a qualitative analysis of how offenders compare imprisonment with non-custodial sanctions. Work presented here attempts to fill that void by presenting aggregated results from a qualitative inquiry of 600 convicted offenders who were asked why they might choose prison over community-based sanctions. By doing so, we hope to more fully explore the ecology of offender decision-making, acquire a better understanding of how offenders experience imprisonment and alternatives, and why many offenders would choose to serve prison even when given the option of a community-based punishment–a decision which runs counter to the conventional belief of the continuum of criminal sanctions and which challenges assumptions central to deterrence.

METHODS AND FINDINGS

Data

The data used in this study were collected in the fall of 2003 from seven state probation and parole offices in Kentucky. Using a sample of offenders under the supervision of community corrections, this study sought to use a qualitative approach to observe offenders' preferences of prison over alternative sanctions. A purposive sampling method was chosen to obtain a large enough sample to have a good proportion of urban, Black, and female offenders to make significant assessments between the parties. The final sample consisted of 618 participants. Of the estimated 27,000 probationer and parolees under supervision in Kentucky at the end of 2003, the sample represented 2.3 percent of that population.[1]

Three in four (77.4%) respondents were male; slightly over half (55.7%) of the respondents were White while one in three (37.9%) respondents were African-American. Although the respondents were not asked to identify the specific crime for which they were sentenced to community supervision, the vast majority of the respondents (86.5%) were currently under community supervision for a felony conviction. Two in five (40.3%) respondents were under community supervision as the result of a drug-related conviction. Roughly half of respondents (47.6%) reported they had served time in prison before, while 52.4% said they had not (a full description of the demographic and contextual characteristics of this sample can be found in May et al., 2005). As expected, far more parolees (91.8%) than probationers (18.7%) had been incarcerated in prison.

Sampling

Members of the research team distributed the questionnaires to those offenders who were at the probation/parole offices to attend to their required appointments. Typically, a research team member was stationed in a vacant office or break room; officers were instructed to send offenders to that area upon completion of the interview. Consequently, the number of respondents available to supply data was dependent upon the support of the officers in sending participants to complete the questionnaire on the day the observers arrived.[2] Respondents were given a letter of consent that: (1) asked for the participant's signature giving informed consent; (2) informed the participants that their involvement was voluntary and that they could answer any, all, or none of the questions; (3) described the purpose of the study; and (4) assured the confidentiality and anonymity of the responses to the questionnaire. The member of the research team then gave respondents the option of completing the questionnaire on their own or having it read aloud to them. Less than one in five (19.0%) declined consent and roughly ten percent of the participants asked that the instruments be read.

Survey

An eight-page questionnaire introduced in several other studies (May et al., 2005; Wood & Grasmick, 1999; Wood & Grasmick, 1995; Wood & May, 2003; Wood et al., 2005) was the instrument administered to collect the data. The respondents were given descriptions of nine alternative sanctions, including boot camp, community service, day reporting, county jail, regular probation, intermittent incarceration, day fines, and halfway houses, after answering a number of demographic questions. After the offenders had completed a series of closed-ended questions (see May et al., 2005 for review), respondents were asked two open-ended questions. Responses to those questions provided the data under analysis here.

First, respondents were asked, "In previous research we have done, we've determined that some people would rather do prison time than any amount of an alternative. Why would someone make that choice?" This question was followed by a second question: "In previous research, we've also determined that some people would rather do an alternative than any length of prison sentence. Why would someone make that choice?"

The responses to these questions were recorded with an audio recorder by the interviewer and later transcribed into electronic text. We then searched the text for words and phrases that regularly appeared in the electronic text. Through this process, we identified a number of responses that were similar for both questions. We then combined like responses into the categories presented below.

Reasons for Choosing Prison

Responses to the first question (hereafter referred to as *Prison Choice*) are presented in Table 1. These responses indicate that the most popular Prison Choice response was that the respondent had no idea why an offender would choose prison over an alternative (17.3%); an additional 9.3% of the respondents said they would rather do the alternative than prison. Thus, over one in four respondents (26.6%), even when asked the question in hypothetical terms where they are responding why *other* offenders would choose prison over alternatives could not explain why someone would make that choice.

Nevertheless, the remainder of the respondents offered a wide variety of reasons why offenders would make a Prison Choice. Over one in four respondents said that prison is easier than the alternative (14.7%) or, similarly, that the alternatives were harder than prison (13.5%). One in six responded that an offender can get out of prison quicker than if they served the alternative (14.4%). Furthermore, 10.1% of the participants

TABLE 1. Why Would Offenders Choose Prison Over an Alternative?

Prison Over Alternatives Category Description	N	%
Respondent had no idea why someone would make that choice	107	17.3%
Prison is easier than the alternative	91	14.7%
Time goes by quicker in prison or a prisoner is released sooner	89	14.4%
The alternative is harder than prison	84	13.5%
There is more freedom in prison than in jail	79	12.7%
People fear being sent back to prison if they fail in the alternative	63	10.1%
I would rather do the alternative sanction	58	9.3%
Some offenders lack life skills to be successful in alternatives	56	8.5%
Prisoners have no responsibilities	48	7.7%
An offender may have already been to prison	39	6.3%
Some choose prison to escape the rules of alternative sanctions	23	3.7%
Some offenders don't want to deal with the probation officer	22	3.5%
Some offenders have no outside support from family or friends	19	3.0%
Prison is better than alternative	15	2.4%
Some offenders don't want to change or get treatment	7	1.1%
An offender has experienced the alternative and doesn't want to do it again	5	0.8%
Other (responses that didn't fit into any particular category)	26	4.5%

said that offenders were afraid of getting into trouble and having the alternative revoked. Despite the use of the term "alternatives" in the research question, some respondents interpreted this to mean jail. One in eight (12.7%) offenders say prison is preferred over an alternative because there is more freedom in prison than in jail. Thus, some offenders compared prison to *jails* as an alternative, in which case they felt that prison provides more programs, opportunities for advancement, and privileges (as presented in the previous statements) than do county or municipal jails. This supports prior work among criminal offenders that finds that jail is consistently viewed as more punitive than prison (Wood & Grasmick, 1999; Wood & May, 2003).

Additionally, almost one in ten (8.5%) respondents stated that some offenders lack the skills necessary to function in society. A number of respondents also said that offenders would make a Prison Choice because they "don't want to face their responsibilities," "they use prison to escape the rules of the alternative sanction," or "they do not want to deal with the probation officers" (7.7% and 3.7%, 3.5%, respectively). Several participants stated that offenders that have had prior experience in prison would be more likely to make a Prison Choice (6.3%) and that offenders make a Prison Choice because they have no outside support to help them stay out of prison (3.0%).

Reasons for Choosing an Alternative

Responses to the second question (hereafter referred to as the *Alternative Choice*) are presented in Table 2. The responses in Table 2 indicate that 5.8% of the sample answered that they didn't know why an offender would make an Alternative Choice. Consequently, unlike with the prison choice, the vast majority of the offenders understood why other offenders would choose an alternative over prison.

The majority of the participants believed that offenders made the Alternative Choice because they can stay on the streets and have freedom and because they can maintain social ties with family and friends (29% and 27.1%, respectively). Moreover, a large percentage of participants insisted that offenders would choose the alternative because they feared prison (13.6%), wanted to be rehabilitated (11.6%), wanted to continue to take advantage of gainful employment (10%), and wanted to maintain the responsibilities they have on the streets (5.5%). Additionally, 9.3% of respondents answered that offenders choose the alternative because they believe that it is easier, yet only 2.9% said that the alternative is better than prison.

TABLE 2. Why Would an Offender Choose an Alternative Over Prison?

Category Description	N	%
Offenders choose alternative for freedom on the streets	185	29.0
Offenders want to maintain social ties	168	27.1
Offenders want to change and be rehabilitated	72	11.6
Offenders are afraid to go to prison	85	13.6
Offenders want to maintain employment	65	10.5
Alternatives are easier than prison	58	9.3
Don't Know	36	5.8
To continue maintaining their responsibilities like family and jobs	34	5.5
Offender has never been to prison	20	3.2
Offender thinks the alternative is better	18	2.9
First-time offenders don't feel they should have to go to prison	16	2.5
Offenders choose alternative because they have never done it	16	2.5
Offenders who are not career criminals will choose the alternative	11	1.7
Offender has experienced prison and doesn't want to go back	10	1.6
Offenders choose alternative to have control over their own actions	8	1.2
Other (responses that didn't fit into any particular category)	7	1.1

Nevertheless, 3.2% of the sample stated that offenders make the Alternative Choice because they don't have any prison experience. Even so, respondents revealed that offenders who are charged with their first offense and who have not experienced the alternative will make the Alternative Choice (2.5% and 2.5%, respectively). However, only 1.2% of the participants stated the people who have experienced prison will make the Alternative Choice in the future.

BIVARIATE RESULTS AND COMMENTS FROM OFFENDERS

Given that prior work finds those with prison experience are more likely to choose prison over alternatives, we examined the impact of previous incarceration in prison on both Prison Choice and Alternative Choice. For each of the categories presented in Tables 1 and 2, respondents who provided an answer that fit into a response category were coded (1) while all other respondents were coded (0). For example, all respondents who stated that offenders would make the Prison Choice because prison is easier than the alternative were coded (1); all other respondents were coded (0). As the results in Table 1 suggest, 91 respondents were coded (1) on the variable representing the "Prison Choice Because It Is Easier" variable; the remaining respondents were coded (0).

Respondents who had been incarcerated in prison were then coded (1) while those who had not been incarcerated were coded (0). Responses were fairly evenly divided between the two groups (47.6% reported they had served time in prison before while 52.4% said they had not). Cross-tabulations were then conducted that examined differences between the variable representing whether or not the respondent had been incarcerated in prison and each category for the Prison Choice and Alternative Choice variables. The statistically significant relationships from those cross-tabulations are presented in Table 3.[3]

Prison Experience and the Choice of Prison v. Alternatives

The respondent's prison experience had a statistically significant relationship with five of the open-ended responses (listed in Table 3). First, respondents who had been to prison were significantly more likely to state that someone might make a Prison Choice because they felt that people ". . . had more freedom in prison than in jail." Although the question was intended to elicit responses about *all* alternative sanctions,

TABLE 3. Categorical Responses Demonstrating Statistically Significant Differences by Prison Experience*

	No Prison Experience		Prison Experience	
	% Yes	% No	% Yes	% No
Offenders choose alternative to have more freedom	9.3%	90.7%	16.7%	83.3%
Offender has experienced prison and doesn't want to go back	0.6%	99.4%	2.8%	97.2%
Offenders want to maintain social ties	30.9%	69.1%	23.0%	77.0%
Offenders are afraid to go to prison	8.7%	91.3%	14.9%	85.1%
Time goes by quicker in prison; Offenders are released sooner	18.3%	81.7%	11.0%	89.0%

* All differences were significant at $p < .05$ or below using the Phi/Cramer's V statistics.

many of the respondents apparently felt that jail was an alternative to prison and thus answered accordingly. For these respondents, the "freedom" that prisoners have (when compared to jails) is an important reason for the choice of a prison sanction over alternative sanctions. This sentiment is evidenced by the following comments:

> 'Cause in prison you can get around, you can move and you got daily activities and in county you can't, you ain't got none of that, got too much to do on probation. I would go to the joint first. (Respondent 161)

> 'Cause in prison, you know, you can probably go outside, you can play basketball, lift weights, smoke cigarettes, whatever. In jail you can't do none of that. (Respondent 3)

> Prison time would be more easy, because once you get inside, you can work, there's a lot of activities; plus you can walk around. (Respondent 12)

> 'Cause prison's just right out easier, you can lay back and you ain't gotta do nothing. (Respondent 35)

Second, those participants who had not experienced prison were significantly more likely to make an Alternative Choice because they feared prison; thus, respondents who had not been to prison may thus be caught up in the disheartening stories they have heard about prison. The following statements exemplify these beliefs:

> They heard of things that may or may not be true, just scared of prison. (Respondent 26)

> Fear of prison fear of jail. (Respondent 403)

> Because some people might be scared of the penitentiary and what they've heard about it. (Respondent 21)

> Uh, to keep from having to go to prison, uh, to keep, I don't know, uh, there's just so many rumors about prison, what happens, what goes on in there, and some people really don't wanna find out what happens, they'd rather try to take care of it otherwise. (Respondent 11)

> Just to some people to keep them from going to prison. I guess it would scare some people. (Respondent 129)

Third, respondents who had not been to prison were significantly more likely to say that offenders would make the Prison Choice because they can complete their sentence more quickly in prison than by completing the alternative. Offenders know that "good time" reduces their prison sentence substantially. This sentiment is noted by the following statements:

> A lot of times the sentencing for prison would be a lot less than probation. (Respondent 403)

> To get it done and over with. If it's a short amount of time in jail then they would rather go ahead and . . . and get it over with but if it's a long time they would rather do it on paper cause your going to be a lot easier. (Respondent 385)

> I've heard that uh prison time is shorter. (Respondent 335)

Furthermore, offenders realize they can follow the rules in prison more easily and earn good time, while alternatives can extend the offenders' sentence through technical violations so that offenders wind up going to prison anyway after possibly serving a majority of their time "on paper."

> People have problem with, uh, their behavior, and they mess up with alternative sanction instead of prison work and go ahead and get it over with and get it out of the way. (Respondent 548)

> Just don't wanna be bothered with it, hassles of the programs. (Respondent 428)

> So just serve it out you don't have to come in and report every day you don't have to take drug tests every time you report you just serve your time out and you're basically a free man or woman opposed to having to still come and see a probation officer. (Respondent 392)

Fourth, those respondents who have been to prison were significantly more likely to say that offenders would make a Prison Choice because they have experienced the alternative before and would rather not deal with the strict rules and probation officers of an alternative sanction. The following comments reflect these feelings:

> 'Cause sometimes the prison time's easier you know you got schedules and things to do and you get in a routine and it's a lot easier than going by all these rules and having to sweat going back to prison and what your parole officer gonna say. (Respondent 146)

> 'Cause they don't like the program. (Respondent 66)

> 'Cause dealing with the parole officers is bad enough, cause if you don't continue the alternative, you're gonna get sent back anyways. (Respondent 567)

Finally, those respondents who have not been to prison were significantly more likely to state that an offender would make the Alternative Choice because they want to continue to have social networks in the community with friends and family. The following statements shed light on these perspectives:

> I made that choice cause I have a son, that I'd rather be with, and I'd rather be out here than in prison. (Respondent 25)

> Uh, personal reasons, family, kids, wife, uh, job, things like that; some people are just physically, there are things about prison, people are afraid of whatever they heard of things that may or may not be true, just scared of prison, but either family, job, kids, or they just afraid of prison. (Respondent 26)

> Because usually they have children, and family, the spouse, the grandparent, mother, father, or someone may be ill. (Respondent 30)

DISCUSSION

Over 600 probationers and parolees were asked for their opinions on why a convicted offender might choose to serve prison rather than an alternative sanction, and vice versa. Responses to this large-scale qualitative inquiry were then analyzed, grouped, and presented in aggregate fashion.

Respondents with prison experience reason that offenders would select prison in order to avoid the terms, strict supervision, and abusive program administrators they might encounter under an alternative sanction. This seems to represent offenders' tendency to choose the least restrictive sanction, and it could also be argued that an offender's decision to choose prison over an alternative is contingent upon whether or not they had a negative experience with that or some other alternative. Qualitative results presented here support findings from quantitative research showing that many offenders would prefer to serve out a prison term and be released with no strings attached rather than invest time in an alternative sanction under restrictive supervision and with a significant likelihood of revocation. What's more, those respondents with prison experience were more likely to say that offenders may choose alternatives over prison because they are afraid to go to prison, and because they are intimidated by the rumors they've heard about prison.

In comparison, respondents who have not been to prison more often stated that offenders might choose the alternative over prison to maintain social ties in the community. This suggests that offenders with strong social bonds in the community may think that with such support, they have a greater probability of successfully completing an alternative program. Finally, those with no prior prison experience more often stated that offenders could choose prison over the alternative because they might get out quicker. Due to the fact that the participants are serving alternative sanctions, they know that penalties for violations of strict conditions of supervision could lead to an extended sentence or revocation. These respondents generally knew that, in prison, offenders can earn "good time" for appropriate behavior and be released earlier than their original sentence.

LIMITATIONS

Although this study was the first to present qualitative findings from probationers and parolees regarding reasons for choosing alternatives over prison (and vice versa), this study is not without limitations. Given that the questions asked were fairly specific, there were a limited number of responses for many answer categories. As such, this reduced the possibility of achieving significant differences in the responses. Therefore, in future studies, rather than asking open-ended questions, researchers should use structured interviews, where they begin a discussion on a particular topic (in this case, reasons for choices of alternatives over prison) and then let the respondent drive the discussion rather than asking focused questions with limited response categories. This approach should allow the respondents the freedom to give answers that represent their exact sentiments in order to obtain richer data.

POLICY IMPLICATIONS

The qualitative results presented here replicate quantitative findings presented in a number of other works (reviewed earlier) and provide some much-needed context in which to view those earlier findings. The findings presented here continue to cast doubt on the value of prison as a specific deterrent mechanism; if anything, prior prison experience makes one *less* fearful of prison and *more* willing to return to prison rather than serve their time under community supervision. The significance of our findings for rational choice/deterrence and social learning theories generates potentially provocative and controversial issues. In fact, as May et al. (2005) have suggested elsewhere, most research on intermediate sanctions determines they are generally no more or less effective than imprisonment in reducing future crime; however, they are potentially less *expensive* than imprisonment. If alternative sanctions are equally effective (or ineffective) as incarceration in prison in reducing recidivism, perceived by offenders as equally punitive, and significantly less expensive than imprisonment, there seems good reason to expand their use.

Our results also continue to raise serious doubts about the validity of a continuum of sanctions bounded by regular probation at one extreme and traditional incarceration at the other. Offenders with personal experience of both imprisonment and alternatives identify several alternatives as more punitive than prison and provide a number of justifications for doing so. Consequently, our findings suggest a more complex decision-making process than that traditionally attributed to criminal offenders, who are uniquely aware of the pitfalls awaiting them should they enroll in certain alternatives. The conventional wisdom of placing regular probation at the low end of a continuum of sanction severity may be valid, but it seems clear many offenders perceive some noncustodial sanctions as more onerous than traditional incarceration. Until policy-makers understand this social fact, incarceration will continue to be used for some offenders in some situations where alternative sanctions might punish more effectively, no matter what rationale for punishment is intended.

REFERENCES

Camhi, M. (1989). *The Prison Experience*. Vermont: Tuttle-ICP.

Crouch, B. M. (1993). Is incarceration really worse? Analysis of offenders' preferences for prison over probation. *Justice Quarterly, 10*, 67-88.

Fleisher, M. S. (1995). *Beggars and thieves: Lives of urban street criminals*. Madison, WI: University of Wisconsin Press.

Flory, C. M., May, D. C., Minor, K.I., & Wood (2006). A comparison of punishment exchange rates between offenders under supervision and their supervising officers. *Journal of Criminal Justice, 34*, 39-50.

Hassine, V. (2004). *Life Without Parole: Living in Prison Today. California: Roxbury Publishing Company.*

Killias, M., Aebi, M., & Ribeaud, D. (2000). Does community service rehabilitate better than short-term imprisonment?: Results of a controlled experiment. *The Howard Jounal, 39*(1), 40-57.

May, D. C., & Wood, P. B. (2005). What Influences Offenders' Willingness to Serve Alternative Sanctions?. *The Prison Journal, 85*, 145-167.

May, D. C., Wood, P. B., Mooney, J. L., & Minor, K. I. (2005). Predicting offender-generated exchange rates: Implications for a theory of sentence severity. *Crime and Delinquency, 51*, 373-399.

Morash, M., & Schram, P. J. (2002). *The Prison Experience: Special Issues of Women in Prison*. Illinois: Waveland Press INC.

Morris, N., & Tonry, M. (1990). *Between prison and probation: Intermediate punishment in a rational sentencing system*. New York: Oxford Press.

National Institute of Justice. (1993). *Intermediate sanctions: Research in brief*. Washington D. C.: U.S. Government Printing Office.

National Institute of Justice. (1995). *National assessment program: 1994 survey results*. Washington D.C.: U.S. Government Printing Office.

Petersen, R. D., & Palumbo, D. J. (1997). The social construction of intermediate punishments. *The Prison Journal, 77*, 77-92.

Petersilia, J. (1990). When Probation becomes more dreaded than prison. *Federal Probation, 54*, 23-27.

Petersilia, J., & Deschenes, E. P. (1994). What punishes? Inmates rank the severity of prison vs. intermediate sanctions. *Federal Probation, 58*(1), 3-9.

Reuss, A. (2003). Taking a long hard look at imprisonment. *The Howard Journal, 42*(5), 426-436.

Rose, D. R., & Clear, T. R. (2004). Who doesn't know someone in jail? The impact of exposure to prison on attitudes toward formal and informal controls. *The Prison Journal, 84*(2), 228-247.

Santos, M. G. (2004). *About prison*. Thomson/Wadsworth Publishing Company.

Spelman, W. (1995). The severity of intermediate sanctions. *Journal of Research in Crime and Delinquency, 32*, 107-135.

Von Hirsch, A., & Ashworth, A. (Eds.). (1992). *Principled sentencing*. Boston, MA: Northeastern University Press.

Wood, P. B. (2006). The Myth that Imprisonment is the Most Severe Form of Punishment. Chapter 22 (pp. 192-200) in *Demystifying Crime and Criminal Justice* by Robert Bohm and Jeffrey Walker (Eds.). Roxbury Publishing Company.

Wood, P. B., & Grasmick, H. G. (1995). Inmates rank the severity of ten alternative sanctions compared to prison. *Journal of the Oklahoma Research Consortium*, (2), 30-42.

Wood, P. B., & Grasmick, H. G. (1999). Toward the development of punishment equivalencies: Male and female inmates rate the severity of alternative sanctions compared to prison. *Justice Quarterly, 16*, 19-50.

Wood, P. B., & May, D. C. (2003). Race differences in perceptions of sanction severity: A comparison of prison with alternatives. *Justice Quarterly, 20*, 605-631.

Wood P. B., May, D. C., & Grasmick, H. G. (2005). Gender differences in the perceived severity of boot camp. *Journal of Offender Rehabilitation, 40*(3-4), 145-167.

NOTES

1. In the state of Kentucky, felony probationers and parolees are supervised by officers that work out of the same office. These officers typically supervise both probationers and parolees as part of their caseload.

2. Our original intention was to interview the probationers and parolees in the waiting area prior to the visit with their supervising officers. Nevertheless, the supervising officers insisted that we interview the respondents after their meeting, rather than before. It is possible that respondents whose visit with their supervising officer went well may have responded that they were more willing to do community sanctions than those whose visit was more unpleasant. While we have no way of knowing the impact that the order of the interview had upon the results of this study, we are confident that its impact was minimal, as most of the respondents had ample experience (both good and bad) with community corrections before the interview date.

3. Because officers in Kentucky typically supervise both parolees and probationers as part of their caseload, and we felt that the incarceration experience was far more important to an individual's perception of the relative punitiveness of prison when compared to alternative sanctions, we originally did not distinguish between parolees and probationers in the analysis reported here. During the review process, we conducted separate analyses for probationers and parolees on the variables under study here and determined that, by and large, there were no substantive differences between probationers and parolees in the relationships reported here. Nevertheless, respondents under parole supervision were significantly more likely than probationers to suggest that time passes more quickly in prison while respondents under probation supervision were significantly more likely than parolees to respond that people fear being sent back to prison if they fail in the alternative. Future research should explore the interaction between type of supervision and prison experience to attempt to determine the complex nature of these relationships.

Community Supervision of Undocumented Immigrants in the United States: Probation and Parole's Role in the Debate

DIANE KINCAID

UNDOCUMENTED IMMIGRANTS IN THE COMMUNITY

The effects of undocumented immigrants (also referred to as "illegal immigrants" or "Illegal aliens" throughout this article) in the U.S. criminal justice system has received much reporting of late; however, for all the media attention on the issue of illegal immigration, little national attention has been placed on the effect of these immigrants on state probation and parole systems. Following requests from several state community corrections officials who were interested in knowing more about the impact of undocumented immigrants in other states, in the summer of 2005, the American Probation and Parole Association (APPA) conducted an informal request for information from its members on the topic of community supervision of unauthorized immigrants in their jurisdictions. The results were not surprising to the field of probation and parole but may be to those who do not recognize the implications of having thousands of offenders whose supervision, for public safety reasons, must be taken as seriously and done as completely as for those offenders who are legal residents of the U.S.

WHO IS HERE ILLEGALLY?

The first hurdle faced by both law enforcement and state judicial systems is in identifying which offenders are unauthorized immigrants. In estimating the unauthorized immigrant population, the Office of Immigration Statistics under the Department of Homeland Security (2006, p. 2) specifies that, "(t)he unauthorized immigrant population is defined as all foreign-born non-citizens who are not legal residents. Unauthorized residents refer to foreign-born persons who entered the United States without inspection or who were admitted temporarily and stayed past the date they were required to leave." The Office of Immigration Statistics (2006) estimates that there were 10.5 million unauthorized immigrants residing in the U.S. in January 2005. While law enforcement and corrections may have access to information in databases such as the Immigration Alien Query (IAQ) through the Law Enforcement Support Center (LESC) or the National Crime Information Center (NCIC), what if the offender does not appear in any of these systems? According to a Fact Sheet produced by the Immigration and Customs Enforcement (ICE) office (2006, p. 1) regarding access and usage of LESC, "(i)n 2004 and 2005, the eleven ICE Special Agents assigned to the LESC lodged a combined total of 27,886 ICE immigration detainers for an average of 1,200 detainers a month. Of the 27,886 detainers, 12,414 were criminals and fugitives who were NCIC hits." These offenders then represent only about 45% of the total number of detainers. It is not clear that these unauthorized immigrants have never committed crimes or simply that they have never been entered into NCIC with the information provided to local authorities at the time of the current NCIC check. There is also the possibility that these offenders have not given the same information to authorities as was logged into the databases through falsification and fear of being deported or simple misunderstandings. Possibilities range from the offender never having encountered authorities who may have entered information into these systems to misunderstandings about cultural naming practices such as those of many from Spanish-American descent. Names from many Spanish speaking nations in Latin America follow a pattern of first name, father's surname then mother's surname. Thus an offender entering the system may give his name using all three names, or perhaps just first and middle if he has learned that in the U.S., most use the father's surname as a last name. There are multiple possibilities for mistaken identity based on this theme. A report by the Urban Institute (Clark, 2000, p. vii) explains additional problems in correctly identifying unauthorized aliens and adds, "(m)isidentification as natives would probably be limited to aliens who are not arrested for immigration offenses and who, among those charged with federal offenses, at least, could produce a social security number." These offenders are also the ones most likely to pass through state level courts and probation/parole offices.

UNDOCUMENTED IMMIGRANTS ON PROBATION AND PAROLE SUPERVISION IN THE COMMUNITY

APPA conducted this request for information on undocumented immigrants on probation or parole as part of its regular "Hot Topics" series. Hot topics are questions on issues of interest to the field of community supervision that are sent via APPA's electronic newsletter published twice each month. The questionnaire was reviewed for accuracy and correct terminology by a senior analyst with the U.S. Department of Homeland Security, Immigration and Customs Enforcement, Office of Detention and Removals prior to being posted on the APPA Web site. The 220 responses came from several levels of community corrections including 34 state chief probation officers or state chief court services officers, 21 state directors, eleven U.S. Probation and Pretrial Services Districts as well as many state level line staff. Of the responses, 33 states were represented including the District of Columbia.

Assuming a court has identified an offender as being in the U.S. illegally, the next question is how serious an offense has this person committed? Respondents revealed that most offenses were misdemeanors and may then qualify the offender to less than one year in jail or more likely, to be placed on probation supervision in the community. Considering the costs to county governments to incarcerate offenders, unless an unauthorized immigrant is considered a high risk to public safety, he or she will more than likely not be sentenced to a jail term. While there is research available on unauthorized immigrants incarcerated in prison (particularly at the federal level), there is little information available on those sentenced to community supervision. The national costs associated with community supervision, counseling and possible treatment for substance abuse, mental illness or to provide victim services are difficult to estimate.

Another question posed to APPA members concerned whether the local probation/parole agency had a formal relationship with a local ICE office. Seventy-four percent of those responding indicated that they did not have such a relationship. Comments came from all areas of the U.S., not only large metropolitan areas. APPA received the responses below from the upper mid-west, one western state and one north-eastern state:

> We don't really have any relationship with what they now call "Homeland Security," they don't care! It took my receptionist four hours to convince Homeland Security that I had an illegal alien on probation that they have been looking for four years to deport.
>
> I've contacted the agency concerning one of the offenders. Their response is rather "stand-offish."
>
> Basically it's a reporting relationship. Due to lack of enforcement, we simply report as needed and proceed as if they will not take any action.
>
> (W)e call them . . . they ignore us.

While others responded with more favorable comments regarding ICE:

> We are able to contact a local agent when there is a concern.
>
> We are in constant contact with the ICE office and often will send them forms identifying who our illegal aliens are. In addition, they often call us when they plan to detain one of our clients. Probably could be a closer relationship.

An audit released by the U.S. Department of Justice (2007, p. iv) reporting on the cooperation of states with ICE officials notes, "we found that local jurisdictions often set the enforcement of state and local law as priority, while sometimes permitting or encouraging law enforcement agencies and officers to work with ICE to some degree on immigration matters."

APPA's data indicates that there is no standardized process within state community corrections systems to notify ICE of unauthorized immigrants who pass through their judicial system. In fact, 66% of respondents indicated that their agency has no policies or arrangements in place for notifying ICE when illegal aliens are placed on probation, parole or community supervision. While responses came primarily from state level officers and officials in community corrections, the system of notification may be no better at the federal level:

> Federal probation authorities in Brooklyn, who currently (2004) have 148 illegal alien felons on their active caseload, have given up trying to coordinate with ICE on deportation. "You send the paperwork over to the INS (Immigration and Naturalization Service), and you never hear back," explains the federal probation official. "We used to have a person assigned to us from the agency, who told us to not even bother sending over forms." (MacDonald, 2004, p. 6)

The previously referenced (2007, p. vi) audit indicates similar frustrations voiced by respondents from jurisdictions receiving SCAAP reimbursements who, "criticized ICE and stated they do not inform ICE about possible undocumented aliens in their custody because they believe ICE will not respond."

STATES TAKING ACTION

Some states have taken a more active roll in enforcing immigration laws. In January 2007, Governor Deval Patrick of Massachusetts announced a plan to train a group of corrections officers in state prisons in Framingham and Concord to initiate deportation proceedings against convicted criminals identified as illegal immigrants. Arizona and several counties in California have similar programs. Such programs are seen as necessary where as noted by Massachusetts Public Safety Secretary, Kevin Burke, "incarcerated illegal immigrants sometimes escape notice because federal authorities lack the resources to check on the immigration status of inmates" (Saltzman, 2007). There is every indication that enforcement of immigration laws is becoming more and more a state issue and cost. While it is correct that the federal system bears the brunt of prosecuting illegal immigration cases, they are involved to a far lesser degree in criminal cases involving undocumented immigrants. The majority of costs incurred from these cases fall upon already stretched state budgets.

If states accept the responsibility of supervising undocumented immigrants, additional resources must be provided and while the federal government allocates funds to states for some costs associated with these offenders through the State Criminal Alien Assistance Program (SCAAP), there are no funds allocated to assist in the costs for community supervision. The Bureau of Justice Assistance (2006, p. 1) administers the SCAAP program and delineates the requirements for reimbursements to states: "SCAAP provides federal payments to states and localities that incurred correctional officer salary costs for incarcerating undocumented criminal aliens with at least one felony or two misdemeanor convictions for violations of State or local law, and incarcerated for at least 4 consecutive days during the reporting period." Incarceration costs are not reimbursed at 100% as indicated in a report prepared by the Office of Strategic Planning & Results Management-Minnesota Department of Administration (2005, p. 13) to Governor Tim Pawlenty in December 2005. Out of the $14 million incarceration price tag in FY 2005, SCAAP payments reimbursed Minnesota for only $1.205 million. In California, "Washington is supposed to reimburse the state for the costs of incarcerating undocumented immigrants convicted of crimes, but it has paid less than a quarter of the costs under the Bush administration" (Sterngold, 2006, p. A1). The costs incurred by prosecuting and then supervising such offenders on probation or parole receive no reimbursement whatsoever from the federal government and must be absorbed by state and local communities.

As follow-up to the question on policies and procedures, APPA asked if agencies had special units created to supervise illegal aliens on probation/parole. The vast majority of responses (90%) indicated that there were no special units created. Similarly, when asked if there were any specialized programs in place (i.e., English as a Second Language (ESL) courses, bi-lingual programs for alcohol or substance abuse, interpreter services) for these offenders, 90% responded that no such programs were in place. Pamela Stowers Johansen (2005, p. 131) recounts her experiences with one case of an undocumented immigrant mother who was offered brochures on parenting and substance abuse, but

"Marina did not tell the worker that she could not read or write in English or Spanish." In many instances, undocumented immigrants in the community on probation or parole find few resources to aid them in complying with court orders to seek substance abuse or other counseling no matter how willing they are to comply.

When asked if the agency had staff with sufficient language diversity to effectively communicate with the client base, 51% indicated that they did not. Responses indicate that the language most available to state probation/parole agencies is Spanish, but that officers fluent in other languages are also needed for communicating with offenders:

> In Michigan we have very diverse cultures but have limited representatives for them. I speak Polish and Spanish, but we could use Arabic, Hmong, Bangladesh, Yugoslavian, numerous Latino members, Indian . . .

> The main office has bilingual officers, however, the satellite offices do not and (it) is very hard to communicate with this population due to that. It is frustrating to supervise this population when they continue to re-offend and the services are not available.

Magdeline Jensen (2002, p. 257) describes the difficulties in working with non-English speakers: "When working through an interpreter, nuances can be missed and intuition based on language clues is frequently lost. At times, cultural differences and misunderstandings by the interpreter interfere with a good interview." Many of the same difficulties recounted by Chief Jensen as a federal probation officer are encountered by state level probation and parole officials when undertaking such tasks as presentence investigations, interviews, intakes, assessments and service referrals. Serious issues involving victims become far more problematic when family members may be the only resource available to officers for translating for an offender. Domestic abuse cases are but one example of such instances.

In a January 2007 article, the Cincinnati Enquirer reports a five-fold increase in cases needing interpreter services in the Clermont County Municipal Court. These services are seen as necessary, not optional, by Judge Joyce Campbell in Fairfield Municipal Court, "When people are in front of me, English-speaking or non-English speaking, legal or illegal, I try to treat them all fairly and impartially. Their legal status in the country really has no bearing on what we do here" (Morse, 2007). Some county courts charge interpreter fees to defendants, while others absorb these costs. Fairfield Municipal Court's interpreter expenses rose to $40,000.00 by 2000 and with needs for such services increasing, the court was forced to pass the costs on to those defendants found guilty.

CONCLUSION: A PLACE AT THE TABLE

The Federal government offers little guidance to states and no financial support for the community supervision of undocumented immigrants while acknowledging the fact that they are responsible for the prosecution and potential deportation of immigrants in the country illegally. The findings in APPA's request for information indicate numerous issues involved in the community supervision of undocumented immigrants in the U.S. The added volume of work required from line officers to notify federal officials, conduct interviews, write reports and attend court hearings often with interpreter services needed, as well as arrange community services such as job training, substance abuse or mental health treatment for offenders who may have little understanding of the judicial system in which they are enmeshed is mind-boggling. Guidance from the federal government on immigration reform cannot come too soon for state level probation and parole officials whose sincere efforts are aimed at public safety and providing supervision of these offenders. Two final comments from respondents to APPA's request for information are telling:

> This Department's staff is becoming increasingly frustrated with the federal government's policy of not dealing with illegal immigration on the local level.
>
> Please note that we are dealing with human beings not "aliens." We also lack cultural understanding in order to deal appropriately with this population. Additionally, as probation officers, we require probationers to comply with conditions which are contradictory to what they are legally able to do, e.g. to be gainfully employed.

This article is not intended to offer a simple solution. Similar to other areas of community corrections policy, there are no simple solutions. Responding to undocumented immigrants is a complex issue, and this article has sought to describe some of the practical issues faced by state community supervision agencies in dealing with undocumented immigrants who commit crimes. The numbers of undocumented immigrants carried on the caseload of probation and parole officers is significant based on the information gathered by APPA. Of those who supplied a figure, estimates ranged from 1% to as high as 85%. Any solution to the problems encountered by state probation and parole professionals in supervising undocumented immigrants will be complex, trying and potentially divisive for the nation; however, such solutions are vital to many sectors of our communities. State probation and parole officials deserve a place at the decision making table regarding issues of public safety whether those under supervision are in the U.S. legally or not.

REFERENCES

Clark, R. L., & Anderson, S. A. (2000, June). *Illegal aliens in federal, state, and local criminal justice systems*. Washington, DC: Urban Institute, p. vii.

Jensen, M. E. (2002, March/April). Reflections of a southwest border probation chief. *Federal Sentencing Reporter, 14*(5), 257.

MacDonald, H. (2004, June). Crime and the illegal alien: The fallout from crippled immigration enforcement. *Backgrounder*. Washington, DC: Center for Immigration Studies, p. 6.

Morse. J. (2007, January 15). Immigrants press courts for interpreters. *Cincinnati Enquirer*.

Office of Immigration Statistics. (2006, August). Department of Homeland Security estimates of the unauthorized immigrant population residing in the United States: January 2005. Washington, DC: Author.

Office of Justice Programs, Bureau of Justice Assistance. (2006). *State criminal alien assistance program: FY 2006 guidelines*. Washington, DC: Author.

Office of Strategic Planning & Results Management, Minnesota Department of Administration. (2005). *The impact of illegal immigration on Minnesota: Costs and population trends*. St. Paul, MN: Author, p. 13.

Saltzman, J. (2007, January 12). Governor rescinds immigration order. *Boston Globe*.

Sterngold, J. (2006, May 4). Bid fails to deport immigrant prisoners–Bill to ease crowding seen as victim of demonstrations. San Francisco Chronicle, p. A1.

Stowers Johansen, P. (2005). Incarcerated mothers: Mental health, child welfare policy, and the special concerns of undocumented mothers. *California Journal of Health Promotion, 3*(2), 130-138.

United States Department of Justice, Office of the Inspector General, Audit Division. (2007, January). *Cooperation of SCAAP recipients in the removal of criminal aliens from the United States: Audit report 07-07*, p. iv.

United States Immigration and Customs Enforcement. (2006, April). *Fact sheet, ICE Law Enforcement Support Center (LESC)*. Washington, DC: Author.

From B. F. Skinner to Spiderman to Martha Stewart: The Past, Present and Future of Electronic Monitoring of Offenders

WILLIAM D. BURRELL
ROBERT S. GABLE

INTRODUCTION

Electronic monitoring of offenders (EM) has an intriguing history in American sentencing and correctional practices. First popularized in the

1980s, EM was used extensively as an alternative to incarceration in jail (primarily) or prison, and as an adjunct to traditional probation or parole supervision. Some two decades later, EM shows renewed popularity with the intense interest of legislatures and policy makers in addressing the problem of sex offenders in the community. Increasingly, jurisdictions are requiring lifetime supervision of sex offenders, monitored with Global Positioning Satellite (GPS) surveillance systems. The involvement of the federal government under the Adam Walsh Child Protection and Safety Act (signed into law in July, 2006) will require every state to re-examine their laws and will certainly accelerate implementation of such systems.

The present article briefly reviews the history of EM, summarizes contemporary research with respect to the impact of EM technology on recidivism rates, and suggests how EM can be used more effectively as a tool in the process of offender rehabilitation. There are many reasons to believe that EM will continue to grow and prosper, at least from a commercial perspective. Questions remain, however, about how much it will contribute to the larger societal goal of public safety.

THE ORIGINS OF ELECTRONIC MONITORING OF OFFENDERS

Although many writers assert that EM began in the 1980s, applications at that time were just the first successful *commercial* endeavors. The first experimental application occurred nearly two decades earlier. It proved to be an economic and sociological failure.

In the early 1960s, a small group of researchers at Harvard University began designing a portable transceiver capable of recording the location of volunteers with criminal records (Schwitzgebel et al., 1964). These researchers were strongly influenced by the psychological perspective of B. F. Skinner (1969). They designed a portable unit, termed "Behavior Transmitter-Reinforcer," that sent two-way messages between a base station and young adult offenders who reported their activities and emotions while in natural social environments. The primary goal was to provide feedback to the offenders for the purpose of rehabilitation and social support.

The inspiration for the system came when the head of the research project, Ralph Kirkland Schwitzgebel, was watching the film, *West Side Story*, in which the hero is killed by an opposing gang member. Schwitzgebel had the idea that if the hero could have received help or a warning, his life would have been saved. Subsequently, all of the monitoring systems of the original Harvard research group included some form of two-way signaling capacity.

Although a few scholarly papers raised appropriate issues of civil liberty, the reactions to the prototype systems were generally negative. The situation was not helped when the editors of the *Harvard Law Review* (1966) chose a witty title ("Dr. Schwitzgebel's machine") for an otherwise serious and insightful article. In addition, inaccurate reporting by a few journalists (e.g., Gordon, 1989) resulted in the myth (still circulating) that a "Schwitzgebel Machine" used brain implants to track offenders and transmit verbal instructions (Everything2.com, 2001/2007). The eminent constitutional law scholar, Laurence Tribe (1973, pp. 331-332), noted that the inventor "attempted for several years to explore the potential abuses of the technology he was developing, but was rebuffed by virtually every professional organization, foundation, and citizen group to which he turned."

It is interesting to speculate why this first EM application failed to gain traction. Several factors seem to have inhibited its adoption. The first had to do with the social acceptance of changing behavior by use of positive reinforcement. At that time, the public was much less familiar with Skinner's concepts of behavior modification, and thus less trusting of the procedures. The second was the use of electronic technology for remote monitoring of individuals. It is not difficult to understand an Orwellian "1984" type of reaction–EM was a tangible manifestation of "Big Brother." Third, the pioneering work was done in the pre-digital era of the mid 1960s. Transistor radios and color televisions were still novelties for many people. The computer age had not yet dawned for the consumer, and the EM technology was a leap that few were ready to make. Lastly, EM was an innovation that was so philosophically and operationally distant from the existing correctional "technology" (Vaill, 1978) that practitioners could not conceive using it. The technology transfer literature shows that in order to be adopted by practitioners, innovations must at least be perceived as feasible (Rogers, 2003). In retrospect, the original EM was probably just a little too "sci fi" for its own good.

WINDS OF CHANGE

The decade of the 1970s saw significant changes in sentencing and correctional policy arenas, as well as in technology. The rehabilitative model of indeterminate sentencing, discretionary parole release, and offender treatment was all but eliminated (Cullen & Gendreau, 2000). The new model was determinate, punitive, and offense-focused. Increasing numbers of offenders were locked up for longer terms, and the jail and prison populations in the U.S. exploded (Langan, 2005). Probation also saw significant increases in their caseloads (Livsey, 2006), and the driving philosophy of community supervision shifted away from rehabilitation to surveillance and enforcement. The system was in crisis and needed help.

In the realm of technology, it was the dawn of the digital age. The microprocessor made possible advances that were unimaginable only a few years before. The range of innovations that appeared in that era transformed almost every aspect of contemporary life, including criminal justice. Improvements in electronic technology and the pressures of jail and prison crowding made the idea of offender monitoring more feasible and more palatable. Two decades after the first system was assembled in Cambridge, Massachusetts, from surplus missile tracking equipment, the dark years of EM came to an end. In this new era, it was a judge (struggling as so many do to find better sentencing options) who saw EM as a potential solution to a growing problem.

In 1983, New Mexico state district judge Jack Love sentenced three offenders to home curfew. This was the culmination of years of effort and consternation during which Judge Love, who had previously served as a Federal public defender, sought ways to keep certain non-violent offenders from going to jail. In 1977, two items in a local newspaper caught his attention. One item showed a photograph of a heifer. A small radio transmitter had been implanted under the skin of the cow, and a hand-held detector received information about the animal's history and diet requirements (Holm et al., 1977). The second newspaper item was a Spiderman cartoon in which the villain clamped a bracelet-style "radar device" on Spiderman in order to track his movements. (The Spiderman cartoon story has attained the status of an urban myth in criminal justice, but Judge Love confirmed its accuracy by showing cartoons that he had filed away [Love, 2006]).

Judge Love subsequently went to several technology companies hoping to sell his idea of electronic monitoring of offenders. All declined to help. However, a computer sales representative at Honeywell, Michael Goss, was convinced. Mr. Goss left Honeywell in 1982, formed a company (NIMCOS–National Incarceration Monitoring and Control Services), secured a $10,000 bank loan, and built several cigarette-pack-size transmitter units designed to be strapped to an ankle. The transmitter propagated a radio signal every 60 seconds that could be picked up by a receiver connected to a telephone line, and then transmitted to a mainframe computer. Loss of the signal occurred at distances greater than approximately 150 feet (45 meters), and could therefore indicate a potential violation of home detention.

In April, 1983, the first of three probationers was sentenced to monitored home detention as a condition of probation. The probationer, a heroin user with a steady job and an infant child, was convicted of writing bad checks. This probationer successfully completed his 30-day sentence on monitored curfew. Unfortunately, 60 days after his curfew ended, he was arrested for shoplifting. The second person, a Vietnam veteran studying to be a computer technician, was placed on 30-day monitored curfew for violating probation after receiving stolen property. Although this probationer did not violate his monitored night-time curfew at a local detention center, on the fifth day of his sentence, he returned to the center intoxicated and was subsequently sentenced to jail. The third individual, a diabetic convicted of a second DUI offense, successfully completed his 30-days of monitoring.

A few months after the initial monitoring experiment, Michael Goss's namesake system (the "GOSSlink") ceased operation because the company had depleted its funds. It should be noted that two of the three offenders sentenced by Judge Love to EM ultimately recidivated; follow-up information for the third is not available. The immediate goal of confinement was achieved, but the longer-term goal of crime reduction was not.

One of the sources of Judge Love's inspiration (i.e., identification tagging of livestock) was not forgotten, however. Mr. Goss made a desperate but timely offer to Boulder Industries (BI) that itself was having difficulties selling several innovative electronic devices–one being an "electronic dairy I.D. system." According to BI's former president and CEO, David Hunter (2006), he asked an assistant to conduct a marketing survey among correctional agency personnel regarding their opinion of EM. The opinion of correctional personnel was reported as follows: "We don't want it" (viz., too much work), "we don't like it" (viz., threatens our jobs), "we've never done it before" (viz., it's too new), and "we don't like you" (viz., a private company shouldn't be involved in probation/parole work). Mr. Hunter's self-described reaction was–"This is a real business opportunity!" Shortly thereafter, BI loaned NIMCOS $250,000, and arranged for Control Data of Minneapolis to be the exclusive marketing agent. The arrangement did not work out (due, in part, to the near-bankruptcy of Control Data as a result of its other diverse operations). All rights and assets of NIMCOS were eventually purchased by BI for another $250,000.

NIMCOS/BI had only one generally recognized competitor during its first year of operation. In December, 1983, Monroe County (FL) judge Allison DeFoor sentenced a 28-year-old carpenter in Key Largo to a weekend of home detention for driving without a license (Shillington, 1983). The 48-hour sentence began when inventor Thomas Moody attached a transmitter anklet to the probationer and installed a receiver in the probationer's trailer. The radio transmitter and the home-based receiver were manufactured by Mr. Moody' company, Controlled Activities Corporation (CONTRAC), located in Key Largo, Florida. The anklet consisted of a 5 × 3 inch plastic transmitter in the shape of a half-cylinder that sent signals every 35 seconds to the receiver that was, in turn, linked via telephone line to a computer at Moody's 24-hour monitoring service, Omni Communications, Inc.

An experimental project testing a full implementation began November, 1984, in Palm Beach as a joint operation between Controlled Activities, the Palm Beach County Sheriff's Department, and Pride, Incorporated, a private nonprofit probation agency that continues to operate a monitoring program to this day. The first probationer, a 20-year-old student convicted of DUI, was permitted to spend nights and weekends at her home and to pay a $250 fee to offset the cost of the experimental program. A follow-up of 415 cases from late 1984 through October, 1989 reported that "ninety-seven percent of the offenders completed their electronic monitoring period successfully, and nearly 80 percent completed their entire term of probation" (Lilly et al., 1992, p. 42).

Between 1986 and 1996, the pool of manufacturers and service providers grew, shrank, consolidated, grew again, and has generally been in flux ever since. In less than three years from the first judicially sanctioned experiments, at least 53 EM programs in 21 states had been initiated (Schmidt, 1987). A newsletter, *Offender Monitoring* (changed in Spring 1989 to *Journal of Offender Monitoring*), was initiated by Professor Marc Renzema in October, 1987. The newsletter listed 10 suppliers, and Renzema (1987) estimated that between 4,000 and 5,000 offenders had worn EM devices. Although there are no comprehensive national data, the current editor of the *Journal of Offender Monitoring* has estimated that approximately 100,000 offenders were on EM in 2006 (Conway, 2006).

This rapid acceptance of EM was followed by the establishment of an information clearinghouse, creation of professional guidelines, and publication of evaluation studies. Some notable events in the development of EM are listed in Table 1. In explaining the popularity of EM, we cannot discount the popular fascination with technological innovation. We in the United States have great faith (largely well placed) in the capacity of technology, primarily computer-based, to solve problems and improve our lives. In a field that is so human capital intensive as corrections, the idea that a "technological fix" could reduce the workload in dealing with the problem of crime is almost irresistible (Corbett & Marx, 1991).

Table 1: Notable Events in Electronic Monitoring, United States, 1964-2006

Year	Event	References
1964	Transceivers used for location monitoring and "behavioral feedback"	Schwitzgebel et al. (1964)
1965	Radio transmitters used for psychotherapy with hyperactive children	Patterson et al. (1965)
1969	Patent issued for wrist-carried transceiver for monitoring offenders	Schwitzgebel & Hurd (1969)
1970	Development of belt-encased two-way vibrotactile transceiver	Schwitzgebel & Bird (1970)
1971	Publication proposes large network of offender-carried transponders	Meyer (1971)
1983	Judge Jack Love sentences three offenders to home detention	Cassidy (1983)
1983	Two companies begin manufacturing and using monitoring systems	Goss (1983); Shillington (1983)
1985	NIJ report describes home confinement, lists six companies offering service	Ford & Schmidt (1985)
1987	*Journal of Offender Monitoring* founded, lists ten suppliers of equipment	Renzema (1987)
1992	Evaluation published of results with first 415 offenders in Florida	Lilly et al. (1992)
1994	National Law Enforcement & Corrections Technology Center established	Community Corrections Technology (2006)
1995	American Correctional Association publishes standards for EM programs	American Correctional Association (1995)
2002	American Probation & Parole Association, with NIJ, publishes a "User's Guide"	Crowe (2002)
2005	Entrepreneur Martha Stewart sentenced. Extensive meta-analysis published	Tyrnauer (2005); Renzema & Mayo-Wilson (2005)
2006	Large study of offenders placed on home confinement in Florida	Padgett, Bales, & Blomberg (2006)

DOES IT WORK?

Evaluation studies of EM programs began almost simultaneously with the spread of the technology, and many of the studies drew a favorable conclusion about the potential of EM. Most of the studies, however, suffered from problems of erratic implementation, equipment malfunction, and weak research design. In a 1997 report to the U.S. Congress, a federally funded research team (Sherman et al., 1997) listed home detention with EM as a crime prevention strategy that "doesn't work." The report's conclusion was based on two carefully designed studies with randomly assigned control groups.

Subsequent studies have reported mixed results. Bonta, Wallace-Capretta, and Rooney (2000) found that EM combined with treatment significantly reduced recidivism among moderately high-risk offenders, but had no effect on lower-risk offenders. Indeed, several studies (Gendreau et al., 2000; Erwin, 1990) suggest that intensive supervision with EM may actually increase recidivism, perhaps as a result of resentment or increased criminal association. A very dramatic reduction in re-conviction rates was reported by the National Audit Office of the U. K. (2006). Their analysis showed that 51 percent of offenders who completed a community-based sentence were re-convicted of another offense within 24 months. Only 12 percent of offenders on EM were re-convicted within 24 months. The audit report notes, however, that some of the difference may have been the result of a selection bias in which those offenders less likely to re-offend were released into the EM programs. This lack of a statistically matched control group is typical of many studies.

The most comprehensive and rigorous meta-analysis of evaluation studies to date "failed to find any convincing evidence that EM is superior to other prison diversion programs" (Renzema & Mayo-Wilson, 2005, p. 17). This does not imply that EM is useless. There is probably some suppression of criminal behavior during the actual monitoring (Padgett, Bales, & Blomberg, 2006), and this provides at least a temporary increase in public safety. Probation, with EM as a condition, also provides an intermediate sanction between prison and traditional community supervision. The degree of inconvenience, discomfort, and restriction that EM can enforce is one way to emphasize to the offender the seriousness of the crime. The most visible example in the United States has been the post-prison supervised release of entrepreneur and TV personality, Martha Stewart. She was sentenced to five months of monitored confinement on her 153-acre estate following five months in prison for lying to federal investigators about insider stock trading. This condition of release was certainly not imposed as a matter of public safety. Nor was surveillance a means of assuring her attendance at a job-training or a social skills class. Rather, Ms. Stewart had become the public whipping girl of corporate malfeasance. Her home confinement with EM was a manifestation of the punitive intent behind her sentencing. In rejecting an appeal for regular parole by Ms. Stewart, U.S. District Judge Miriam Cedarbaum (2005, p. 2) wrote: "In my opinion, the sentence I imposed was particularly needed to reflect the seriousness of the offense, to promote respect for the law and to provide just punishment."

As previously noted, the growth of EM is being encouraged by sex offender legislation. However, sentences such as life-time supervision with GPS have the potential for creating catastrophic consequences in community corrections (DeMichele, Payne, & Button, 2007). First, there will be unrelenting growth in sex offender caseloads because these cases will never (at least for the foreseeable future) be terminated from supervision. Second, given the high priority that these offenders are suppose to receive, probation and parole agencies are likely to assign them to small caseloads with increased levels of supervision. This will compound the caseload growth by giving each sex offender's case added weight in calculating staffing needs. Lastly, the GPS technology works around the clock, seven days a week, monitoring and reporting violations whenever they occur. At present, it is impossible to know the volume of alerts that will be generated, or their distribution over time, but it is not unreasonable to expect significant numbers of alerts both day and night. Some alerts will be real (intentional violations of restricted areas such as playgrounds), others could be more circumstantial (unintended violations while traveling to a legitimate location), and still others could be false alarms or technological glitches.

Another increasingly popular use of GPS monitoring that should be mentioned is the protection of victims of domestic abuse. In domestic abuse cases, an offender may be prohibited from coming within approximately 300 feet (100 meters) of a victim's home or workplace. Regardless of the nature of a GPS violation, the expectation of policy makers and elected officials is certainly that someone (be it a probation/parole officer or law enforcement officer) will respond as soon as possible to a GPS alert. The integrity of the entire program requires that violations receive a timely and appropriate response. If offenders can violate the terms of their supervision and no one takes note, those terms and the supervision lose credibility. Failure to respond in a timely manner also exposes the agency and staff to the possibility of a liability claim for negligent supervision. Changes in policies concerning hours of work, schedules, after-hours work, and overtime pay have now become issues that need to be addressed.

An unfortunate result of increased staff burden is the tendency to resort primarily to surveillance and punishment. However, research and experience of the last two decades strongly suggest that the most effective means to reduce re-offending by criminals and delinquents is not to just incapacitate and punish them, but to address the motivation for their law-violating behavior, their *criminogenic risk factors* (Andrews & Bonta, 2006). Incapacitation and punishment are legitimate goals for sentencing, but they have limited utility in achieving the "super-ordinate function" of the criminal justice system–protecting citizens from victimization by reducing long-term crime (Flanagan, 1996, p. 5).

Inasmuch as EM in most of its present forms does not address the criminogenic risk factor of offender motivation, monitoring alone is not likely to affect public safety after the offender is no longer under the jurisdiction of a correctional agency. Although EM can document an offender's location, it does not tell us what the offender is doing. A sex offender, for example, might be victimizing a child in the offender's home or the victim's home. Data suggest that this is the scenario for the vast majority of child victim sex offenses. A U.S. Department of Justice survey reported that 46 percent of all sexual crimes against children were committed by persons related to their victims; only seven percent of child sexual assaults were committed by complete strangers (Langan, Schmitt, & Durose, 2003). GPS programs appear to be promising more than they can deliver (DeMichele, Payne, & Button, 2007). Add to such unrealistic promises the stress placed on community corrections agencies, and the picture looks very grim indeed.

AN ALTERNATIVE FUTURE

Rehabilitation has returned to the marketplace of ideas in public policy. This renewed discourse is being driven by a compelling body of empirical evidence that some types of correctional treatment of offenders are effective (Andrews & Bonta, 2006). This research, now called "evidence-based practice," is being considered by policy-makers who are frustrated by the lack of effectiveness of "get tough" approaches, hamstrung by ever-increasing costs, and intrigued by the success of the overtly treatment-oriented drug courts (Cooper, 2001). Even in such a notoriously punitive state as Texas, legislators are endorsing rehabilitation programs over prison construction (Ramshaw, 2007).

Central to this new evidence-based approach to corrections is the same analysis of social contingencies that informed the inventors of EM some 40 years ago. Psychologist B. F. Skinner (1969) emphasized that social behavior is shaped and maintained by the specific nature and timing of consequences. Akers (1994), Bandura (1977) and others subsequently incorporated Skinnerian behaviorism, along with other theories such Sutherland's differential association theory, into a well-known social learning theory of crime. No theory adequately describes all the principles necessary for successful intervention, but substantial research over several decades indicates moderately strong support for the differential reinforcement aspects of the social learning theory of crime (e.g., Brezina & Piquero, 2003; Jessor & Jessor, 1977; Winfree, Vigil-Backstrom & Mays, 1994). In the review of principles of effective correctional treatment enunciated by Andrews and Bonta (2006), social learning theory serves as the predominate theoretical model. Also, behavioral techniques drawn from social learning theory and operant conditioning are reportedly used in the majority of probation service programs in the U.K. (Vennard, Sugg, & Hedderman, 1977). It appears that EM need no longer be an ideological orphan; evidence-based practice utilizing social reinforcers can provide a good home.

Probably the best examples of the use of positive reinforcement in criminal justice are the drug courts. They have recognized, embraced, and greatly expanded the use of small, seemingly insignificant rewards for offenders who exhibit and maintain sober, law-abiding behaviors. The Henrico (VA) County Drug Court (2006, p. 1), for example, includes in its brochure given to offenders the following statement:

> A variety of rewards will be awarded weekly during Drug Court in an attempt to quickly recognize the positive actions of participants. Incentives will be used to recognize completion of assignments, phase progression, periods of sobriety, etc. Incentives will include gift certificates or gift cards, prizes from local merchants, movie passes, bus passes, certificates and medallions, etc.

Cooper (2001) has provided a detailed listing of different types of incentives used in more than 30 drug court programs. The Bureau of Justice Assistance (2004, p. 11) *Drug Court Discretionary Grant Program* guidelines has required applicants to "indicate what graduated incentives and sanctions are used in the [proposed] program."

The hundreds of drug courts currently operational in the U.S. have developed their own, somewhat unique approach based on an accepted and established set of principles for drug courts (NADCP, 1997). It is useful to begin this limited exploration of an alternative future for EM by articulating several elements or principles that should form the foundation for an incentive-based model of EM. These principles would help guide those pioneers who seek to implement new programs and explore the potential of this new paradigm.

An incentive-based EM program would include the following elements:

1. *Clearly articulated principles of social learning theory.* Well-documented developmental studies report that parents, teachers, and peers are routinely provoked by antisocial children and adolescents into administering excessive punishment that, in turn, prompts still more antisocial behavior (Church, 2006). A classroom observation showed that only 11% of a teacher's interaction with troublesome students involved approval for desired behavior while 89% involved negative responses for inappropriate behavior. Conversely, normal students received about 80% supportive interactions and only 20% negative interactions (Walker & Buckley, 1973).

Thus, based on such observation, positive reinforcers should outnumber sanctions in the normal course of supervision, and be given contingent on gradual improvements of an offender's behavior (a procedure known as "shaping" in operant conditioning). Although immediate and front-loaded reinforcement is usually more effective in the early stages of a learning process, this may not be practical in a supervisory context. In fact, an increased interval between response and reinforcement is preferable toward the end of training (Van Camp, Borrero, & Vollner, 2003). A technically accurate and realistic description of strategies for administering rewards and sanctions to felony drug clients has been provided by Marlowe (2007).

2. *Gradual changes in agency procedures.* Ideally, positively oriented EM would be guided by feedback of relevant offender behavior over a period of one to three years. Establishing an incentive program is, unfortunately, a front-loaded task where start-up costs are immediate and possible benefits are delayed.

An innovative probation incentive program in Pinal County (AZ) found that getting staff buy-in, not acquiring appropriate incentives for the clients, was the most difficult aspect of establishing the service (McBride, 2007). Many officers see their primary responsibility as holding offenders accountable for compliance with probation or parole conditions. Attempting to develop prosocial behavior among offender clientele, particularly after supervision has ended, is not only difficult but may go unrewarded by supervisors. White (2006) has outlined practical steps for developing an office culture supportive of evidence-based, behavior-change practices.

3. *Incremental fade-out of monitoring restrictions.* In order to increase the probability of long-term behavior change, an offender's EM restrictions should be slowly replaced by variable rewards for prosocial behavior produced by the natural social environment. This program element is not easily achieved. Too often, as a result of very limited options, offenders are released into the same or similar social environment that encouraged the original problem behavior. Thus, while the usual goals of finding employment, starting a hobby, and developing law-abiding friendships are desirable, the goals must be broken into small intermediate steps (e.g., learning to arrive promptly at job interviews appropriately dressed). The Community Reinforcement Approach is one reportedly effective behaviorally oriented program that attempts to develop familial, social, recreational, and vocational incentives in an offender's natural environment (Finney & Monahan, 1996). This approach is illustrated in a study of violent criminal offenders with alcohol problems in which employment levels were significantly improved (Funderburk et al., 1993).

The practice of giving rewards of varying degrees of value at unpredictable intervals of time (technically termed a "variable ratio–variable interval" schedule of reinforcement) is a common strategy for sustaining behavior. Lotteries and raffles rely on such ambiguity. People who purchase a ticket are not sure when or how much, if anything, they might win. Checking e-mail is another behavior that is maintained by the varied nature of the consequences. In probation or parole, for example, a variable reward schedule could be easily implemented with low-risk offenders who use a computer kiosk check-in system.

Similarly, positive reinforcers could be delivered in conjunction with alcohol monitoring systems. One well-known system uses a tamper-resistant ankle bracelet (SCRAM®, Secure Continuous Remote Alcohol Monitor) that tests perspiration excreted through the skin. Because the monitoring agency can set the intervals at which the bracelet does the testing, a detailed pattern of alcohol use or abstinence can be obtained. Other remote alcohol testing devices that use a standard telephone line (e.g., iSecureTrac 2000VB®, Sobrietor®) are particularly amenable to re-design to the extent that they could permit immediate positive feedback at remote locations for clean tests or other desired behavior.

The future of EM will continue to change with advances in electronics, particularly cellular and battery technology. Bluetooth-enabled cell phones can be used to verify the location of willingly tagged individuals. A network of transceivers might be installed and periodically moved in order to create an "electronically enriched" urban area where offenders could become eligible for a reward if they spontaneously exhibited cooperative rather than aggressive social behavior. Social psychologists have developed numerous strategies for unobtrusively measuring helping and cooperative behavior in a wide range of social settings (e.g., Levine, 2003).

CONCLUSION

In the past 40 years, much has changed in the EM environment. Most of the original service providers have disappeared or been replaced. Equipment has become smaller, more dependable and sophisticated. Some legislators have adopted EM as an "effective intermediate sanction tool" for high-risk offenders (Prouty, 2005, p. 2). Nonetheless, as a technology for promoting humane rehabilitation, it has yet to demonstrate its efficacy. Electronic monitoring remains as Professor Renzema (1987, p. 1) described it in the first issue of his newsletter–"an oddity with great potential."

The challenge is how to realize the rehabilitation potential of EM. The answer lies in going beyond the technology, to the underlying science of human behavior (Burrell, 2006). As applied to date, EM has generally lacked the science and a credible theoretical construct to guide its use. In her discussion of officer-offender contacts in supervision, Taxman (2002) noted that contacts are just tools for the officer to apply.

They have no inherent value; they are atheoretical. Firmly anchored in a well-grounded theory, these tools can be applied effectively to achieve the goals of supervision. Absent those anchors, tools such as supervisory contacts and EM are destined to uselessly absorb valuable time, resources, and energy. The appeal of technology such as EM should be tempered by a pragmatic concern for sound science to guide its use. Social learning theory and evidence-based practices provide such a guide.

REFERENCES

Akers, R. L. (1994). *Criminological theories: Introduction and evaluation*. Los Angeles, CA: Roxbury.

American Correctional Association. (1995). *Standards for electronic monitoring programs*. Laurel, MD: author.

Andrews, D. A. & Bonta, J. (2006). *The Psychology of criminal conduct*, 4th ed. Cincinnati: Anderson Publishing.

Bandura, A. (1977). *Social learning theory*. Englewood Cliffs, NJ: Prentice-Hall.

Bonta, J., Wallace-Capretta, S., & Rooney, J. (2000). Can electronic monitoring make a difference? An evaluation of three Canadian programs. *Crime and Delinquency*, 46, 61-75.

Brezina, T. & Piquero, A. R. (2003). Exploring the relationship between social and non-social reinforcement in the context of social learning theory, pp. 265-288, in R. L. Akers & G. F. Jensen (Eds.), *Social learning theory and the explanation of crime: A guide for the new century*. New Brunswick, NJ: Transaction Publishers.

Bureau of Justice Assistance. (2004). *Drug court discretionary grant program: FY 2005 resource guide for drug court applicants*. Washington, DC: author.

Burrell, W. D. (2006). Science, technology and community corrections. *Community Corrections Report*, 13, 83-85, 94.

Cassidy, J. (1983, March 18). District judge tests electronic monitor. *Albuquerque Journal*, No.77, p. A-1.

Cedarbaum, M. G. (2005, April 11). *United States of America against Martha Stewart and Peter Bacanovic*. Memorandum opinion, 03 Cr. 717.

Church, J. (2006). *Church report–The definition, diagnosis and treatment of children and youth with severe behaviour difficulties*. Christchurch, N.Z.: University of Canterbury.

Community Corrections Technology Newsletter. (2006). Denver, CO: National Law Enforcement and Community Corrections Technology Center–Rocky Mountain. Retrieved December 29, 2006, from http://www.nlectc.org/nlectcrm/

Conway, P. (2006, June 13). Personal communication with William Burrell.

Cooper, C. S. (2001, May). Juvenile drug court programs. *JAIBG Bulletin*. Rockville, MD: Office of Juvenile Justice and Delinquency Prevention.

Corbett, R. & Marx, G. T. (1991). Critique: No soul in the new machine: Technofallacies in the electronic monitoring movement. *Justice Quarterly*. 8, 399-414.

Crowe, A. H. (2002). *Offender supervision with electronic technology*. Lexington, KY: American Probation and Parole Association.

Cullen, F. T. & Gendreau, P. (2000). Assessing correctional rehabilitation: Policy, practice and prospects. In J. Horney (Ed.), NIJ *Criminal Justice, 2000. Changes in decision making and discretion in the criminal justice system*, pp. 109–175. Washington, DC: National Institute of Justice.

DeMichele, M., Payne, B., & Button, D. (2007, January). A call fore vidence-based policy: Sex offender electronic monitoring has advantages, problems. *State News*, 26-29.

Erwin, B. (1990). Old and new tools for the modern probation officer. *Crime and Delinquency*, 36, 61-75.

Everything2.com (2001). Schwitzgebel machine. Retrieved January 29, 2007, from http://everything2.com/index.pl?node_id=1082991

Finney, J. W. & Monahan, S. C. (1996). The cost-effectiveness of treatment of alcoholism: A second approximation. *Journal of Studies on Alcohol*, 57, 229-243.

Flanagan, T.J. (1996). Community corrections in the public mind. *Federal Probation*, 60, 3-9.

Ford, D. F. & Schmidt, A. K. (1985). Electronically monitored home confinement. *NIJ Reports (*SNI 194).Washington, D.C.: National Institute of Justice.

Funderburk, F. R., Mackenzie, A., Dehaven, G. P., Stefan, R., & Allan, R. P. (1993). Evaluation of the Multiple Offender Alcoholism Project, Quasi-experimental evaluation strategy with a focus on individual disorders. *Evaluation and Program Planning,* 16, 181-191.

Gendreau, P., Goggin, C., Cullen, F. T., & Andrews, D. A. (2000). The effects of community sanctions and incarceration on recidivism. *Forum on Corrections Research*, 12, 10-13.

Gordon, T. (1989). *Journey into madness: The true story of secret CIA mind control and medical abuse.* New York, NY: Bantam Books.

Goss, M. T. (1983). *The GOSSlink.* Albuquerque, NM: National Incarceration Monitor and Control Services, Inc., (pamphlet), 4 pages.

Harvard Law Review. (1966). Anthropotelemetry: Dr. Schwitzgebel's machine. 80, 403–421.

Henrico County Drug Court. (2006). *Expectations of participants*. Richmond, VA:Author. Retrived July 11, 2006, from http://www.co.henrico.va.us/drugcourt/expectations.html

Holm, D. M., Bobbett, R. E., Koelle, A. R., Landt, J. A., & Depp, S. W. (1977). *Electronic identification* (Progress report, 1 Jul. 1976-30 Sep. 1977). Los Alamos, NM: Los Alamos Scientific Laboratory.

Hunter, D. (2006, December 19). Telephone interview with Robert Gable.

Jessor, R. & Jessor, S. L. (1977). *Problem behavior and psychological development.* New York, NY: Academic Press.

Langan, P. A. (2005). Crime and punishment in the United States, 1981-1999. In M. Tonry & D. Farrington (Eds.), *Crime and punishment in western countries*, 1980-1999, pp. 123-159. Chicago: University of Chicago Press.

Langan, P. A., Schmitt, E. L., & Durose, M. R. (2003). *Recidivism of sex offenders released from prison in 1994.* Washington, D. C.: Bureau of Justice Statistics.

Levine, R. V. (2003). Measuring helping behavior across cultures. In W. J. Lonner (Ed.). *Online readings in psychology and culture* (Unit 15, Chapter 9). Bellingham, WA: Western Washington University at http:www.wwu.edu/~culture

Lilly, J. R., Ball, R. A., Curry, G. D., & Smith, R. C. (1992). The Pride, Inc., Program: An evaluation of 5 years of electronic monitoring. *Federal Probation*, 56, 42-47.
Livsey, S. (2006). *Juvenile delinquency probation caseload, 1985-2002.* Washington, D. C.: Office of Juvenile Justice and Delinquency Prevention.
Love, J. (2006). In-person interview with Robert Gable, Albuquerque, NM, November 29, 2006.
Marlowe, D. B. (2007). Strategies for administering rewards and sanctions. In J. Lessenger & G. Roper (Eds.), *The drug court handbook.* New York, NY: Springer-Verlag.
McBride, D. (2007, March 20). Program administrator, Pinal County Juvenile Court, Florence, AZ. E-mail correspondence with R. Gable.
Meyer, J. A. (1971). Crime deterrent transponder system. *IEEE Transactions on Aerospace and Electronic Systems*, 7, 2-22.
National Association of Drug Court Professionals (NADCP). (1997). *Defining drug courts: the key components.* Washington, DC: Bureau of Justice Assistance.
National Audit Office. (2006). *The electronic monitoring of adult offenders.* London, U.K: The Stationery Office.
Padgett, K. G., Bales, W. D., & Blomberg, T. G. (2006). Under surveillance: An empirical test of the effectiveness and consequences of electronic monitoring. *Criminology and Public Policy*, 5, 61-92.
Patterson, G., Jones, R., Whittier, J., & Wright, M. A. (1965). A behavior modification technique for the hyperactive child. *Behavior Research and Therapy*, 2, 217-226.
Prouty, D. (2005). *Electronic monitoring of sex offenders.* Des Moines, IA: State Capital, Iowa Legislative Services Agency.
Ramshaw, E. (2007, January 4). Smart approach to prisons sought. Dallas Morning News.com, p. 1.
Renzema, M. (1987). Editorial: Monitoring for better or worse. *Offender Monitoring*, 1, 1.
Renzema, M. & Mayo-Wilson, E. (2005). Can electronic monitoring reduce crime for moderate to high-risk offenders? *Journal of Experimental Criminology*, 1, 1-23.
Rogers, E. M. (2003). *The diffusion of innovations* (5th ed.). New York: Free Press.
Schmidt, A. K. (1987). The use of electronic monitoring by criminal justice agencies. N.I.J. Discussion Paper No. 2-87 (typescript). Washington, D.C.: National Institute of Justice.
Schwitzgebel, R. K. & Hurd, W. S. (1969). Behavioral supervision with a wrist-carried transceiver. U. S. Patent Office, No. 3,478,344.
Schwitzgebel, R. K., Schwitzgebel, R. L., Pahnke, W. N., & Hurd, W. S. (1964). A program of research in behavioral electronics. *Behavioral Science*, 9, 233-238.
Schwitzgebel, R. L. & Bird, R. M. (1970). Sociotechnical design factors in remote instrumentation with humans in natural environments. *Behavior Research Methods and Instrumentation,* 2, 99-105.
Sherman, L. W., Gottfredson, D. C., MacKenzie, D. L., Eck, J., Reuter, P., & Bushway, S. D. (1997). *Preventing crime: What works, what doesn't, what's promising.* Report to Congress. Washington, D. C.: National Institute of Justice.
Shillington, P. (1983, December 17). Electronic 'jailkeeper' gets a tryout. *Miami Herald,* p. 2.

Skinner B. F. (1969). *Contingencies of reinforcement: A theoretical analysis.* New York, NY: Appleton-Century-Crofts.

Taxman, F. S. (2002). Supervision–Exploring the dimensions of effectiveness. *Federal Probation*, 66, 14-27.

Tribe, L. H. (1973). *Channeling technology through law.* Chicago, IL: Bracton Press.

Tyrnauer, M. (2005, August). The prisoner of Bedford. *Vanity Fair.* No. 540, 110-118, 175-180.

Vaill, P. B. (1978). Notes on technology. In M. R. Weisbord (Ed.). *Organizational diagnosis: A workbook of theory and practice* (pp. 153-159). Reading, MA: Addison-Wesley.

Van Camp, C. M., Borrero, J. C., & Vollmer, T. R. (2003). The family safety/applied behavior analysis initiative: An introduction and overview. *Behavior Analyst Today*, 3, 389-404.

Vennard, J., Sugg, D., & Hedderman, C. (1997). *Changing offenders' attitudes and behaviour: what works?* London: Research and Statistics Directorate, Home Office.

Walker, H. M. & Buckley, N. K.(1973). Teacher attention to appropriate and inappropriate classroom behavior: An individual case study. *Focus on Exceptional Children*, 5, 5-11.

White, T. (2006). Evidence-based practice in probation and parole: The implementation challenge. *Perspectives* (American Probation and Parole Association), 30, 22-27.

Winfree, L. T., Vigil-Backstrom, T., & Mays, G. L. (1994). Social learning theory, self–reported delinquency, and youth gangs, a new twist on a general theory of crime and delinquency. *Youth and Society*, 26, 147-177.

Electronic Monitoring of Sex Offenders: Identifying Unanticipated Consequences and Implications

MATTHEW DEMICHELE
BRIAN K. PAYNE
DEEANNA M. BUTTON

INTRODUCTION

Sex offenders present unique challenges to the policymaking and community corrections fields. There are few crimes that elicit as much public concern and policy reaction as sexually related crimes. These offenses are typically presented by the news media in sensational formats that ignore important contextual factors such as the frequency with which sex crimes are committed among people knowing one another–as it is with other forms of predation, sex offenders tend to victimize people they know (Kappeler, Blumberg, & Potter, 2000; Simon, 2000). This is not to ignore the importance of preventing stranger perpetrated offenses, but rather to highlight the context in which most sex crimes take place among people knowing one another as family members, friends, or acquaintances such as a friend's stepfather or co-worker.

Electronic monitoring of sex offenders is a recent legislative concern, with every state in the U.S. using some form of electronic monitoring. It appears that the policymaking community is potentially blurring the issues of electronic monitoring and sex offenses (DeMichele, Button, & Payne, 2007). That is, much of the recent policy development guiding community corrections practices involve the electronic monitoring of sex offenders. Recent federal legislation, the Adam Walsh Act of 2006, stipulates that all sex offenders are to be supervised with electronic monitoring devices, with states encouraged to comply within three years of passage of the act. This suggests that electronic monitoring of sex offenders is a significant issue that will shape community corrections sex offender supervision practices.

Unfortunately, very little research has been done on how electronic monitoring can be used for this offender group and community corrections practitioners have been provided little guidance and insight into ways to apply this sanction, which was historically reserved for less serious offenders, to sex offenders. Experts from two divergent areas (e.g., those working with and studying community based corrections and those working with and studying sex offenders) are now expected to merge these areas in a way that will allow for effective supervision of sex offenders. Indeed, those working in one of these areas may not be familiar with the history or assumptions of the other area. In an effort to merge these two areas, in the current article attention is given to (1) sex offending, (2) electronic monitoring, (3) the deterrent potential of electronic monitoring, (4) efforts to apply the electronic monitoring sanction to sex offenders, (5) the potential unintended consequences stemming from the monitoring policies, and (6) recommendations for practitioners involved with the sanction and researchers studying the topic.

SEX OFFENDERS

The term "sex offender" is often used in a rather general way to refer to a diverse set of sexually related offenses, with the typical image centering on child molesters (Simon, 1998; Cole, 2000). Sex offenses cause untold harm and suffering to their victims, families, and the community, and it is estimated that about 235,000 individuals convicted of sex offenses are under the supervision of the criminal justice system (Greenfeld, 1997). The bulk of these sex offenders (60 percent) are not institutionalized in a jail or prison, but instead are supervised in the community (Greenfeld, 1997). "Sex offender" is an imprecise term in that the offense classification may refer to several different levels and types of crimes that vary by state and local jurisdiction. For example, half of the states in the U.S. do not use the term rape at all, but instead employ other statutory language to designate this specific sex crime (Langan, Schmitt, & Durose, 2003, p. 3).

Sex offending exists across a wide continuum of behaviors. To make sense of this phenomenon, scholars have developed various typologies to differentiate offenders according the age and gender of their victim(s), the amount of force used, offender motivations, and the relationship between the victim and offender (see Cumming & McGrath, 2005; Gebhard, Gagnon, Pomeroy, & Christenson, 1965). Typologies work to organize information to ease cognitive processing by classifying offenders (or other social and physical phenomena) according to similar characteristics to provide some sense of the probability of future behaviors. Cummings and McGrath (2005) identify six different kinds of typologies: adult male child molesters (e.g., Knight, 1999; Lanning, 1986), adult male rapists (e.g., Groth, 1979; Hazelwood, 1995), adult male hands-off, adult male child pornographers (Hernandez, 2000), adult female offenders (Matthews, Matthew, & Speltz, 1989), and adult male sexual abusers (Worling, 2001).

There has been much discussion regarding criminal typologies and the debate between general and specialist offenders (see Guay et al., 2001). Some scholars claim that offenders are general criminals willing to engage in a diverse set of criminal and deviant behaviors that can range from petty theft to sex offending, and result from a lack of self-control and weak social bonds (Gottfredson & Hirschi, 1990). Others, however, suggest there is more stability in offending patterns especially with regards to sex offenders (Hanson, Scott, & Steffy, 1995; Soothill et al., 2000). A more helpful approach for community corrections practitioners and policymakers is to consider a sport's analogy adapted from Soothill et al. (2000) in which it is possible for a person to enjoy playing several sports such as football, baseball, and basketball, but to emphasize (or specialize in) football and spend most of their time with this specific sport, and as opportunities present themselves they might play other sports as well. Similarly, individuals convicted of sex offenses may commit other forms of criminality (e.g., burglary, drug offenses) depending on opportunity structures, as well as possessing multiple paraphilia, and victimize across age and gender (see Abel et al., 1987; Soothill et al., 2000).

Sex offenders represent varying levels of risk of committing a new sex or other crime (Andrews et al., 1990). It may seem counterintuitive to claim that any sex offender is low risk when considering the potential for victim harm or seriousness of the offense. This notion of severity, however, is not what is meant by risk in this context. Known recidivism patterns for sex offenders tend to be lower than for other forms of criminal behavior (Hanson & Bussiere, 1998). Sex offender supervision and legislation are based on the idea that sex offenders are a persistent offending population that poses a greater likelihood of recidivating than non-sex offenders. The bulk of recidivism studies do not support this contention. Sample and Bray (2003) compare 146,918 offenders arrested in Illinois between 1990 and 1997 to determine the relative level of risk between sex and non-sex offenders. The authors found that at one, three, and five year follow-ups robbery offenders were the group most likely to reoffend for any offense, with burglary, larceny, and non-sexual assault offenders close behind. Langan, Schmitt, and Durose (2003) compared 9,691 sex offenders released from 15 states at three year follow-up and found that about 5.3 percent of sex offenders and 1.3 percent of non-sex offenders were rearrested for a sex crime.

Because of the persistent, albeit erroneous, belief that sex offenders have higher rates of recidivism than other offenders, recent laws have called for the use of electronic monitoring to supervise sex offenders released from prison. Some state laws have even stipulated that sex offenders must be supervised for the remainder of their lives.

ELECTRONIC MONITORING: SUPERVISION TOOL

Electronic monitoring is estimated to be used with more than 100,000 offenders (inclusive of various monitoring and tracking technologies) (Conway, 2003; Renzema & Mayo-Wilson, 2005). Some speculate that electronic monitoring is a criminal justice tool that adds to the system's ability to structure offenders' lives. Electronic monitoring technologies emerged in the mid-1980s as a way to accomplish several justice system goals of punishing, supervising, and potentially contributing to rehabilitating offenders, and reducing prison and jail populations (see Crowe, Sydney, & Bancroft, 2002).

Probation and parole agencies have created many programs to improve their ability to supervise sex offenders in the community, with the incorporation of electronic monitoring beginning about two decades ago with general offenders (initially in Florida and New Mexico). Electronic monitoring is perceived to offer several benefits to the justice system such as alleviating the burden on jails and prisons, and providing additional supervision to areas of offenders' lives otherwise undetectable (Papy & Nimer, 1991). Despite these potential benefits, there is little rigorous research documenting the crime reducing impact of electronic monitoring programs (Renzema & Mayo-Wilson, 2005).

Electronic monitoring technologies generally include either radio frequency (RF) or global positioning systems (GPS). The RF system allows a computer to receive a signal (i.e., radio signal) from a transmitter connected to an offender's telephone that can receive radio signals from a bracelet worn by the offender to indicate whether the offender is at home (within a certain range of the receiver) during required times. The offender's proximity to the receiver is constantly monitored and transmitted via telephone lines sending data to a central computer. If the offender moves too far away from the transmitter during prohibited times officials are notified via the telephone connection. Similarly, if the offender is detected by the receiver when he or she should not be within range (e.g., when he or she should be at work or treatment) the monitoring agency will notify appropriate individuals (Crowe et al.,

2002; Nellis, 1991, p. 166). Handheld or drive-by devices have been developed for this technology to enable community corrections officers to drive past a location, such as a treatment provider or workplace, and utilize the handheld device to detect the radio signal emitted from the anklet.

More recent technologies have led to the development of electronic monitoring devices relying on GPS. In some jurisdictions, the use of satellite tracking allows for the "monitoring of movement rather than just single locations" (Nellis, 2005). With this type of technology, offenders carry a GPS signal receiver, portable tracking device ensuring the GPS signal remains with the offender, and a cell phone to relay information to a central monitoring agency. The offender's location is derived by calculating distance and time away from global positioning satellites operating above the Earth's surface by the U.S. Department of Defense (Crowe et al., 2002). The monitoring agency can be notified of locations the offender is allowed to and prohibited from going, known as inclusion and exclusion zones, respectively. If the offender and his or her transmitter are detected in an unauthorized area (e.g., near a victim's home) the monitoring agency generates an alert.

Electronic Monitoring and Crime Reduction

Renzema and Mayo-Wilson (2005) provide the most thorough assessment of research measuring the relationship between electronic monitoring and offender performance. They identify only three published studies meeting their inclusion criteria of comparison groups and analysis of multiple outcome indicators, and conclude "that applications of [electronic monitoring] as a tool for reducing crime are not supported by existing data. Properly controlled experiments would be required to draw stronger conclusions about the effects of [electronic monitoring]" (p. 220).

Bonta, Wallace-Capretta, and Rooney (2000a) compared court-based and corrections-based electronic monitoring programs with inmates and probationers in Canada. Their research found little crime reducing impact for either type of electronic monitoring program, suggesting that electronic monitoring does little more than "net-widening" or increasing surveillance without altering underlying criminal attitudes and behaviors. Bonta et al. (2000a, p. 61) point out that electronic monitoring "added little value to more traditional forms of community control." They did find that offenders on electronic monitoring had more favorable attitudes toward staff (e.g., empathy, trust), and had significantly higher program completion rates (see also Bonta, Wallace-Carpetta, & Rooney, 2000b).

Finn and Muirhead-Steves (2002) compared 128 high-risk parolees on electronic monitoring with 158 similar parolees not on electronic monitoring. Their results indicated that "electronic monitoring had no direct effect on the likelihood of recommitment to prison or time until failure" (p. 293). Although this analysis found little crime reduction among the general sample, the authors did indicate that sex offenders on electronic monitoring had significantly longer times until arrest and smaller probabilities of returning to prison than similar offenders not on electronic monitoring. The authors concluded that electronic monitoring needs further scientific scrutiny of the interactions between treatment completion and electronic monitoring as well as investigating the mechanisms involved with the crime reducing effects on subgroups of high-risk offenders (i.e., sex offenders).

The most recent evaluation of both RF and GPS technologies to enforce home detention orders used data from more than 75,000 offenders in Florida. Padgett, Bales, and Blomberg (2006) found offenders monitored with either technology to have significantly lower probabilities for revocations for technical violations or new crimes as well as lower absconding rates. This is the only evaluation of electronic monitoring technologies in a community corrections setting to uncover such optimistic findings. However, the authors offer little in the way of an explanation. It seems counterintuitive that increased surveillance of offenders (in this case with electronic devices) would result in significant reductions in technical violations. That is, Petersilia and Turner (1991) are well-known for finding a strong positive relationship between increased surveillance and technical violations in an intensive supervision experiment. Padgett et al. (2006) have contributed significantly to understanding electronic monitoring, but further research needs to uncover the relationship between electronic monitoring and technical violations (and other offender behaviors) to identify the causal mechanisms related to offender performance. Furthermore, their research focused on quantitative offender data to understanding the probability and timing of three offender outcomes, but did not include a process evaluation to determine how electronic monitoring tools were used.

Other evaluations, with less rigorous methodology, show that electronic monitoring programs have the ability to effectively treat DUI offenders, drug offenders, and other non-violent offenders (Clayton, 1998; Courtright, Berg, & Mutchnick, 1997; Jolin & Stipak, 1992). When used prior to trial, electronic monitoring has been shown to be an effective strategy for pretrial detention (Cadigan, 1991; Cooprider, 1992; Cooprider & Kerby, 1990). With pretrial detention occurring in the home rather than in jail, suspects are potentially avoiding the criminogenic environment found in many jails.

Rehabilitation theories posit that programs will be successful when offenders are assigned treatments that target their specific criminogenic needs (Andrews et al., 1990). Like other treatment programs, electronic monitoring programs are not successful in treating all offenders, but this does not mean that they are useless; rather, other goals of the justice system may be attained even if the offender is not rehabilitated. Studies have focused on factors associated with program completion and recidivism among offenders sentenced to house arrest with electronic monitoring.

THE UNANTICIPATED CONSEQUENCES OF MONITORING POLICIES FOR SEX OFFENDERS

Legislation mandating electronic monitoring of sex offenders may work to improve community supervision, but it might also be the case that there are numerous unanticipated consequences reducing the effectiveness of electronic monitoring of sex offenders. Consider that there is an assortment of potential outcomes stemming from various social policies as there "is a range of consequences, any one of which may follow the act in any given case" (Merton, 1936, p. 899). Robert Merton (1936, p. 899) claimed that policymakers, administrators, and social scientists may be able to narrow the "limits of the range of possible consequences . . . but it is impossible to predict with certainty the results in any particular case." Joan McCord (2003, p. 17) suggests that often social policy interventions are passed with little interest in reporting that "some treatments cause harm." McCord (2003) worked from Merton's idea of unanticipated consequences of social interventions that in some cases the intervention itself leads to further harm.

In a similar way, Roger Roots (2004) discussed the unintended consequences of public policy as laws backfire. Roots (2004) argued that often governmental responses to various social problems are created in a hurried context in which immediate and rather straightforward solutions are expected to solve some longstanding complex social problem. Roots described several occasions in which well articulated policy arguments for such social issues as labor legislation, progressive taxation, and public education programs have backfired as they did not bring about better working conditions, more egalitarian tax structure, or more effective teaching programs.

Combining the sex offender literature with research on electronic monitoring and other community based sanctions, potential unintended consequences from these policies can be identified. In particular, the following unintended consequences are possible: (1) a false sense of security among the public, (2) sanction stacking, (3) restructured workloads, (4) anomic conditions in the electronic monitoring program, and (5) isolation.

A false sense of security is one potential unintended consequence from these policies (see Fine, 2006; McCord, 2003; Merton, 1936; Roots, 2004). Given that nearly 95 percent of all sex crimes involving a victim less than 18 years of age involve a known offender (Langan et al., 2003) electronic monitoring policies may not be providing much direct protection to the community. This is not to suggest that electronic monitoring of sex offenders cannot be an effective tool when combined with other supervision tools (e.g., treatment, risk assessment, polygraph) with some offenders. In fact, it might be the case that electronic monitoring assists in providing an effective source of external criminal justice control and increases the likelihood of treatment completion, avoidance of exclusionary zones, sobriety, and other conditions.

Another unintended consequence has to do with sanction stacking. Sex offenders supervised in the community previously had to abide by a number of different conditions. Offenders typically have numerous supervision conditions that structure their time in the community, such as substance abuse treatment, paying restitution, urinalysis, employment, training, curfews, and electronic monitoring. Adding electronic monitoring to the supervision tools used to monitor sex offenders will result in another set of conditions. This creates a situation in which community corrections officers supervise many offenders with high expectations regarding the type and number of conditions of supervision. "Sanction stacking" occurs when probationers and parolees are exposed "to a number of punitive and rehabilitative controls, which often leads to violations and returns to the correctional system" (Lucken, 1997, p. 367). It may be the case that electronic monitoring and sex offender legislation also contain unanticipated consequences such as unrealistic expectations, lack of concern for officer workload, neglecting objective needs for sex offenders, and other consequences that are unconceivable.

Another potential unintended consequence has to do with the restructured workloads of probation and parole officers. Certainly, probation and parole officer workloads are greatly restructured when adding a GPS component to supervision. Despite the tendency for technology to improve workplace efficiency, GPS supervision increases per offender workload by lengthening the enrollment phase for an offender, as officers must provide them information related to operating the device, informing offenders of how to handle lost signals, recharging batteries, emergency response considerations, equipment failure, and other problems. It also takes considerable time for officers to fit, clean, replace, and maintain equipment. Consider that GPS units are normally worn by an offender for between 60 and 90 days, something adding to the amount of time needed to clean and sanitize the equipment.

A related unintended consequence can be labeled anomic conditions in sex offender supervision units. Durkheim uses the concept of anomie to refer to instances of normlessness that potentially arise during periods of rapid change in which social actors are unable to determine the rules for appropriate behavior. Merton (1938) broadened the application of the concept to refer to the experience of being unable to meet one's goals due to blocked opportunity structures. If unrealistic expectations are placed on probation and parole officers in their efforts to supervise sex offenders, and they are provided little guidance in their supervision efforts, the potential for normlessness and frustration in the officer's caseload escalates. Having problems with one particular offender will make it difficult to supervise other offenders as well. For professors, just as one or two students can ruin a college course, one or two offenders can make the probation or parole officer's caseload unbearable.

Finally, the potential for isolation is another unintended consequence of applying the monitoring sanction to sex offenders. This technological trend could push probation and parole officers further away from face-to-face interaction with offenders as they become more accustomed to reviewing GPS location tracking sheets and corresponding with monitoring agencies to discern whether a probationer or parolee violated his or her curfew.

IMPLICATIONS FOR PROBATION/PAROLE OFFICERS AND FUTURE RESEARCH

Currently, community corrections agencies are responsible for supervising nearly five million adults (Glaze & Bonczar, 2006). Increasingly, probation and parole policies are being developed for the supervision of individuals convicted of sex offenses (Farkas & Stichman, 2002; Zevitz & Farkas, 2000). These new policies have evolved so quickly that empirical research has been noticeably scant on the topic. Using the prior research discussed earlier as a backdrop, recommendations for probation/parole practice and future research can be made to help ensure that probation and parole officers are ably equipped to supervise sex offenders with electronic monitoring strategies.

Six general recommendations for probation and parole officers can be made. First, probation and parole officers must recognize that electronic monitoring is nothing more than a tool. Just as a contractor uses several tools to build a house, probation and parole officers need several tools to supervise sex offenders. It is important to realize that each sanction or condition should be perceived as a supervision tool that may accomplish little when used alone, but when these tools are appropriately linked together they create an overall supervision strategy to provide external control to an offender's life (English, 1998). Incorporating several supervision tools to structure offenders' lives is essential to avoiding the problematic nature of sanction stacking, and potentially reduces the likelihood that an offender will be unsuccessful while on supervision.

Second, probation and parole officers must recognize the diverse nature of sex offenders. Although the category of child molesters, no doubt, incites fear into many citizens, there are numerous other sorts of offenders defined as sex offenders across the U.S. These offenders have diverse sets of needs, support structures, and risks that work to either push them away from reoffending or pull them closer to committing another sex crime (Hanson, 1998; Hanson & Bussiere, 1998). The evidence-based practices literature argues that each offender poses varying levels of risk (i.e., static factors), criminogenic needs (i.e., dynamic antisocial attitudes, criminal associates, and motivations), and if reductions in criminal behavior are sought, interventions must be individualized to address each offender's specific combination of risks and needs (see Andrews et al., 1990; Andrews & Bonta, 1998; Lowenkamp & Latessa, 2004; Taxman & Thanner, 2006). Meta-analyses of correctional program effectiveness have recently reported that when treatment interventions are based upon the three evidence-based principles–risk, need, and responsivity–there is a significant reduction in recidivism (Dowden & Andrews, 1999a, 1999b) and analogous behaviors (Wilson, Lipsey, & Derzon, 2003). What this means is that supervision strategies for sex offenders must be tailored to specific sex offenders.

Third, probation and parole officers must be sensitive to the dynamics of sex offending while supervising sex offenders. This mean that officers must consider the differences in reabuse patterns across sex offender types and recognize that most sex crimes, especially those against children, are committed by someone the victim knew beforehand (see Farkas & Stichman, 2002). Sex offender response strategies must address the realities of sex offender patterns (Edwards & Hensley, 2001; English, 1998; LaFond, 1998; Zevitz & Farkas, 2000).

Fourth, probation and parole officers, and their supervisors, must make sure that they are adequately prepared to use electronic monitoring strategies to supervise sex offenders. Participating in various training programs on sex offenders and electronic monitoring is a starting point for such preparation.

Fifth, to address the possibility of isolation, probation and parole officers must make sure that they are a part of a supportive environment that will help them overcome the consequences of isolation. Working with sex offenders, in and of itself, can result in burnout for any human services professional. Working in an environment characterized by anomie and isolation only increases the potential for burnout among probation and parole officers. Paying attention to the risk of burnout can help protect officers from experiencing it in the first place.

Sixth, probation and parole officers must work with researchers to make sure that response strategies are evidence-based and not emotionally charged, irrational responses. The need for research on this topic is evident. Policies demanding electronic monitoring of sex offenders, despite their intentions, are sometimes passed without fully considering the potential for unintended consequences or even worsening the problem by reducing supervision effectiveness (Fine, 2006; Robinson, 2003; Roots, 2004). Community supervision of sex offenders must be rooted in scientifically proven approaches that avoid mythical notions of sex offenders (Cole, 2000; Sample & Bray, 2003; Simon, 2003).

Electronic monitoring programs are fast appearing as a way to accomplish justice system goals and ease public safety concerns. There has yet to emerge, however, a large body of scientific research documenting the crime reduction impacts of electronic monitoring. Instead, much of this research fails to incorporate adequate controls, ignores department level contextual factors, and analyzes small samples.

There is little research empirically verifying the effectiveness of electronic monitoring technologies to change offender behaviors, and there has been next to nothing mentioned about the everyday implications of utilizing electronic monitoring technologies as part of offender supervision (Ibarra, 2005). It is essential for crime and justice researchers to take a close look at electronic monitoring in the community as prisons and jails have reached their limits, as federal, state, and local budgets are stretched thin, and as more offenders are sentenced to community supervision (Petersilia, 2003; Taxman, Shephardson, & Byrne, 2004).

Before mandating the use of electronic monitoring with sex offenders or other types of offenders, it is necessary to identify the direct and indirect effects of such technologies on offender community performance. Do electronically monitored offenders remain compliant longer in the community? Do these offenders have a greater incidence of completing treatment? And, are there any unanticipated consequences for community corrections agencies and officers? How will lifetime GPS policies be funded? How will electronic monitoring change workload allocations for officers? Electronic monitoring may prove to be an effective *tool* for community corrections officers to improve offender behavior. Or, conversely, it could be found that electronic monitoring programs do not result in significant reductions in violating or criminal behaviors (see Mair, 2005).

Also, because a multitude of factors contribute to explaining variation in criminal recidivism, both between and within criminal types, researchers and practitioners must work toward identifying the underlying sources of this variation. Identifying combinations of offender characteristics that are routinely found to co-occur with various types of criminal behavior does nevertheless provide researchers and practitioners with a strong footing to target interventions. Risk differentiation is essential for developing supervision conditions targeted toward each offender to reduce unintended negative consequences. Failing to address these unintended consequences has the potential to harm probation and parole officers, community members, and supervised sex offenders.

REFERENCES

Abel, G., Becker, J., Mittleman, M., Cunnigham-Ratherner, J., Rouleau, J., & Murphy, W. (1987). Self-reported sex crimes of nonincarcerate paraphiliacs. *Journal of Interpersonal Violence, 2*, 3-25.

Andrews, D., & Bonta, J. (1998). *The psychology of criminal conduct* (2nd ed.). Cincinnati, OH: Anderson Publishing.

Andrews, D., Zinger, I., Hoge, R., Bonta, J., Gendreau, P., & Cullen, F. (1990). Does correctional treatment work? A clinically relevant and psychologically informed meta-analysis. *Criminology, 28*(3), 369-404.

Bonta, J., Wallace-Capretta, S., & Rooney, J. (2000a). Can electronic monitoring make a difference? *Crime and Delinquency, 46,* 61-75.

Bonta, J., Wallace-Capretta, S., & Rooney, J. (2000b). A quasi-experimental evaluation of intensive rehabilitation supervision probation. *Criminal Justice & Behavior, 27*(3): 312-329.

Cadigan, T. P. (1991). Electronic monitoring in federal pretrial release. *Federal Probation*, *55*(2), 26-30.

Clayton, S. (1998). Implementing innovative approaches to community corrections. *Corrections Today, 60,* 26.

Cole, S. (2000). From the sexual psychopath statute to Megan's law: Psychiatric knowledge in the diagnosis, treatment, and adjudication of sex criminals in New Jersey, 1949-1999. *Journal of the History of Medicine, 55,* 292-314.

Conway, P. (2003). A survey of agencies using electronic monitoring reveals a promising future. *Journal of Offender Monitoring, 16*(2), 18-23.

Cooprider, K. W. (1992). Pretrial bond supervision: An empirical analysis with policy implications *Federal Probation, 56* (3), 41-49.

Cooprider, K. W., & Kerby, J. (1990). A practical application of electronic monitoring at the pretrial stage. *Federal Probation, 54* (1), 28-35.

Courtright, K., Berg, B. L., & Mutchnick, R. (1997). The cost effectiveness of using house arrest with electronic monitoring for drunk drivers. *Federal Probation, 61,* 19-22.

Crowe, A., Sydney, L., & Bancroft, P. (2002). *Offender supervision with electronic technology: A user's guide.* National Institute of Justice, U.S. Department of Justice, Washington, D.C.

Cumming, G., & McGrath, R. (2005). *Supervision of the sex offender: Community management, risk assessment, and treatment, second edition.* Brandon, Vermont: Safer Society Press.

DeMichele, M., Payne, B., & Button, D. (2007). Sex offenders and electronic monitoring: A call for evidence-based policy. Council of State Governments, *State News,* January.

Dowden, C., & Andrews, D. (1999a). What works for female offenders: A meta-analysis. *Forum on Corrections Research, 11,* 21-24.

Dowden, C., & Andrews, D. (1999b). Effective correctional treatment and violent reoffending: A meta-analysis. *Canadian Journal of Criminology,* 449-467.

Edwards, W., & Hensley, C. (2001). Contextualizing sex offender management legislation and policy: Evaluating the problem of latent consequences in community notification laws. *International Journal of Offender Therapy and Comparative Criminology, 45*(1), 83-101.

English, K. (1998). The containment approach: An aggressive strategy for the community management of adult sex offenders. *Psychology, Public Policy, and Law, 4*(1/2), 218-235.

Farkas, M., & Stichman, A. (2002). Sex offender laws: Can treatment, punishment, incapacitation, and public safety be reconciled? *Criminal Justice Review, 27*(2), 256-283.

Fine, G. (2006). The chaining of social problems: Solutions and unintended consequences in the age of betrayal. *Social Problems, 53*(1), 3-17.

Finn, M. A., & Muirhead-Steves, S. (2002). The effectiveness of electronic monitoring with violent male parolees. *Justice Quarterly, 19,* 293-312.

Gebhard, P., Gagnon, J., Pomeroy, W., & Christenson, V. (1965). *Sex offenders: An analysis of types.* New York: Harper and Row.

Glaze, L., & Bonczar, T. (2006). *Probation and parole in the United States, 2005.* Bureau of Justice Statistics, Office of Justice Programs, U.S. Department of Justice, Washington, D.C.

Gottfredson, M., & Hirschi, T. (1990). *A general theory of crime*. Stanford, CA: Stanford University Press.

Greenfeld, L. (1997). *Sex offenses and offenders: An analysis of rape and sexual assault.* U.S. Department of Justice, Office of Justice Programs, Bureau of Justice Statistics. Washington, D.C.

Groth, A. (1979). *Men who rape: The psychology of the offender*. New York: Plenum.

Guay, J., Proulx, J., Cussen, M., & Ouimet, M. (2001). Victim-choice polymorphia among serious sex offenders. *Archives of Sexual Behavior, 30*(5), 521-533.

Hanson, K. (1998). What do we know about sex offender risk assessment?' *Psychology, Public Policy, and Law, 4*, 50-72.

Hanson, K., & Bussiere, M. (1998). Predicting relapse: A meta-analysis of sexual offender recidivism studies. *Journal of Consulting and Clinical psychology, 66*, 348-362.

Hanson, K., Scott, H., & Steffy, R. (1995). A comparison of child molesters and nonsexual criminals: Risk predictors and long-term recidivism. *Journal of Research in Crime and Delinquency, 32*, 325-337.

Hazlewood, R. (1995). Analyzing rape and profiling the offender. In R. Hazlewood & A. Burgess (Eds.), *Practical aspects of rape investigation: A multidisciplinary approach* (pp. 155-181). New York: CRC Press.

Hernandez, A. (2000). *Effective management of sex offenders in the community*. Presentation at the Federal Correctional Center, Butner, N.C.

Ibarra, P. (2005). Red flags and trigger control: The role of human supervision in an electronic monitoring program. *Crime, Law, and Deviance, 6*, 31-48.

Jolin, A., & Stipak, B. (1992). Drug treatment and electronically monitored home confinement: An evaluation of a community-based sentencing option. *Crime and Delinquency, 38*(2), 158-170.

Kappeler, V., Blumberg, M., & Potter, G. (2000). *The mythology of crime and criminal justice.* Prospect Heights, IL: Waveland Press, second edition.

Knight, R. (1999). Validation of a typology for rapists. *Journal of Interpersonal Violence, 14*, 297-323.

LaFond, J. (1998). The costs of enacting a sexual predator law. *Psychology, Public Policy, and Law, 4*(1/2), 468-504.

Langan, P., Schmitt, E., & Durose, M. (2003). *Recidivism of sex offenders released from prison in 1994.* U.S. Department of Justice, Office of Justice Programs, Bureau of Justice Statistics. Washington, D.C.

Lanning, K. (1986). *Child molesters: A behavioral analysis for law enforcement officers investigating cases of child sexual exploitation.* Washington, DC: National Center for Missing and Exploited Children.

Lowenkamp, C., & Latessa, E. (2004). Understanding the risk principle: How and why correctional interventions can harm low-risk offenders. *Topics in Community Corrections*, 1-8.

Lucken, K. (1997). The dynamics of penal reform. *Crime, Law, & Social Change, 26*, 367-384.

Mair, G. (2005). Electronic monitoring in England and Wales: Evidence-based or not? *Criminal Justice, 5*(3), 257-277.

Matthew, R., Matthew, J., & Speltz, K. (1989). *Female sex offenders: An exploratory study.* Orwell, VT: Safer Society.

McCord, J. (2003). Cures that harm: Unanticipated outcomes of crime prevention programs. *Annals of American Political and Social Science, 587*, 16-30.

Merton, R. (1936). The unanticipated consequences of purposive action. *American Sociological Review, 1*, 894-904.

Nellis, M. (1991). The electronic monitoring of offenders in England and Wales: Recent developments and future prospects. *British Journal of Criminology, 31*(2), 165-185.

Nellis, M. (2005). Out of this world. *Howard Journal of Criminal Justice, 44*, 125-150.

Padgett, K., Bales, W., & Blomberg, T. (2006). Under surveillance: An empirical test of the effectiveness of electronic monitoring. *Criminology & Public Policy, 5*(1), 61-92.

Papy, J. E., & Nimer, R. (1991). Electronic monitoring in Florida. *Federal Probation, 55*(1), 31-33.

Petersilia, J. (2003). *When prisoners come home: Parole and prisoner reentry*. NY: Oxford University Press.

Petersilia, J., & Turner, S. (1991). An evaluation of intensive probation in California. *Journal of Criminal Law & Criminology, 82*(3), 610-658.

Renzema, M., & Mayo-Wilson, E. (2005). Can electronic monitoring reduce crime for moderate to high-risk offender? *Journal of Experimental Criminology, 1*, 215-237.

Robinson, L. (2003). Sex offender management: The public policy challenges. *Annals of New York Academy of Science, 989*, 1-7.

Roots, R. (2004). When laws backfire: Unintended consequences of public policy. *American Behavioral Scientist, 47*(11), 1376-1394.

Sample, L., & Bray, T. (2003). Are sex offenders dangerous? *Criminology and Public Policy, 3*(1), 59-82.

Simon, J. (1998). Managing the monsters: Sex offenders in the new penology. *Psychology, Public Policy, and Law, 4*(1/2), 452-467.

Simon, J. (2003). Managing the monstrous: Sex offenders and the New Penology. In B. Winick and J. LaFond (Eds.), *Protecting society from sexually dangerous offenders: Law, Justice, and Therapy* (pp. 301-316). Washington, D.C. American Psychological Association.

Simon, L. (2000). An examination of the assumptions of specialization, mental disorder, and dangerousness in sex offenders. *Behavioral Sciences & the Law, 18*, 275-308.

Soothill, K., Francis, B., Sanderson, B., & Ackerly, E. (2000). Sex offenders: Specialists, generalists–or both? A 32-year criminological study. *British Journal of Criminology, 40*, 56-67.

Taxman, F., Shephardson, E., & Byrne, J. (2004). *Tools of the trade: A guide to incorporating science into practice*. National Institute of Corrections, U.S. Department of Justice, Office of Justice Programs.

Taxman, F., & Thanner, M. (2006). Risk, need, and responsivity (RNR): It all depends. *Crime and Delinquency, 52*(1), 28-51.

Wilson, S., Lipsey, M., & Derzon, J. (2003). The effects of school-based intervention programs on aggressive and disruptive behavior: A meta-analysis. *Journal of Consulting and Clinical Psychology, 71*, 136-149.

Worling, J. (2001). Personality-based typology of adolescent male sexual offenders: Differences in recidivism rates, victim-selection characteristics, and personal victimization histories. *Sexual Abuse: A Journal of Research and Treatment, 13*, 149-166.

Zevitz, R., & Farkas, M. (2000). The impact of sex-offender community notification on probation/parole in Wisconsin. *International Journal of Offender Therapy and Comparative Criminology, 44*(1), 8-21.

Zimring, F. (2004). *An American Travesty: Legal response to adolescent sexual offending*. Chicago: University of Chicago Press.

Understanding the Decision to Pursue Revocation of Intensive Supervision: A Descriptive Survey of Juvenile Probation and Aftercare Officers

NATHAN C. LOWE
CHERIE DAWSON-EDWARDS
KEVIN I. MINOR
JAMES B. WELLS

INTRODUCTION

As an intermediate sanction, intensive supervision programs (ISPs) lie along the continuum of dispositional alternatives between probation and incarceration (Harris, Petersen, & Rapoza, 2001; Lurigio, 1987; Tonry & Lynch, 1996). Intermediate sanctions were developed to offer money-strapped, overcrowded corrections and juvenile justice departments, as well as fear-stricken communities, with sanctioning alternatives that combine supervision, treatment, and punishment. Theoretically, these sanctions are meant to accommodate competing goals of the community and the criminal justice system by offering "lower cost, community-based alternatives that impose 'tough time' in the community without jeopardizing public safety" (Byrne, 1990; Harris et al., 2001, p. 308).

Intermediate sanctions encompass the traditional philosophical underpinnings of adult corrections in the U.S., including retribution, incapacitation, deterrence, and rehabilitation. More recently, there has been a move to incorporate these sanctions (especially ISP) into juvenile justice, even though the underpinning of juvenile justice has historically been *parens patriae* which emphasizes furthering the best interests of the child through individualized justice (Cavender & Knepper, 1992). Despite manifestations of the "get tough" movement, juvenile justice has continued to reflect a rehabilitative model that posits the youthful offender to be "treatable" as opposed to (or sometimes in addition to) being in need of punishment (Curtis & Reese, 1994; Goodstein & Sontheimer, 1997; McGarrell, 1991).

The Juvenile Justice & Delinquency Prevention Act of 1974 stressed the development of "critically needed alternatives to institutionalization" and provided funding for community-based alternatives to juvenile detention facilities (Josi & Sechrest, 1999, p. 54). Juvenile ISPs now serve as an alternative to traditional detention and residential placements in an effort to control the rising costs of institutionalization (Goodstein & Sontheimes, 1997). As an offshoot of adult ISPs that were revamped and became popular in the 1980s (Lurigio, 1987), juvenile ISPs were a response to increased juvenile violence that was predicted by some criminologists and evidenced by statistical trends in the early to mid-1990s (Corbett, 1999). In theory, ISPs emphasize: (1) reduced caseloads; (2) closer surveillance and monitoring; and (3) relatively less focus on treatment (Armstrong, 1991). Although goals of ISPs vary across state programs, they generally include increased public safety, reduced institutional overcrowding, accessible rehabilitation programs for the offender, and reduced costs (Clear & Hardyman, 1990; Fulton, Latessa, Stichman, Travis, Corbett, & Harris, 1997).

One concern with both adult and juvenile ISPs is the high rate of technical violations frequently leading to revocation and incarceration. Both current and earlier studies have shown that persons in ISPs, and to a lesser extent even those on traditional probation and parole, are often sent to institutions because of technical violations, as opposed to further criminal behavior (e.g., Banks, Porter, Rardin, Sider, & Unger, 1977; Carter & Wilkins, 1976; Fulton et al., 1997; Neithercutt & Gottfredson, 1975; Wilson, 2005). A common explanation is that these violations reflect the stringent rules and conditions placed on offenders in combination with heightened surveillance (Altshuler & Armstrong, 2001). Violations may also be indicative of the inadequacy of the services provided in ISPs. However, as writers have suggested (e.g., Altschuler & Armstrong, 2001), more research is needed to determine where the problem lies.

Types of Intensive Supervision Programs

As with many criminal justice programs, definitional issues hinder the study of ISPs. Both programs and research studies vary significantly in operational definitions of the goals, components, and implementation of ISPs; however, the common trait is that ISPs are considered a more "intense" alternative than traditional community supervision (Petersilia & Turner, 1993). Some states differentiate between front-end intermediate sanctions, like intensive supervision probation, and back-end ones, like intensive parole or aftercare. Other states, including Kentucky, offer a variety of relatively distinct programs and incorporate ISP with these. For example, Kentucky offers both traditional juvenile probation and aftercare services, but at certain points during the probation or reentry process, intensive supervision can be combined with either of these services (Kentucky Department of Juvenile Justice, n.d.).

Clear and Drammer (2000) identify three types of ISPs: institutional diversion, probation enhancement, and early release. The distinction mentioned between front-end and back-end programs corresponds to Clear and Drammer's typology. Front-end programs include those that focus on diverting offenders from institutional placements as well as enhanced probation. The former deals with juvenile offenders whose offenses were serious enough to warrant incarceration, but circumstances warranted them eligible for participation in an ISP. Enhanced probation increases the level of supervision and services for probated offenders.

By contrast, back-end ISPs involve the early release of offenders into enhanced community supervision. Similar to adult corrections, research has suggested that the exorbitant numbers of confined juveniles being released back into communities are in need of aftercare (Altschuler & Armstrong, 2001). Therefore, upon release from a detention center or longer-term facility, juveniles deemed "high risk" may be placed in an intensive aftercare program as a transition and reintegration period (Altschuler & Armstrong, 2001). An important goal of back-end programs is to reduce the costs of juvenile institutions (Clear & Drammer, 2000). However, Altschuler and Armstrong (2001) identified an apparent contradiction in the intensive aftercare framework. They report that juvenile aftercare programs attempt to reduce "the high rates of failure and relapse usually experienced" by high risk juveniles (p. 73); yet studies have found the conditions of intensive aftercare programs are often unrealistic, difficult to attain, and unenforceable (Altschuler & Armstrong, 1994a; Krisberg, Rodriguez, Baake, Neuenfeldt, & Steele, 1989).

Officer Orientation and the Impact on Modification or Revocation Decisions

Clear, Harris, and Baird (1992) reported that research has only shown a "vague portrait" of the attitudes and responses community supervision officers have toward technical violations. Researchers have discovered that officers are given a significant amount of discretion, and even intra-agency officer responses to technical violations vary widely (Clear et al., 1992; McCleary, 1975). Officer attitudes affect their interactions with offenders, and those attitudes reflect both individual characteristics and organizational conditions (Whitehead & Lindquist, 1992). Other research suggests that officers sometimes modify their decisions to gain approval from their immediate supervisors (Clear et al., 1992; Rosecrance, 1985).

In the early 1990s, some researchers suggested that detailed research on officer responses to violations was missing from the literature (Clear et al., 1992). Thereafter, a few empirical studies (e.g., Cavender & Knepper, 1992) addressed this issue (see below). However, these studies began to dissipate around the mid-1990s. Rather than focusing on officers' attitudes and responses, most evaluations of the effectiveness of ISPs have examined either: (a) the rates and causes of technical violations and new offenses, often as compared with other sanctions (e.g., Petersilia & Turner, 1993; Turner & Petersilia, 1992) or (b) the impact of technical violations on revocation (e.g., Gray, Fields, & Maxwell, 2001).

Role and Goal Conflict in the Juvenile Justice System

Studt (1973) is credited with introducing the concepts of service and surveillance to describe the role of community supervision officers (see Whitehead & Lindquist, 1992). She suggested that as "jacks of all trades," officers have several sets of attitudes towards parolees and must take on a range of tasks that include both service and surveillance (Studt, 1973, p. 37). Curtis and Reese (1994) suggested that a conflict exists between service and surveillance, where offering juvenile offenders a second chance is often viewed synonymously with endangering the community and the child. Steiner, Roberts, and Hemmens (2003) found past literature to be unreliable in describing and revealing the true duties of juvenile probation officers and suggested that they remain somewhere between "law enforcement versus counselor" (p. 272).

Lawrence (1984) found that most officers claimed they were "working more for the court than for the client"; this implies a control or community protection orientation over an offender rehabilitative orientation (Whitehead & Lindquist, 1992, p. 15). In contrast, Petronio (1982) reported that courts felt probation officers should emphasize community protection, while officers articulated more concern for juveniles. Other research has confirmed this goal conflict between juvenile probation officers (JPOs) and the sentencing judges with whom they work (Asquith, 1983; Bortner, 1984; Curtis & Reese, 1994). In a study of determinants of adult probation and parole officer professional orientation, Whitehead and Lindquist (1992) found that even officers from conservative states do not necessarily support a pure, punitive orientation; they found that officers believed rehabilitation should be emphasized to some degree.

Other literature has compared the perceptions of adult and juvenile probation officers on their role in the juvenile justice system. Sluder and Reddington (1993) found that adult probation officers aligned their role with law enforcement, while JPOs preferred a more supportive role. Shearer (2002) found similar results in a comparison of adult and juvenile probation officer trainees, which revealed that JPOs identified with a casework or resource brokerage typology, while adult officers preferred the law enforcer role.

Factors in the Decision to Commit or Revoke a Juvenile Offender

Curtis and Reese (1994) offer one of the best examples of research that attempts to examine how juvenile justice officers' recommendations correspond with their justifications for those recommendations. Utilizing a causal attribution approach, they identified three dominant research areas in the literature related to factors that contribute to criminal justice attributions: (1) case effects; (2) decision maker effects; and (3) contextual effects. They used a self-administered questionnaire that included various measures relating to the officer's background characteristics, causal explanations for delinquency, and evaluation of the effectiveness of juvenile justice and internal agency programs and objectives. The instrument also included an actual department case that represented actions equating to a mid-range, "high nuisance" case (Curtis & Reese, 1994, p. 249). Eighty-two JPOs provided recommended dispositions for the case. Overall, the researchers found the officers' recommendations were not affected by their attitudes toward their department's effectiveness, though previous research suggested the existence of such a relationship (see Batson, Jones, & Cochran, 1979; Forst & Wellford, 1981). Curtis and Reese also found conflicting views toward the intent of treatment, though an organizational commitment to rehabilitation was apparent.

In another approach to understanding revocation decisions, Cavender and Knepper (1992, p. 387) applied the "gestalt of justice" decision making model, which emphasizes the "social production of decisions" (Drass & Spencer, 1987). This approach suggests that the critical components of the revocation decision include "case sequence and flow, decision maker/client interactions, professional norms, organizational goals and situational contexts" (Cavender & Knepper, 1992, p. 387; Emerson, 1983; Maynard, 1982). Specifically, the gestalt perspective emphasizes three areas of decision-making: (1) theory of office; (2) organizational context; and (3) accounts.

First, the working ideology or "theory of office" of decision makers comprises typologies and related outcomes that are obtained through the professionalization process (Cavender & Knepper, 1992; Drass & Spencer, 1987). The gestalt of justice model posits that a client/ case typology is developed through the decision-maker's reliance on legal factors, attitudinal impressions, training, and experience (Cavender & Knepper, 1992; Sudnow, 1965). The decision maker then seeks out information that serves as confirmation to the developed typology and the accompanying "appropriate case outcome" (Cavender & Knepper, 1992, p. 388; Rosecrance, 1988). Second, the organizational context includes the performance of certain tasks to achieve the goals of the agency. For example, community supervision officers may dispose of a case due to organizational considerations such as bed space and the availability of other organizational resources. "Accounts," the final aspect of the gestalt perspective, are the "language people use to make actions intelligible to evaluative inquiry" (Cavender & Knepper, 1992, p. 388; Scott & Lyman, 1968, p. 46). They argue that criminal justice decision makers offer accounts by "emphasizing some aspects of a situation and de-emphasizing others" (Cavender & Knepper, 1992, p. 388). Accounts operate in the process of professional socialization of decision makers by confirming the theory of office (Cavender & Knepper, 1992; Drass & Spencer, 1987; Spencer, 1983).

Cavender and Knepper (1992) tested the gestalt of justice through examining 114 hearings conducted by a state juvenile parole board. The juveniles in the study were being charged with parole violations that could have been either technical violations or a new criminal offense. The study found that actions by decision makers in the revocation hearing followed the predetermined outcomes for the particular case typology being heard. They also reported that actions "consistently invoked the language of individualized justice" with a combination of individual responsibility. Overall, the researchers concluded that they observed "a theory of office, its organizational context, and accompanying accounts as integrated features of the decision-making gestalt" (Cavender & Knepper, 1992, p. 397).

In recent years, researchers have devoted less attention to juvenile ISPs generally and revocation decisions in particular. There are at least three interrelated considerations surrounding our understanding the dynamics of juvenile ISPs. First, the operational definitions of these programs vary significantly both in applied programs and empirical research studies. This is not only a significant issue in regard to ISPs, but it is problematic among community corrections in general (Mays & Winfree, 2003). Second, since the mid-1990s, researchers have largely ignored surveying community juvenile justice workers in order to study attitudes and perceptions toward aspects of ISPs, such as their perceptions of and responses to technical violations. And third, it is evident that further research is needed to gain better insight into officers' attitudes toward their roles as workers as well as departmental and program goals.

The present study addresses these issues through surveying juvenile justice ISP officers in Kentucky. The study investigates research questions pertaining to: (a) officers' perceptions of the goals of intensive supervision, (b) their perceptions of the frequency of various violations, and (c) the degree of importance officers assign to several different factors in deciding to recommend the unsuccessful termination of a case from intensive supervision. The latter two questions are addressed for both probated and aftercare cases. Additionally, we extend the focus of previous literature by addressing a fourth question that has received little if any attention heretofore, namely the likelihood with which officers might pursue specific avenues or alternatives in hopes of averting a decision to recommend unsuccessful termination of intensive supervision.

THE KENTUCKY JUVENILE INTENSIVE SUPERVISION TEAM PROGRAM

The Kentucky Department of Juvenile Justice's (DJJ's) Juvenile Intensive Supervision Team (JIST) Program was created in 1998. It was originally designed to be a variation of a youth program in Boston, Massachusetts called "Operation Night Light," which was created in an attempt to decrease gang violence among inner-city youth (Boston Police Department, 1996). However, unlike Boston's program, JIST was created as a new community-based placement for: (a) committed (aftercare) youth who no longer require the level of supervision and care provided by state juvenile facilities but who need more intensive supervision than provided by traditional probation or aftercare, and (b) probated youth considered to be at high risk of out-of-home placement.

Since its inception, the program has been administered through a team effort between local law enforcement officers and DJJ community workers. Teams make regular home, school, and work visits to enforce youths' conditions of probation or supervised community placement. These contacts allow teams to accomplish three things: (1) establish whether or not the juvenile is in compliance with curfew and other restrictions; (2) reinforce the importance of strict observance of all conditions of probation/aftercare; and (3) inquire of family members about the behavior of the juvenile, both at home and in the community. In addition, the JIST Program intends to strengthen relationships between local law enforcement and DJJ, involve families in the youth's progress, and provide awareness to other youth of the juvenile justice system's seriousness about promoting safe communities (Kentucky Department of Juvenile Justice, n.d.).

Unlike Boston's program, the JIST Program has not primarily focused on gang violence among inner-city youth. In its contemporary practice, as described above, it more closely resembles ISPs for juvenile offenders in other states. For instance, the Anchorage Coordinated Agency Network (CAN) Program in Alaska also utilizes local law enforcement officers to help supervise juvenile probationers in the community. Another objective of the CAN Program is to provide supplemental mentors to juvenile probationers who are deemed high-risk (Giblin, 2002); this feature also resembles the JIST Program in that the team maintains consistent contact with both the youth and his/her family. Whether operated by local or state juvenile justice agencies, ISPs like the JIST Program, attempt to closely monitor youth in the community in an attempt to reduce and/or prevent further delinquency.

As in other juvenile ISPs, juveniles are selected to participate in the JIST program through one of two ways: (1) probated youth who are court-ordered by a judge as a means to avert commitment, or (2) probated or aftercare youth who are selected by their community worker. The criteria vary for a youth to be selected to participate in JIST. Similar to other juvenile ISPs, however, youth selected for JIST often have a history of offenses, repeated violation of conditions of probation or supervised community placement, or have displayed other problems related to their personal and home life.

DJJ currently operates JIST programs in 11 areas throughout the state. Five programs operate at the county level, and six operate at the city level. Each program operates somewhat differently, since they are coordinated in a way that local JIST staff deem best and most convenient for accomplishing objectives (see Kentucky Department of Juvenile Justice, n.d.).

METHOD

Participants

Participants in this study were employees of the Kentucky DJJ's Community Services Branch. Only community workers who had some type of association with JIST programs in their district areas were selected to participate. Each supervisor of every district having JIST programs was contacted via e-mail to determine the community workers associated with JIST. Based on this, a total of 81 individuals (including district supervisors) were initially contacted to participate in the study. Nine of those individuals declined to participate for various reasons or were removed from the distribution list for administrative reasons. Of the 72 remaining persons, a total 66 returned completed surveys. This represented an 81.5 percent response rate.

Respondents' ages ranged from 25 to 60 years, with the mean age being about 38. Nearly 60 percent ($n = 38$) of the respondents were female. In addition, 42 were White, 15 were Black, and 3 were of other ethnic origin. All respondents indicated they had at least earned a bachelor's degree, and 48 said that a bachelor's degree was their highest level of education. A majority had earned their bachelor's degrees in social work ($n = 15$), criminal justice ($n = 12$), psychology ($n = 9$), or sociology ($n = 6$). Sixteen respondents indicated a master's degree was their highest level of education.

Respondents were asked to provide their current job title and describe their role with the JIST Program. Based on current job title, respondents were divided into three categories: "direct line community workers," "case specialists," and "district supervisors." Most of the participants ($n = 46$) noted they were direct line community workers whose role was to either: (a) conduct the main duties of the JIST Program (e.g., curfew checks) in their district area, (b) make referrals for JIST monitoring without conducting any of the main duties of the program, or (c) perform a dual role involving both conducting the main duties and making referrals. Nine respondents were categorized as case specialists. These individuals made referrals for JIST monitoring and coordinated the caseloads of the direct line community workers. In some instances, case specialists may have cases of their own to manage. Lastly, nine respondents were categorized as district supervisors. They oversaw the direct line community workers and case specialists, and they did not have a caseload of youth for JIST monitoring.

Participants were also asked how long they had been working for DJJ, as well as how long they had been working in the Division of Community Services. The range of time working for DJJ was between 3 months and 26 years, with the median being slightly over 7 years. The range of time working in the Division of Community Services was between 1 month and 26 years, with the median being about 5.5 years. Additionally, respondents were asked to describe the geographical area within their district in which the majority of their JIST work was conducted. Since Kentucky is predominantly a rural state, unsurprisingly, most of the respondents indicated the majority of their JIST work was done in rural areas or mid size cities; there are only three urban areas in Kentucky in which JIST programs exist (i.e., Louisville, Lexington, and the Northern Kentucky area outside Cincinnati, Ohio). Finally, respondents were asked to indicate how many youth they currently had on their caseload, as well as how many youth on their caseload were under JIST supervision. Reported caseloads ranged from 0 to 38, with a mean of approximately 15. The number of JIST cases ranged from 0 to 19, with a mean of about 2. Those respondents who reported having no JIST cases were in supervisory positions, and their job duties did not involve direct case management. These respondents were associated with the JIST program in an administrative capacity.

Date Collection Procedure

Data for the study were collected through an e-mail survey distributed between December, 2006 and March, 2007. E-mail was the preferred method because all respondents had access, and this method was convenient and cost efficient. Further, e-mail allowed for easy tracking of surveys and consent forms, as well as recording of the dates of correspondence. The methodology used in contacting the subjects and administering the surveys was a variation of Dillman's (2006) method. Participants were initially contacted via e-mail to explain the purpose of the study and to provide surveys and consent forms as attachments. While the intent was to have the respondents complete and return surveys on their work computers, some surveys were returned via fax or postal mail. Subjects who had not returned surveys were contacted every two weeks via e-mail until they offered correspondence as to whether or not they were participating in the study. After three contact attempts via e-mail, subjects were then contacted via telephone. Finally, as a last resort, a representative of DJJ's Division of Program Services, the division in which research studies are authorized, was contacted in hopes of encouraging any employees who had not yet participated in the study to do so.

Measures

In addition to containing the demographic and background variables mentioned above, the survey instrument contained items designed on the basis of the four research questions posed earlier: (1) What is the perceived function of JIST; (2) What is the perceived frequency of violations committed by probated and aftercare youth who are monitored by JIST; (3) What is the perceived importance of various factors that contribute to the decision to pursue commitment of probated youth or revocation of aftercare youth who are monitored by JIST; and (4) What avenues of intervention are likely to be utilized to avert commitment of probated youth or revocation of aftercare youth who are monitored by JIST? These questions and corresponding survey response options and formats appear in the appendix.

For the first research question (item 1 in the appendix), workers were presented with DJJ's official description of JIST (i.e., the program was developed to provide intensive surveillance of delinquent youth, facilitate rehabilitation, reduce recidivism rates, and safeguard the community). Based on that information, they were asked to rank order the four functions listed in the appendix.

The remaining three research questions enabled comparison of how workers perceived probated and aftercare youth. Similar to other juvenile justice systems, in Kentucky "probated" youth are those who have been adjudicated as delinquent and allowed to remain in the community subject to compliance with conditions set forth by DJJ and the court. On the other hand, in Kentucky, aftercare youth are commonly referred to as "committed" youth, meaning they have been paroled from a residential placement after being committed to DJJ. Following successful completion of residential placement, these youth return to the community under the supervision of DJJ community workers and must comply with conditions set forth by DJJ. As such, community workers and case specialists, may have both probated and aftercare youth on their caseloads.

For the second research question (items 2a and 2b in the appendix), felonies and misdemeanors were considered new offenses, whereas term violations were considered actions in violation of the technical conditions of probation or supervised placement. Though not involving additional charges, term violations may lead to a probation violation or aftercare revocation hearing. Examples of such violations include positive drug screens, breaking curfew, accumulation of unexcused absences from school, or not reporting to a worker as directed. The appendix items corresponding to the third research question (items 3a and 3b), as well as those corresponding to the fourth question (items 4a and 4b) are self-explanatory.

RESULTS

Means and standard deviations pertaining to the first research question are presented in Table 1. While most respondents ($n = 51$) rank ordered the functions and thus answered the question using the proper response format, some respondents provided the same response for multiple functions. For instance, one person gave two of the four functions a "1"; another person gave three of the four functions a "1" and the remaining function a "4." In other cases, respondents correctly ranked two of the four functions but then gave the remaining two functions a "1." Returned surveys in which such errors existed were classified as missing data. For the properly formatted responses, Table 1 shows minimal differences in what participants perceived as the main functions of JIST–

Table 1: Means and Standard Deviations of Community Workers' Perceived Main Function of JIST Programs

Variable	M	SD
Provide supervision/surveillance to detect violations	2.06	1.01
Promote rehabilitation by providing services or referrals	3.49	0.78
Deter violations by sanctioning infractions	2.47	0.99
Ensure safety and security within the community	1.98	1.01

Range of Mean: 1 = Least Function . . . 4 = Greatest Function
N = 51

ensuring safety and security as well as providing supervision/surveillance to detect violations. The function of deterring violations by sanctioning infractions was also perceived as relatively important. The function perceived as least important was that of promoting rehabilitation.

A Friedman Test, which is the nonparametric analog to a repeated measures analysis of variance, was conducted on the rank orderings of the four functions. The Friedman Test does not require normality of data, and it tests for significant differences among the ranking of repeated variables (Gibbons, 1993). The test showed significant differences in the manner respondents rank ordered the functions ($\chi^2 = 44.25$, df = 3, $p = .00$).

Table 2, along with Figures 1 and 2, depict respondents' perceptions of the categorical frequencies of felonies, misdemeanors, and term violations among both probated and aftercare youth; higher scores indicate greater perceived frequency. It can be seen that among both probated and aftercare youth, respondents perceived term violations as being committed most frequently, followed by misdemeanors, and then felonies. There were only slight differences between probated and after-

Table 2: Number of Cases, Means, and Standard Deviations of Community Workers' Perceptions of the Frequency of Violations Among Probated and Aftercare Youth

	Probated			Aftercare		
Variable	N	M	SD	N	M	SD
Felonies	66	2.42	0.90	64	2.36	0.90
Misdemeanors	66	2.94	0.86	64	2.78	0.81
Term Violations	64	3.70	0.97	65	3.42	0.97

Range of Mean: 1 = Very Infrequent; 2 = Infrequent; 3 = Moderate; 4 = Frequent; 5 = Very Frequent

Figure 1: Means of Community Workers' Perceived Frequency of Violations Among Probated Youth

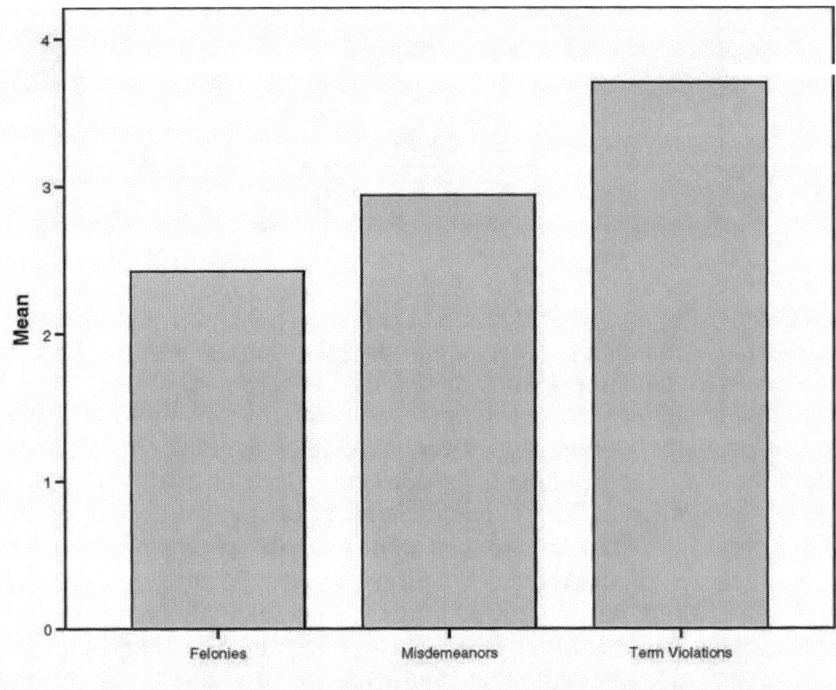

care youth. Probated youth were perceived as committing felonies, misdemeanors, and term violations slightly more frequently than aftercare youth.

Survey items for the remaining research questions (i.e., items 3a-4b in the appendix) asked respondents to rate lists of variables. Where a respondent provided multiple responses for the same variable, or when a response was not provided at all, the variable was coded as missing. Therefore, the number of cases differed slightly per variable (see Tables 3 and 4).

For the third research question, participants were asked to rate 23 factors in terms of importance to workers' decisions to pursue commitment of probated youth and revocation of aftercare youth who have been under JIST monitoring and in some way violated their term conditions. Similar

Figure 2: Means of Community Workers' Perceived Frequency of Violations Among Aftercare Youth

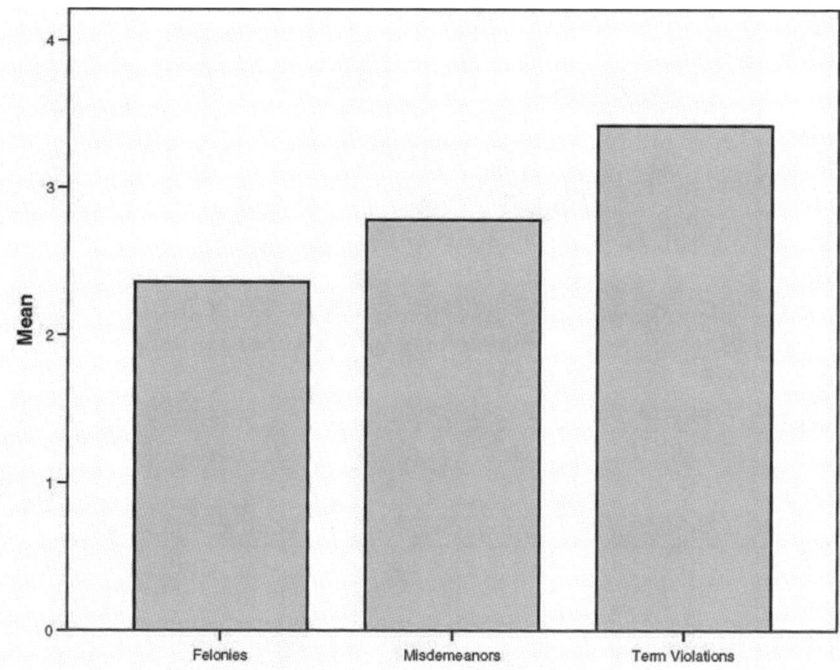

Range of Mean: 1=Very Infrequent, 2=Infrequent, 3=Moderate, 4=Frequent, 5=Very Frequent

Refer to Table 2 for the number of cases per variable.

to how respondents perceived the frequency of violations among probated and aftercare youth, there was not much difference in how participants perceived the importance of factors among both populations of youth. As can be seen in Table 3 and Figures 3 and 4, the distribution of means of the corresponding factors are quite similar for both probated and aftercare youth. For probated youth, the top five most important factors in deciding to pursue commitment were: seriousness of current offense that led to DJJ probation, seriousness of prior offenses before DJJ probation, seriousness of term violations after JIST involvement, number of term violations after JIST involvement, and substance abuse issues. The only other item with a mean rating that exceeded 4.0 was perceived

Table 3: Number of Cases, Means, and Standard Deviations of Community Workers' Perceptions of the Importance of Factors in Pursuit of Commitment or Revocation Among Probated and Aftercare Youth

	Probated			Aftercare		
Variable	N	M	SD	N	M	SD
Age of youth	66	2.70	0.96	64	2.61	1.06
Gender of youth	64	1.66	0.80	62	1.74	0.79
Number of prior offense(s) before DJJ probation or commitment	63	3.98	0.81	63	3.70	0.99
Seriousness of prior offense(s) before DJJ probation or commitment	63	4.40	0.81	63	4.06	1.06
Seriousness of current offense(s) that led to DJJ probation or commitment	66	4.50	0.77	63	4.38	0.92
Number of term violations before JIST involvement	66	3.79	0.90	64	3.81	1.01
Seriousness of term violations before JIST involvement	66	3.95	0.90	62	4.02	0.95
Number of term violations after JIST involvement	66	4.36	0.72	64	4.36	0.76
Seriousness of term violations after JIST involvement	66	4.39	0.74	64	4.41	0.71
Length of time under DJJ supervision	63	3.78	0.83	63	3.63	0.89
Attitude towards DJJ intervention	66	3.53	1.10	62	3.56	0.97
Responsiveness to past rehabilitative efforts	63	4.02	0.87	62	3.94	0.87
Projected responsiveness to future rehabilitative efforts	63	3.68	0.90	59	3.59	0.99
Availability of resources in the community	66	3.77	0.93	64	3.84	0.93
Home environment	66	3.79	0.94	64	3.86	0.94
Employability skills	66	2.94	0.89	64	3.06	0.92
Peer group associations	65	3.68	0.71	63	3.62	0.89
Leisure/recreation activities	65	3.35	0.94	63	3.38	1.02
School performance	66	3.71	0.80	64	3.77	0.90
Mental health issues/needs	66	3.89	0.88	62	3.87	1.03
Substance abuse issues	66	4.15	0.83	62	4.26	0.75
Attitude toward DJJ community worker	61	2.72	1.19	62	2.71	1.22
Conclusion that the youth has had sufficient chances to succeed	66	3.98	0.97	63	4.14	0.98

Range of Mean: 1 = Not Important at All; 2 = Not Important; 3 = Moderate; 4 = Important; 5 = Very Important

Figure 3: Means of Community Workers' Perceived Importance of Factors That Contribute to the Decision to Pursue Commitment Among Probated Youth

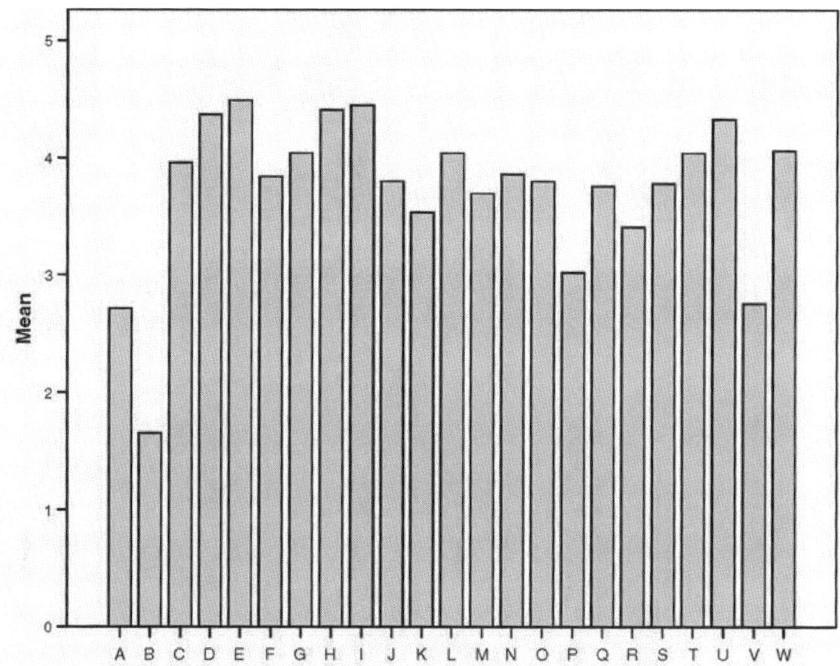

See Question 3a in the appendix for the corresponding variable names.

Range of Mean: 1=Not Important at All, 2=Not Important, 3=Moderate, 4=Important, 5=Very Important

Refer to Table 3 for the number of cases per variable.

responsiveness to past rehabilitation efforts. For aftercare youth, the top five were: seriousness of term violations after JIST involvement, seriousness of current offense that led to DJJ commitment, number of term violations after JIST involvement, substance abuse issues, and the conclusion that the youth has had sufficient chances to succeed. Only two other factors received mean ratings in excess of 4.0 (i.e., seriousness of pre-commitment offenses and seriousness of pre-JIST term violations). In contrast, respondents rated the gender of the youth as the least important factor for both probated and aftercare youth. Age, attitude toward DJJ worker, and employability skills were also perceived as relatively unimportant.

Figure 4: Means of Community Workers' Perceived Importance of Factors That Contribute to the Decision to Pursue Revocation Among Aftercare Youth

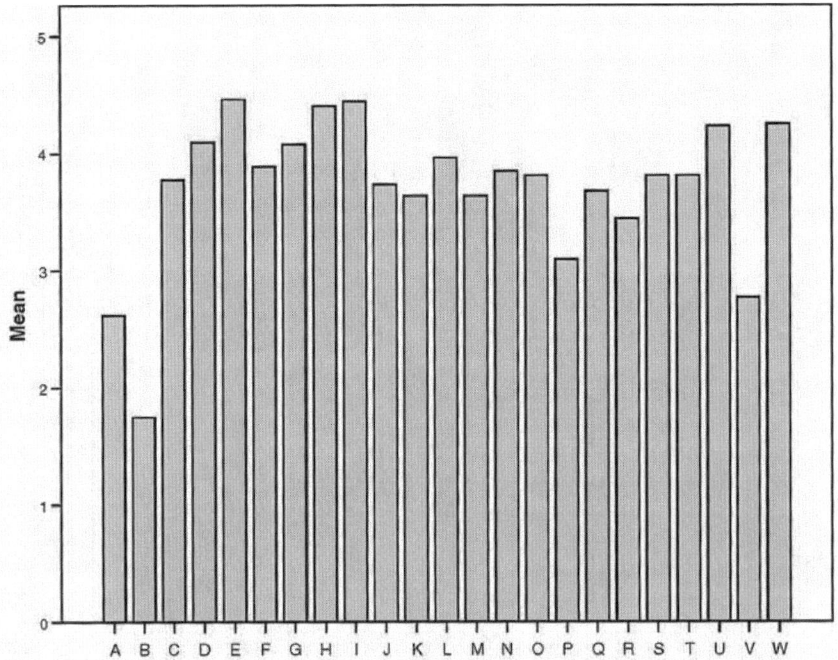

See Question 3b in the appendix for the corresponding variable names.

Range of Mean: 1=Not Important at All, 2=Not Important, 3=Moderate, 4=Important, 5=Very Important

Refer to Table 3 for the number of cases per variable.

As noted above, the fourth and final research question asked respondents to rate the likelihood that they might pursue each of 16 avenues of intervention to avert the decision to commit probated youth or revoke aftercare youth who have been under JIST surveillance and in some way violated their term conditions. The similarity with which participants perceived probated and aftercare cases continued regarding the avenues of intervention. In viewing Table 4 and Figures 5 and 6, it can be seen that the corresponding means of probated and aftercare youth are nearly identical. For both probated and aftercare youth, electronic monitoring, designation of an earlier curfew time, increased drug testing, home detention, and meeting with family and youth were rated as the top five most likely avenues to be utilized to avert commitment or revocation. Both in-home and outpatient counseling also received relatively high mean ratings. By contrast, assignment of homework and emergency shelter placement were the avenues rated by the respondents as less likely to be used to avert commitment or revocation for both populations of youth.

The 16 avenues were divided into two categories: (1) those oriented toward monitoring, controlling, and deterring offenders (items A-I in the appendix), and (2) those oriented toward rehabilitation (items J-P). For the first category, the overall mean rating (i.e., mean of means) for probated youth was 4.04, while that for aftercare cases was 4.03. For the rehabilitation category, the mean for probated cases was 3.70, while that for aftercare youth was 3.76.

DISCUSSION

This study yielded a number of interesting findings. First, officers perceived rehabilitation as the least important function of the JIST Program, behind the functions of ensuring community safety, detecting violations through monitoring, and deterrence through sanctioning infractions. This finding is consistent with the manner in which ISPs have widely been viewed as "tough" on crime and oriented toward law enforcement (Byrne, 1990; Harris et al., 2001; Whitehead & Lindquist, 1992). Although youth involved in JIST are referred by community workers in a final attempt to "help" them before pursuing commitment or revocation, respondents did not seem to perceive rehabilitative services as a main priority of the program. As such, a contradiction may exist in terms of how JIST and similar programs are broadly conceptualized in the policy realm (i.e., as a last chance to demonstrate improvements before commitment or revocation) and how the programs operate in practice (i.e., with a premium on monitoring, control, and deterrence). In turn, this may help contribute to high rates of revocation for technical violations.

It was not surprising to find that technical violations were perceived by respondents as the most frequently committed violations. For both probated and aftercare cases, technical violations were rated as occurring on a moderately frequent to frequent basis, while misdemeanors and felonies were rated as less common. Previous research on ISPs has shown that technical violations are quite prevalent among offenders (see Banks et al., 1977; Carter & Wilkins, 1976; Fulton et al., 1997;

☐ *Table 4: Number of Cases, Means, and Standard Deviations of Community Workers' Perceptions of the Avenues of Interventions to Avert Commitment or Revocation Among Probated and Aftercare Youth*

	Probated			Aftercare		
Variable	N	M	SD	N	M	SD
Assign homework	64	2.89	1.13	63	2.83	1.23
Designate an earlier curfew time	64	4.58	0.64	65	4.62	0.63
Increase frequency of drug testing	66	4.50	0.75	64	4.61	0.77
Voice monitoring	66	3.88	1.30	63	4.19	1.13
Electronic monitoring	66	4.59	0.72	64	4.70	0.61
Home detention	64	4.50	0.85	64	4.50	0.89
Community service	66	3.59	1.02	64	3.44	1.11
Alternative school placement	66	3.88	1.06	64	3.84	0.98
Time at juvenile detention center	66	3.95	0.94	63	3.57	1.17
Meeting with family and youth	65	4.46	0.83	64	4.53	0.69
Vocational training program	65	3.02	0.93	64	3.25	0.99
After school mentoring program	65	3.35	1.01	61	3.28	1.02
In-home counseling services	65	4.14	0.81	64	4.08	1.00
Outpatient counseling services	65	4.20	0.73	63	4.25	0.72
Inpatient treatment program	65	3.94	0.86	63	3.92	0.94
Emergency placement shelter	63	2.79	1.08	63	2.98	1.06

Range of Mean: 1 = Not Likely at All; 2 = Unlikely; 3 = Possibly; 4 = Likely; 5 = Very Likely

Figure 5: Means of Community Workers' Perceived Likelihood to Utilize Avenues of Intervention to Avert Commitment of Probated Youth

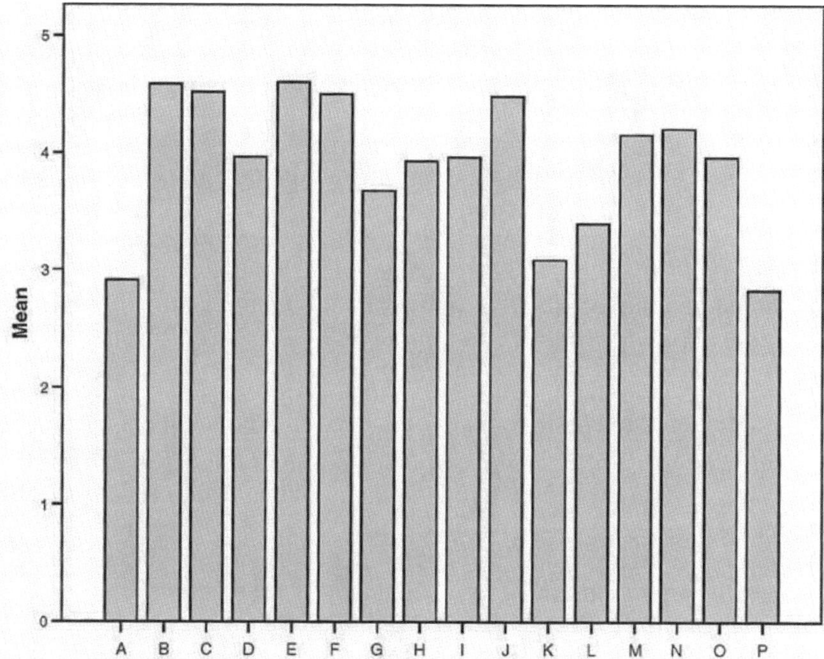

See Question 4a in the appendix for the corresponding variable names.

Range of Mean: 1=Not Likely at All, 2=Unlikely, 3=Possibly, 4=Likely, 5=Very Likely

Refer to Table 4 for the number of cases per variable.

Neithercutt & Gottfredson, 1975). As Altschuler and Armstrong (2001) observe, these violations are more easily detected as a result of more intense supervision and the more stringent conditions placed on offenders. Furthermore, the perception that technical violations are relatively common, may lead officers to expect and be on guard for these violations (i.e., officers may find what they are looking for).

The factors that officers said they consider most important in deciding whether to pursue revocation were virtually identical for probated and aftercare cases and included the number and seriousness of prior and current offenses as well as substance abuse. This finding indicates that the legal status of a youth was largely irrelevant in how community

Figure 6: Means of Community Workers' Perceived Likelihood to Utilize Avenues of Intervention to Avert Revocation of Aftercare Youth

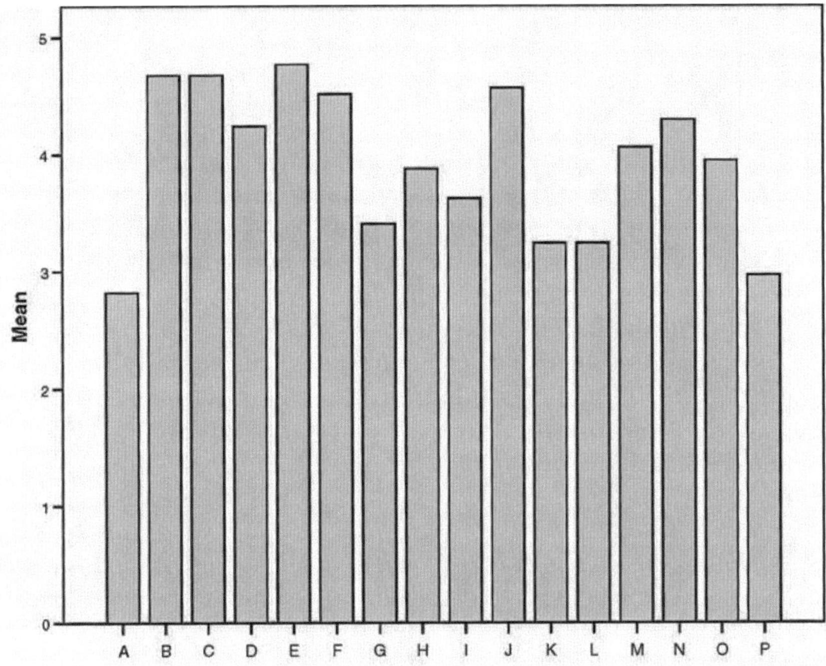

See Question 4b in the appendix for the corresponding variable names.

Range of Mean: 1=Not Likely at All, 2=Unlikely, 3=Possibly, 4=Likely, 5=Very Likely

Refer to Table 4 for the number of cases per variable.

workers weighed factors when considering revocation. This is true despite the fact that, by definition, aftercare cases would have spent more time under DJJ supervision and, in many instances, almost certainly have demonstrated less responsiveness overall to rehabilitative efforts. However, respondents did not rate these factors much differently between the two groups of youth.

For both probated and aftercare cases, the seriousness of the current charge that led to DJJ probation or aftercare was seen as very important in deciding whether to pursue commitment or revocation of youth who have violated their conditions. Seriousness of prior offenses was also rated high, particularly for probated youth. This finding suggests that even once aftercare youth have returned to the community following stays at long-term residential placements, they remain judged to an important extent by the original charges that led to commitment and by charges before that. In some cases, the time period between an original charge and placement of a youth under JIST surveillance in the community could be up to three years. In such instances, the current behaviors of youth in the community leading up to additional problems or issues seem more relevant than the charge resulting in commitment or prior charges.

Overall, respondents rated the number and seriousness of term violations after JIST placement as fairly important for both probated and aftercare youth. This indicates that respondents give serious consideration to how youth behave after entering JIST, especially with regard to technical violations. This seems consistent with the research noted above in that technical violations not only occur more frequently among offenders in ISPs, but, at least in this sample, they are deemed relatively important by community workers in the decision to violate or revoke an offender.

Substance abuse issues were rated as fairly important by respondents as well. As Snyder and Sickmund (2006) suggest, illicit drug use among adolescents has continued to be an area of concern in the U.S., particularly among those adolescents who simultaneously engage in other delinquent acts. Therefore, it is not surprising that respondents rated this factor so important. An additional reason for the high rating of this factor may be related to agency-wide initiatives of DJJ. A comprehensive substance abuse education and treatment initiative has been in place since 2005, and this initiative has been at the forefront of the agency's goals and objectives. This is consistent with the aforementioned mentioned research (Cavender & Knepper, 1992; Curtis & Reese, 1994; Whitehead & Lindquist, 1992) in that community supervision officers are to some degree affected by organizational imperatives and conditions.

Some factors were rated as relatively unimportant by respondents. These included youths' gender, age, and attitude toward the community worker. With regard to gender and attitude toward workers, it may be that respondents were attempting to remain objective in their decision-making. However, age would seem to have more direct relevance to such decision-making. For instance, it is typically not ideal to pursue commitment of a probated youth who is near 18 years old unless he/she commits a rather serious offense, even if the youth has been involved with the JIST program. In contrast, it would seem more probable to pursue commitment of a youth who is 15 or 16 years old under the same set of conditions. Although such instances regarding age of youth are not written in policy, they are commonly practiced by agents of the juvenile justice system. The thinking behind such practice is that younger juvenile offenders will benefit more from the services provided by the juvenile justice agency than those who are closer to 18 years old. Legal reasons may also deter juvenile justice agents from pursuing commitment of older youth, because in most cases, legal authority of juvenile justice agents is relinquished once a youth turns 18 years old.

Finally, respondents rated 16 avenues of intervention on the likelihood that they would utilize each to avoid commitment or revocation. Except for family meetings, all of the avenues respondents rated as the most likely to pursue related to monitoring and control, rather than rehabilitation. However, the overall average rating for avenues pertaining to control and monitoring was only slightly higher than that for avenues geared more toward rehabilitation. Consistent with past research, this suggests that while intensive supervision officers prioritize control, monitoring, and deterrence over rehabilitation, these officers are also concerned to some degree with rehabilitation (e.g., Curtis & Reese, 1994; Steiner et al., 2003; Whitehead & Lindquist, 1992).

The findings from this study provide a description of the perceptions of intensive supervision officers working in the juvenile justice system. An obvious limitation of the study is the sample itself. The study was conducted in a single state, and therefore, generalizations cannot necessarily be made regarding juvenile ISPs in other jurisdictions. In addition, the sample size was quite small. However, the 66 respondents comprised over 81 percent of all JIST officers in the state and can therefore be considered reasonably representative of the population. Although the small sample size restricted the use of inferential statistics, a very solid case can be made that such statistics are unnecessary anytime data are available on such a high proportion of the population.

Future research in other jurisdictions could seek to confirm or replicate the pattern of findings presented here, especially with respect to the sub-prioritization of rehabilitation, the salience officers attach to technical violations, and the minimal distinction drawn between probation and aftercare cases. In addition, it would be fruitful for such research to examine a broader range of factors (e.g., organizational and contextual variables) that officers might consider in deciding to pursue revocation of those thought to have violated conditions of intensive supervision.

REFERENCES

Altschuler, D. M., & Armstrong, T. L. (1994). *Intensive aftercare for high-risk juveniles: An assessment report.* Washington, DC: Office of Juvenile Justice and Delinquency Prevention, Office of Justice Programs, U.S. Department of Justice.

Altschuler, D. M., & Armstrong, T. L. (2001). Reintegrating high-risk juvenile offenders into communities: Experiences and prospects. *Corrections Management Quarterly, 5*(3), 72-88.

Armstrong, T. L. (Ed.). (1991). *Intensive interventions with high-risk youths: Promising approaches in juvenile probation and parole.* New York: Criminal Justice Press.

Asquith, S. (1983). *Children and justice: Decision-making in children's hearings and juvenile justice courts.* Edinburgh, Scotland: Edinburgh University Press.

Bortner, M. A. (1984). *Inside a juvenile court: The tarnished ideal of individualized justice.* New York: New York University Press.

Banks, J., Porter, A., Rardin, R., Sider, R., & Unger, V. (1977). *Evaluation of intensive special probation projects. Phase I report* (Grant No. 76 NI-99-0045). Washington DC: U.S. Department of Justice.

Batson, C. D., Jones, C. H., & Cochran, P. J. (1979). Attributional bias in counselors' diagnoses: The effect of resources. *Journal of Applied Psychology, 9*, 377-393.

Boston Police Department. (1996). *Youth violence: A community-based response one city's success story.* Washington, DC: National Criminal Justice Reference Service, Office of Justice Programs, U.S. Department of Justice.

Byrne, J. M. (1990). The future of intensive probation supervision and the new intermediate sanctions. *Crime & Delinquency, 36*, 6-41.

Carter, R., & Wilkins, S. L. (1976). Caseload: Some Conceptual Models. In R. Carter and L. Wilkins (Eds.), *Probation, parole and community corrections* (pp. 391-401). New York: Wiley and Sons.

Cavender, G., & Knepper, P. (1992). Strange interlude: An analysis of juvenile parole revocation decisionmaking. *Social Problems, 39*(4), 387-399.

Clear, T., & Drammer, H. (2003). *The offender in the community*. Belmont, CA: Thomson/Wadsworth.

Clear, T. R., Harris, P. M., & Baird, S. C. (1992). Probationer violations and officer response. *Journal of Criminal Justice, 20*(1), 1-12.

Clear, T., & Hardyman, P. (1990). The new intensive supervision movement. *Crime & Delinquency, 36* (1), 42–60.

Corbett, R. P., Jr. (1999). Juvenile probation on the eve of the next millennium. *Federal Probation, 63*, 78-86.

Curtis, R. L., Jr., & Reese, W. A., II. (1994). Framed attributions and shaped accounts: A study of dispositional process in juvenile justice. *Criminal Justice Review, 19*(2), 244-270.

Dillman, D. (2006). *Mail and Internet surveys: The tailored design method–2007 update with new Internet, visual, and mixed-mode guide*. Hoboken, NJ: John Wiley & Sons, Inc.

Drass, K., & Spencer, W. (1987). Accounting for pre-sentence recommendations: Typologies and probation officers' theory of office. *Social Problems, 34*, 156-171.

Emerson, R. (1983). Holistic effects in social control decision-making. *Law and Society Review, 17*, 425-455.

Forst, B., & Wellford, C. (1981). Punishment and sentencing: Developing sentencing guidelines empirically form principles of punishment. *Hofstra University Law Review, 9,* 799-837.

Fulton, B., Latessa, E., Stichman, A., Travis, L., Corbett, R., & Harris, M. (1997). A review of research for practitioners. *Federal Probation, 62*(4), 65–75.

Gibbons, J. D. (1993). *Nonparametric statistics: An Introduction.* Newbury Park, CA: Sage.

Giblin, M. J. (2002). Using police officers to enhance the supervision of juvenile probationers: An evaluation of the Anchorage CAN program. *Crime & Delinquency, 48*(1), 116-137.

Goodstein, L., & Sontheimer, H. (1997). The implementation of an intensive supervision aftercare program for serious juvenile offenders: A case study. *Criminal Justice & Behavior, 24*(3), 332-359.

Gray, M. K., Fields, M., & Maxwell, S. R. (2001). Examining probation violations: Who, what, and when. *Crime & Delinquency, 47*(4), 537-557.

Harris, P. M., Petersen, R. D., & Rapoza, S. (2001). Between probation and revocation: A study of intermediate sanctions decision-making. *Journal of Criminal Justice, 29*, 307-318.

Josi, D. A., & Sechrest, D. K. (1999). A pragmatic approach to parole aftercare: Evaluation of a community reintegration program for high-risk youthful offenders. *Justice Quarterly, 16*(1), 51-80.

Kentucky Department of Juvenile Justice. (n.d.). *Intensive supervision.* Retrieved April 9, 2007 from http://www.djj.ky.gov/programs/jist/

Krisberg, B., Rodriguez, O., Baake, A., Neuenfeldt, D., & Steele, P. (1989). *Demonstration of post-adjudication non-residential intensive supervision programs: Assessment report.* San Francisco, CA: National Council on Crime and Delinquency.

Lawrence, R. (1984). *Probation officers' role perceptions.* Paper presented at the annual meeting of the Academy of Criminal Justice Sciences, Chicago, IL.

Lurigio, A. J. (1987). Introduction. *Crime & Delinquency, 33*(4), 3-5.

Maynard, D. (1982). Defendant attributes in plea bargaining: Notes on the modeling of sentencing decisions. *Social Problems, 29,* 347-360.

Mays, G. L., & Winfree, L. T., Jr. (2005). *Essentials of Corrections* (3rd edition). Belmont, CA: Thomson Wadsworth.

McCleary, R. (1975). How structural variables constrain the parole officer's use of discretionary power. *Social Problems, 23*, 209-225.

McGarrell, E. F. (1991). Differential effects of juvenile justice reform on the incarceration rates of the states. *Crime & Delinquency, 37*, 262-280.

Neithercutt, M. G., & Gottfredson, D. (1975). *Caseload size variation and differences in probation/parole performance.* Washington, DC: National Center for Juvenile Justice.

Petersilia, J., & Turner, S. (1993). Intensive probation and parole. In M. Tonry (Ed.). *Crime and Justice: A Review of Research*, *17*, 281-335.

Petronio, R. J. (1982). Role socialization of juvenile court probation officers. *Criminal Justice & Behavior, 9*(2), 143.

Rosecrance, J. (1985). The probation officer's search for credibility: Ballpark recommendations. *Crime & Delinquency, 31,* 539-554.

Rosecrance, J. (1988). Maintaining the myth of individualized justice: Probation presentence reports. *Justice Quarterly, 5,* 235-256.

Scott, M., & Lyman, S. (1968). Accounts. *American Sociological Review, 33,* 46-62.

Shearer, R. (2002). Probation strategies of juvenile and adult pre-service trainees. *Federal Probation, 66*(1), 33-38.

Sluder, R., & Reddington, F. (1993). An empirical examination of the work ideologies of juvenile and adult probation officers. *Journal of Offender Rehabilitation, 20* (1-2), 115-137.

Snyder, H., & Sickmund, M. (2006). *Juvenile offenders and victims: 2006 national report.* Washington, DC: U.S. Department of Justice, Office of Justice Programs, Office of Juvenile Justice and Delinquency Prevention.

Spencer, J. W. (1983). Accounts, attitudes, and solutions: Probation officer-defendant negotiations of subjective orientations. *Social Problems, 30*, 570-581.

Steiner, B., Roberts, E., & Hemmens, C. (2003). Where is juvenile probation today? The legally prescribed functions of juvenile probation officers. *Criminal Justice Studies, 16*(4), 267-281.

Studt, E. (1993). *Surveillance and supervision in parole: A report of the parole action study.* Washington, DC: National Institute of Corrections.

Sudnow, D. (1965). Normal crimes: Sociological features of the penal code in a public defender office. *Social Problems, 12*, 255-270.

Tonry, M., & Lynch, M. (1996). Intermediate sanctions. In: M. Tonry (Ed.), *Crime and justice: A review of research, 20* (pp. 99-144). Chicago: University of Chicago Press.

Turner, S., & Petersilia, J. (1992). Focusing on high-risk parolees: An experiment to reduce commitments to the Texas Department of Corrections. *Journal of Research in Crime & Delinquency, 29*, 34-61.

Whitehead, J. T., & Lindquist, C. A. (1992). Determinants of probation and parole officer professional orientation. *Journal of Criminal Justice, 20*(1), 13-14.

Wilson, J. A. (2005). Bad behavior or bad policy? An examination of Tennessee release cohorts, 1993-2001. *Criminology and Public Policy, 4,* 485-518.

APPENDIX. Survey Items Corresponding to Research Questions

Perceived Main Function of JIST Programs

1. The JIST program was developed to provide intensive surveillance of delinquent youth, to facilitate rehabilitation, reduce recidivism rates, and safeguard the community. Based on this information, rank order the following functions from 1 to 4 (1 = greatest function . . . 4 = least function) by typing a number in the field to the right of each function.

a Provide supervision/surveillance to detect violations ____
b Promote rehabilitation by providing services or referrals ____
c Deter violations by sanctioning infractions ____
d Ensure safety and security within the community ____

Perceived Frequency of Violations Among Probated and Aftercare Youth

2a. By checking the desired box in the following table, rate your perception of the general **frequency** of the violations listed below among **probated youth** who are under JIST surveillance in your district. Although any additional charge is technically a violation of a youth's probation conditions, consider the following actions as "term violations": positive drug screen, breaking curfew, not attending school, not reporting in with worker as directed, etc. These are violations in which a youth may not receive an additional charge but may lead to a probation violation charge. **Select only ONE response for each type.**

☐ ***Frequency of Violations Among Probated Youth Under Jist Surveillance***

Violations	Very Frequent	Frequent	Moderate	Infrequent	Very Infrequent
(A) Felonies	☐	☐	☐	☐	☐
(B) Misdemeanors	☐	☐	☐	☐	☐
(C) Term Violations	☐	☐	☐	☐	☐

2b. By checking the desired box in the following table, rate your perception of the general **frequency** of the violations listed below among **aftercare youth** who are under JIST surveillance in your district. Although any additional charge is technically a violation of a youth's conditions of supervised placement, consider the following actions as "term violations": positive drug screen, breaking curfew, not attending school, not reporting in with worker as directed, etc. These are violations in which a youth may not receive an additional charge but may lead to a revocation hearing. **Select only ONE response for each type.**

Perceived Importance of Factors that Contribute to the Decision to Pursue Commitment or Revocation among Probated and Aftercare Youth

3a. By checking the desired box in the following table, rate the **factors** listed below in terms of their **importance** in your own decision to pursue **commitment of a probated youth** who has been under JIST surveillance and in some way violated his/her term conditions. **Select only ONE response for each factor.**

☐ ***Frequency of Violations Among Aftercare Youth Under JIST Surveillance***

Violations	Very Frequent	Frequent	Moderate	Infrequent	Very Infrequent
(A) Felonies	☐	☐	☐	☐	☐
(B) Misdemeanors	☐	☐	☐	☐	☐
(C) Term Violations	☐	☐	☐	☐	☐

☐ ***Importance of Factors Among Probated Youth in Pursuit of Commitment***

Factors	Very Important	Important	Moderate	Not Important	Not Important at All
(A) Age of Youth	☐	☐	☐	☐	☐
(B) Gender of Youth	☐	☐	☐	☐	☐
(C) Number of Prior Offenses **before** DJJ Probation	☐	☐	☐	☐	☐
(D) Seriousness of Prior Offense(s) **before** DJJ Probation	☐	☐	☐	☐	☐
(E) Seriousness of Current Offense(s) **that led** to DJJ Probation	☐	☐	☐	☐	☐
(F) Number of Term Violations **before** JIST Involvement	☐	☐	☐	☐	☐
(G) Seriousness of Term Violations **before** JIST Involvement	☐	☐	☐	☐	☐
(H) Number of Term Violations **after** JIST Involvement	☐	☐	☐	☐	☐
(I) Seriousness of Term Violations **after** JIST Involvement	☐	☐	☐	☐	☐
(J) Length of Time under DJJ Supervision	☐	☐	☐	☐	☐
(K) Attitude towards DJJ Intervention	☐	☐	☐	☐	☐
(L) Responsiveness to **past** Rehabilitative Efforts	☐	☐	☐	☐	☐
(M) Projected Responsiveness to **future** Rehabilitative Efforts	☐	☐	☐	☐	☐
(N) Availability of Resources in the Community	☐	☐	☐	☐	☐
(O) Home Environment (family, neighborhood, etc.)	☐	☐	☐	☐	☐
(P) Employability Skills	☐	☐	☐	☐	☐
(Q) Peer Group Associations	☐	☐	☐	☐	☐
(R) Leisure/Recreation Activities	☐	☐	☐	☐	☐
(S) School Performance	☐	☐	☐	☐	☐
(T) Mental Health Issues/Needs	☐	☐	☐	☐	☐
(U) Substance Abuse Issues	☐	☐	☐	☐	☐
(V) Attitude towards DJJ Community Worker	☐	☐	☐	☐	☐
(W) Conclusion that the Youth has had Sufficient Chances to Succeed	☐	☐	☐	☐	☐

3b. By checking the desired box in the following table, rate the **factors** listed below in terms of their importance in your own decision to pursue **revocation of an aftercare youth** who has been under JIST surveillance and in some way violated his/her term conditions. **Select only ONE response for each factor**.

☐ ***Importance of Factors Among Aftercare Youth in Pursuit of Revocation***

Factors	Very Important	Important	Moderate	Not Important	Not Important at All
(A) Age of Youth	☐	☐	☐	☐	☐
(B) Gender of Youth	☐	☐	☐	☐	☐
(C) Number of Prior Offenses **before** Commitment with DJJ	☐	☐	☐	☐	☐
(D) Seriousness of Prior Offense(s) **before** Commitment with DJJ	☐	☐	☐	☐	☐
(E) Seriousness of Current Offense(s) **that led** to Commitment w/DJJ	☐	☐	☐	☐	☐
(F) Number of Term Violations **before** JIST Involvement	☐	☐	☐	☐	☐
(G) Seriousness of Term Violations **before** JIST Involvement	☐	☐	☐	☐	☐
(H) Number of Term Violations **after** JIST Involvement	☐	☐	☐	☐	☐
(I) Seriousness of Term Violations **after** JIST Involvement	☐	☐	☐	☐	☐
(J) Length of Time under DJJ Supervision	☐	☐	☐	☐	☐
(K) Attitude towards DJJ Intervention	☐	☐	☐	☐	☐
(L) Responsiveness to **past** Rehabilitative Efforts	☐	☐	☐	☐	☐
(M) Projected Responsiveness to **future** Rehabilitative Efforts	☐	☐	☐	☐	☐
(N) Availability of Resources in the Community	☐	☐	☐	☐	☐
(O) Home Environment (family, neighborhood, etc.)	☐	☐	☐	☐	☐
(P) Employability Skills	☐	☐	☐	☐	☐
(Q) Peer Group Associations	☐	☐	☐	☐	☐
(R) Leisure/Recreation Activities	☐	☐	☐	☐	☐
(S) School Performance	☐	☐	☐	☐	☐
(T) Mental Health Issues/Needs	☐	☐	☐	☐	☐
(U) Substance Abuse Issues	☐	☐	☐	☐	☐
(V) Attitude towards DJJ Community Worker	☐	☐	☐	☐	☐
(W) Conclusion that the Youth has had Sufficient Chances to Succeed	☐	☐	☐	☐	☐

Perceived Likelihood to Utilize Avenues of Intervention to Avert Commitment or Revocation of Probated or Aftercare Youth

4a. By checking the desired box in the following table, rate the **likelihood** that you might pursue each avenue of intervention to avert the decision to **commit a probated youth** who has been under JIST surveillance and violated his/her term conditions. **Select only ONE response for each avenue.**

☐ ***Likelihood to Utilize Avenues to Avert Commitment of Probated Youth***

Avenues of Intervention	Very Likely	Likely	Possibly	Unlikely	Not Likely at All
(A) Assign Homework	☐	☐	☐	☐	☐
(B) Designate an Earlier Curfew Time	☐	☐	☐	☐	☐
(C) Increase Frequency of Drug Testing	☐	☐	☐	☐	☐
(D) Voice Monitoring	☐	☐	☐	☐	☐
(E) Electronic Monitoring	☐	☐	☐	☐	☐
(F) Home Detention	☐	☐	☐	☐	☐
(G) Community Service	☐	☐	☐	☐	☐
(H) Alternative School Placement	☐	☐	☐	☐	☐
(I) Time at Juvenile Detention Center	☐	☐	☐	☐	☐
(J) Meeting with Family and Youth	☐	☐	☐	☐	☐
(K) Vocational Training Program	☐	☐	☐	☐	☐
(L) After School Mentoring Program	☐	☐	☐	☐	☐
(M) In-Home Counseling Services	☐	☐	☐	☐	☐
(N) Outpatient Counseling Services	☐	☐	☐	☐	☐
(O) Inpatient Treatment Program	☐	☐	☐	☐	☐
(P) Emergency Shelter Placement	☐	☐	☐	☐	☐

4b. By checking the desired box in the following table, rate the **likelihood** that you might pursue each avenue of intervention to avert the decision to **revoke an aftercare youth** who has been under JIST surveillance and violated his/her term conditions. **Select only ONE response for each avenue.**

☐ ***Likelihood to Utilize Avenues to Avert Revocation of Aftercare Youth***

Avenues of Intervention	Very Likely	Likely	Possibly	Unlikely	Not Likely at All
(A) Assign Homework	☐	☐	☐	☐	☐
(B) Designate an Earlier Curfew Time	☐	☐	☐	☐	☐
(C) Increase Frequency of Drug Testing	☐	☐	☐	☐	☐
(D) Voice Monitoring	☐	☐	☐	☐	☐
(E) Electronic Monitoring	☐	☐	☐	☐	☐
(F) Home Detention	☐	☐	☐	☐	☐
(G) Community Service	☐	☐	☐	☐	☐
(H) Alternative School Placement	☐	☐	☐	☐	☐
(I) Time at Juvenile Detention Center	☐	☐	☐	☐	☐
(J) Meeting with Family and Youth	☐	☐	☐	☐	☐
(K) Vocational Training Program	☐	☐	☐	☐	☐
(L) After School Mentoring Program	☐	☐	☐	☐	☐
(M) In-Home Counseling Services	☐	☐	☐	☐	☐
(N) Outpatient Counseling Services	☐	☐	☐	☐	☐
(O) Inpatient Treatment Program	☐	☐	☐	☐	☐
(P) Emergency Shelter Placement	☐	☐	☐	☐	☐

☐

Recidivism Among Juvenile Offenders Following Release from Residential Placements: Multivariate Predictors and Gender Differences

KEVIN I. MINOR
JAMES B. WELLS
EARL ANGEL

INTRODUCTION

Some youthful offenders can be expected to recidivate upon release from out-of-home placements, such as juvenile institutions and community-based residential facilities. Nonetheless, recidivism levels are often higher than expected and thereby frustrate hopes for what juvenile corrections should be accomplishing, both during residential placements and in the community thereafter.

It is unusual for recidivism levels to reach as high as the 85 percent rearrest figure recently reported by Trulson, Marquart, Mullings, and Caeti (2005) in a five-year follow-up study of serious offenders released to parole/aftercare from residential facilities. On the other hand, it is rare in the literature (though not entirely unheard of) to find studies reporting juvenile recidivism rates of less than one-third or one-quarter, irrespective of how recidivism is operationalized or the disposition under study (see Howell, 2003). It is fair to say, then, that while juvenile court and correctional agencies are not a total failure, there is room for improvement.

Fundamental to achieving less recidivism in juvenile corrections is identifying, understanding, and targeting the variables associated with it. The present study examines variables predictive of recidivism among juveniles released from out-of-home placements, with an eye toward how findings might be used to improve the prospects of success in the community following release from placement.

Past studies of recidivism in juvenile corrections have tended to focus on re-offending associated with specific and often relatively novel residential programs, such as boot camps (e.g., Kurlychek & Kempinen, 2006; Wells, Minor, Angel, & Stearman, 2006) and special probation or aftercare programs (e.g., Josi & Sechrest, 1999; Lane, Turner, Fain, & Sehgal, 2005; Minor & Elrod, 1990). This is in contrast to recidivism associated with those standard, routine dispositions that Lipsey (1999) refers to as "practical programs." While there have been studies of the latter (e.g., Minor, Hartmann, & Terry, 1997; Trulson et al., 2005; Wooldredge, 1988), the emphasis has been considerably less. The present study addresses this slanted focus by analyzing a diverse array of possible predictors of recidivism across an 18-month follow-up period among juveniles released from standard out-of-home placements administered by the Kentucky Department of Juvenile Justice (DJJ).

While much recidivism research in juvenile corrections has focused on community programs for in-home placements, there are at least three interrelated reasons why it is equally important to study residential placements and subsequent re-offending, as was done in this research. First, in general these placements are the most restrictive and expensive dispositions available to judges. Second, residential facilities contain the more serious cases, frequently cases in which in-home program placements, such as diversion and probation, have been ineffective at controlling re-offending. Finally, because residential placements tend to involve more serious, higher risk cases, they are sometimes associated with greater levels of recidivism.

Table 1 summarizes significant predictors of juvenile recidivism following residential placement and other standard court dispositions, as these have been reported in 11 previous studies. While variation is apparent, taken collectively, these studies also point to some fairly consistent predictors. Age is the most consistent predictor across studies, followed by prior legal record. Gender, substance abuse/use (including alcohol), gang involvement, and length of facility stay are also relatively stable predictors. Other variables reported to be significantly predictive of recidivism in at least three studies include educational deficits, race/ethnicity, as well as test scores and mental health problems.

In a meta-analysis of 22 studies published between 1983 and 2000, Cottle, Lee, and Heilbrun (2001) found offense history variables to be the strongest predictors of recidivism among adjudicated juvenile offenders. Other reasonably good predictors included family problems, social variables (including use of leisure time and peers), as well as mental health problems. Cottle et al. distinguished between static and dynamic predictor variables in an effort to separate those factors that are (e.g., family relations) and are not (e.g., gender) subject to change through correctional intervention. They found that both sets of variables were useful in predicting re-offending.

Trulson et al. (2005) conducted separate analyses for males and females and found a divergence in predictors by gender; there were fewer significant predictors for females. The predictors of male recidivism included age, length of placement, prior felony adjudications, gang membership, institutional conduct, and mental health problems. For females, the only significant predictors were institutional conduct and special education needs.

Similarly, Funk (1999) compared variables predictive of recidivism among males and female placed on juvenile probation. Predictors for males included family financial hardships, school problems, peer group affiliations, age of onset, placement in detention facilities, and prior offenses against the person. Only the last two of these variables were also significant predictors of recidivism among females. Additional predictors

Table 1: Significant Predictors of Juvenile Recidivism in Previous Studies

Study	*Nature of Sample*	*Operationalization of Recidivism and Overall Rate (when available)*	*Significant Predictors of Recidivism*
Archwamety & Katsiyannis (1998)	238 females, age 12 to18, committed to a state facility	Facility recommitment within three years following initial commitment (40.3%)	Age at first offense and first commitment educational deficits, gang affiliation, abuse history, location of residence, and length of facility stay
Benda et al. (2001)	414 adolescents (age 17) released from facility for serious offenders	Entry into the adult correctional system within two years of release (65.2%)	Prior incarceration, age at first offense, gang membership, age at which drug/alcohol use began, test scores (MMPI, chemical abuse, Jesness Inventory, and Carlson Psychological Inventory), and gender
Dembo et al. (1998)	9,176 youth, age 12 to 19, processed at a juvenile assessment center	Re-admission to the juvenile assessment center following their first registration (40%)	Age, race, gender, ethnicity, physical abuse/neglect history, and delinquency referral history
Katsiyannis & Archwamety (1997)	294 males (147 recidivist and 147 non-recidivists), age 12 to 18, committed to a state facility	Facility recommitment within three years following initial commitment	Age at first offense and first commitment, educational deficits, gang affiliation, length of facility stay, type of crime, special education background, and risk assessment score
McMackin et al. (2004)	162 juveniles, approximately 13 to 18 years old, released from private residential facility	Reconviction taking place one year following release	Prior offending and length in placement

Minor et al. (1997)	475 first-time referrals to juvenile court, 6 to 17 years old	Re-referral to court two years after initial court referral (33.1%)	Age at referral, gender, and custodial arrangement (mother only versus other)
Myner et al. (1998)	138 male juveniles convicted of criminal offenses	Reconviction after first offense and prior to age 18	Age at first conviction, alcohol abuse, status conviction, length of first incarceration, group home placement, and birth order
Niarhos & Routh (1992)	234 males, age 8 to 18, arrested and evaluated at a court administered clinic	Return to court or detention within 1 year of current violation (49.6%)	Prior arrests, academic achievement, and history of drug use
Ryan & Yang (2005)	90 males released from residential care facility	Re-arrest and conviction after release–2.64 years average follow-up period (36%)	Age, race, and family contact
Stoolmiller & Blechman (2005)	505 juveniles with at least one arrest prior to age 18	Re-arrest after initial arrest (872 day average follow-up period)	Parental and youth reported drug/alcohol use, ethnicity, and substance use
Trulson et al. (2005)	2,436 serious violent offenders, age 12 to 21, released from a correctional facility	Rearrest within five years of release (85%)	Gender, age, prior legal background, gang membership, poverty, and mental health problems

for females included being a victim of child abuse and a history of being a runaway. Also studying a sample of juvenile offenders assigned community-based sentences, Schwalbe, Fraser, Day, and Cooley (2006) found the utility of a risk assessment instrument for predicting recidivism to vary by gender. Most of the risk factors in the instrument predicted male recidivism for both African American and White juveniles. However, fewer factors predicted recidivism among African American females (prior referrals, school problems, peer relations, and parental supervision), and only one factor (record of prior assaults) was predictive among White females.

These three studies aside, most previous studies of juvenile recidivism have not compared predictors for male and female sub-groups. The present study includes such a comparison.

METHOD

Participants

The sampling frame for the study consisted of over 2,000 youth released from out-of-home placements across a two-year period, 2000-2001. In Kentucky, out-of-home placements include two types of facilities operated by DJJ. The first type, youth development centers (YDCs), are relatively small juvenile institutions or training schools ranging from low to high security levels; most are medium security. The second type is low security group homes. Out-of-home placements also include low security residential facilities and foster care placements that are administered by private child care agencies under contract with the state. Excluded from the sampling frame were youths who were waived to adult court and sex offenders; the latter received specialized placements and treatment.

A random sampling approach was employed to select males for inclusion in the study. Every fourth male on the list of releases making up the sampling frame was included in the sample (n = 467). Every female in the frame (n = 113) was included in the sample in order to insure an adequate number of female cases for analysis. Thus, the total number of cases was 580, with 80.5 percent being male. Likewise, 70.3 percent of the sample was white. Age at commitment ranged from 12 to 18 years, with a mean of 15.8 years. Kentucky is a predominately rural state, and 64.5 percent of the sample had resided in rural counties prior to placement.

Just over 68 percent had completed the ninth grade at the time of commitment, while the remainder had completed the tenth grade or higher.

Data Source and Variables

The data source for this research included both automated and hardcopy case history and tracking databases maintained by DJJ, the Kentucky Administrative Office of the Courts, and the Kentucky Department of Corrections. The latter source was used in instances were individuals turned 18 (the age of majority in Kentucky) at some point during the 18-month follow-up period.

Much of the case history data were based on self-reports of juveniles and/or interpretations of caseworkers collecting the information. Hence, the reliability and validity of these data depend on the honesty of juveniles as well as the judgments and accuracy of caseworkers. At the same time, both self-report and officially recorded data sources have a long history of use in delinquency research. Additionally, case history information represents the main source of data staff members have at their disposal for guiding decisions. It is therefore important to examine the extent to which such data predict post-release recidivism.

The dependent or predicted variable in this study was dichotomous and consisted of whether any Class A misdemeanor or any felony taking place within 18 months of release from residential placement resulted in a new adjudication. Besides the demographic variables mentioned above, data were collected on a wide range of other independent or predictor variables. These variables are listed in Table 2; frequencies are also provided for these variables.

RESULTS

Overall, 52.2 percent of the 580 youth experienced adjudication for a Class A misdemeanor or a felony crime that took place within 18 months of release from residential placement. Year of release from placement (2000 or 2001) was not significantly associated with recidivism. Hence, data were pooled across the two years for the remaining analyses described below.

Given the dichotomous dependent variable, logistic regression was performed to identify the combination of variables from Table 2 that best predicted the likelihood of recidivism. The recommendations of Tabachnick and Fidell (2000) were followed when performing diagnostics

Table 2: Predictor Variables and Frequencies

Variable	*Sample n*	*Sample %*
Documented Evidence of Family Conflict		
No	138	23.8
Yes	441	76.2
Documented History of Crime for Either Parent		
No	130	22.5
Yes	449	77.5
Documented History of Incarceration for Either Parent		
No	149	25.7
Yes	430	74.3
Documented History of Substance Abuse for Either Parent		
No	123	21.2
Yes	456	78.8
Documented History of Crime for any Sibling		
No	464	80.1
Yes	115	19.9
Documented History of Incarceration for any Sibling		
No	492	85.0
Yes	87	15.0
Documented History of Substance Abuse for any Sibling		
No	528	91.2
Yes	51	8.8
Documented Victimization History		
Physical Abuse		
No	330	57.0
Yes	249	43.0
Sexual Abuse		
No	393	67.9
Yes	186	32.1
Emotional Abuse		
No	335	57.9
Yes	244	42.1
Abandonment		
No	397	68.6
Yes	182	31.4
Documented Special Education Needs		
No	359	62.0
Yes	220	38.0
Documented Behavior Problems in School		
No	75	13.0
Yes	504	87.0
Documented History of Truancy		
No	212	36.6
Yes	367	63.4

Variable	*Sample n*	*Sample %*
Documented History of Sexually Inappropriate Behavior		
No	473	81.7
Yes	106	18.3
Documented History of Substance Abuse		
No	185	32.0
Yes	394	68.0
Documented History of Assaultive Behavior		
No	108	18.7
Yes	471	81.3
Documented History of Gang Involvement		
No	456	78.8
Yes	123	21.2
Documented History of Mental Health Treatment		
No	291	50.3
Yes	288	49.7
Documented History of Substance Abuse Treatment		
No	279	48.2
Yes	300	51.8
Any Prior Adjudication(s)		
No	67	11.6
Yes	511	88.4
Prior Felony Adjudication(s)		
No	300	51.9
Yes	278	48.1
Previous Supervised In-Home Placements/Probation		
No	220	37.9
Yes	360	62.1
Previously Charged with Violation of Probation, Aftercare, or Court Order		
No	423	72.9
Yes	157	27.1
Previous Out-Of-Home Placement(s)		
No	391	67.4
Yes	189	32.6
Most Serious Instant Offense		
Misdemeanor, Status Offense, or Code Violation	316	54.5
Felony	264	45.5
Instant Offense Drug/Alcohol Related		
No	434	75.0
Yes	145	25.0
Facility of Discharge		
Youth Development Center	314	54.1
Group Home or Foster Care	266	45.9
Facility of Discharge		
Public	344	59.3
Private	236	40.7

for the regression model. Specifically, the variables were tested for multicollinearity as well as univariate and multivariate outliers. The ratio of cases to variables was sufficient for the analysis, and no more than 20 percent of the categorical variable cells had expected frequencies less than 5. Discrete variables had no dichotomous splits where one category had 10 percent or fewer cases. Post hoc inspection of the standard errors of the standardized regression coefficients revealed that none exceeded a value of 1. Based on these diagnostics, two variables in Table 2 were excluded from the logistic regression analysis (i.e., history of incarceration for either parent and history of substance abuse for any sibling).

Regression of 18-month recidivism on variables in Table 2 resulted in the significant predictors shown in Table 3. The overall model was easily significant ($\chi^2 = 82.650$, $df = 33$, $p = .000$). The goodness of fit test was not significant, suggesting that the model provided an adequate fit to the theoretical model of perfect prediction.

Gender was a strong predictor of recidivism. As the datum in the odds column of Table 3 reveals, males were over two times more likely than females to recidivate. Likewise, for each year of age, a youth was 1.3 times more likely to recidivate. The probability of recidivism was also greater among youth with histories of abandonment as well as those with special education needs. However, those with a documented history of sexual abuse were 44.6 percent less likely to recidivate than those without such a history.

Collectively, the combination of significant predictors accounted for 18.2 percent of the total variability in recidivism. The model correctly

Table 3: Significant Predictors of 18-Month Recidivism for Combined Sample

Predictor	*B*	*S.E.*	*Wald*	*p*	*Odds*
Gender	.748	.285	6.904	.009	2.113
Age at Commitment	.263	.083	10.052	.002	1.300
Victimization History–Sexual Abuse	–.809	.318	6.473	.011	.446
Victimization History–Abandonment	.717	.341	4.406	.036	2.047
Special Education Needs	.418	.202	4.298	.038	1.519

Constant for model = –4.720.

classified 65.5 percent of the cases overall. It was more accurate at correctly classifying recidivists (71.0% correct) than non-recidivists (59.6% correct).

Based on the findings of previous research, separate recidivism models were estimated for males (n = 465) and females (n = 113) incorporating the variables (other than gender) that were significant in the combined model shown in Table 3. The separate models are shown in Table 4. Only the overall model for males was significant ($\chi^2 = 25.499$, $df = 4$, $p = .000$). The goodness of fit test was not significant for either model.

All of the variables that were significant in the combined model remained significant in the model for males except for special education needs, which only approached significance. However, none of the variables were significant in the model for females. In the male model, the combination of significant predictors accounted for 7.2 percent of the variability in recidivism, correctly classifying 83.5 percent of the recidivists but only 33.7 percent of the non-recidivists.

Table 4: Logistic Regression Models of 18-Month Recidivism for Males (Panel A) and Females (Panel B) Using Variables Significant in the Combined Model

Panel A

Predictor of Male Recidivism	*B*	*S.E.*	*Wald*	*p*	*Odds*
Age at Commitment	.298	.079	14.137	.000	1.347
Victimization History–Sexual Abuse	–.847	.320	7.001	.008	.429
Victimization History–Abandonment	.660	.318	4.314	.038	1.934
Special Education Needs	.362	.197	3.357	.066	1.436

Constant for model = –4.403.

Panel B

Predictor of Female Recidivism	*B*	*S.E.*	*Wald*	*p*	*Odds*
Age at Commitment	.156	.155	1.009	.315	1.169
Victimization History–Sexual Abuse	–.786	.577	1.857	.173	.456
Victimization History–Abandonment	.873	.596	2.142	.143	2.393
Special Education Needs	–.036	.541	.004	.947	.965

Constant for model = –3.032.

Since none of the four variables from the combined model were predictive of female recidivism, an additional multivariate model was estimated for females incorporating the variables that were significantly associated with female recidivism in bivariate analyses. This model is displayed in Table 5. The overall model was significant ($\chi^2 = 11.592$, $df = 4$, $p = .021$), and the goodness of fit test was not. The model accounted for 13.7 percent of the variation in female recidivism, and consisted of one significant predictor; females who had experienced previous out-of-home placement were one-third *less* likely to recidivate than those without such placements. This model correctly classified 67.3 percent of all the cases, correctly classifying 88.3 percent of the recidivists but only 22.27 percent of the non-recidivists.

DISCUSSION

The 52.2 percent rate of recidivism found in this study is higher than those rates sometimes reported in studies involving predominately community-based dispositions for less serious offenders (e.g., Minor et al., 1997) and comparable to those reported in other such studies (e.g., Lane et al., 2005) . The rate is on par with, or lower than, figures reported in many studies of more serious juvenile offenders returning to the community from residential placements (Benda et al., 2001; Grissom & Dubnov, 1989; Niarhos & Routh, 1992; Trulson et al., 2005). Obviously, the 52.2% figure would have been higher had recidivism been operationalized in terms of new arrests rather than new adjudications and/or if the definition had incorporated less serious offenses (i.e., lower level misdemeanors, status offenses, and technical violations).

Table 5: Logistic Regression Model of 18-Month Recidivism for Females Using Variables Significant in Bivariate Analyses

Predictor	*B*	*S.E.*	*Wald*	*p*	*Odds*
Age at Commitment	.228	.168	1.824	.177	1.255
Race	.553	.452	1.498	.221	1.738
History of Assaultive Behavior	1.177	.696	2.857	.091	3.245
Previous Out-of-Home Placements	-1.106	.531	4.337	.037	.331

Constant for model = –5.066.

While a higher proportion (58.6%) of those released from institutions (YDCs) than those released from group homes or foster care placements (44.7%) were reconvicted, the type of out-of-home placement was not a significant predictor in the multivariate model. Furthermore, comparable proportions of juveniles released from public (51.7%) and private (53.0%) facilities were reconvicted. Thus, classification by kind of placement did little to predict the likelihood of recidivism.

Including the two variables related to kind of placement, the present study examined 33 possible predictors of recidivism, many of which have been found to predict recidivism in previous research (see Table 1). However, only five of these variables were significantly predictive of reconvictions. As in most past studies, recidivism was found to be predicted by age (cf. Archwamety & Katsiyannis, 1998; Benda et al., 2001; Dembo et al., 1998; Katsiyannis & Archwamety, 1997; Minor et al., 1997; Myner et al., 1998; Ryan & Yang, 2005; Trulson et al., 2005) and by gender (cf. Benda et al., 2001; Dembo et al., 1998; Minor et al., 1997; Trulson et al., 2005). Consistent with the work of Archwamety and Katsiyannis (1998) as well as Katsiyannis and Archwamety (1997), recidivism was predicted by the presence of special education needs. And as in the studies by Archwamety and Katsiyannis (1998) as well as by Dembo et al. (1998), recidivism was predicted by victimization history, specifically a history of being abandoned or neglected and a history of being sexually abused.

Interestingly, the data revealed that juveniles with a documented history of sexual abuse were *less* likely to recidivate than those lacking such a record. Based upon follow-up interview data gathered from DJJ treatment staff concerning this finding, the most tenable explanation pertains to the intervention received by these particular youth during the course of residential placement. Delinquent behavior among sexually abused youth is conceptualized by treatment staff as a reaction to the trauma associated with the abuse. Once these youth have been identified, the emphasis is on teaching them the coping skills needed to deal effectively with trauma and having the youth practice these skills.

The findings of a recent study by Lemmon (2006) are consistent with this logic. He found that the provision of out-of-home placement services was associated with reduced frequency and seriousness of delinquent conduct among youth having a history of maltreatment. Lemmon concluded that "placement services afford maltreated children the opportunity to forge bonds with competent and caring adults that can reduce maltreatment's effect on delinquency" (p. 25). At the same time, the relationship between exposure to abuse and delinquent behavior is not clear cut. Past research had demonstrated that the relationship can vary by the type of delinquency and by the type of abuse (see Lemmon, 2006 for a review). The present study supported this caveat. Neither a history of exposure to physical abuse or exposure to emotional abuse was predictive of recidivism. However, a history of abandonment or neglect was associated with an increased likelihood of recidivism, but only among males.

As is often true in research, the non-significant findings of this study are important. Probably the main anomaly with past research is the lack of relationship between prior legal record and recidivism. Some investigators (e.g., Cottle et al., 2001; McMackin et al., 2004) point to prior record as the single most robust predictor of recidivism, and an ample number of studies have demonstrated the relationship (e.g., Benda et al., 2001; Dembo et al., 1998; Niarhos & Routh, 1992; Trulson et al., 2005). Similarly, other studies have found that substance abuse history is predictive of recidivism (Myner et al., 1998; Stoolmiller & Blechman, 2005).

The present study analyzed several proxies for prior record including history of behavior problems in school, truancy, sexually inappropriate activity, substance abuse, and assaultive behavior. Additional proxies included previous treatment for mental health or substance abuse problems, prior court adjudications, prior in-home and out-of-home placements for offending, and prior violations of court orders (including orders related to probation and aftercare). With a single exception, none of these variables were found to be significantly predictive of recidivism; the exception was the prior out-of-home placement variable (see below). Likewise, although gang involvement has been found to be predictive of recidivism in past studies (Benda et al., 2001; Katsiyannis & Archwamety, 1997; Trulson et al., 2005), this was not true in the present study.

Another important finding in this study is that, consistent with the limited amount of previous research conducted (e.g., Funk, 1999; Schwalbe et al., 2006; Trulson et al., 2005), the predictors of recidivism among males were inadequate at predicting recidivism among females. None of the variables predictive of recidivism in the male sample (age, history of sexual abuse, or history of abandonment) predicted female recidivism. Because of this, another multivariate model was estimated based on the significant bivariate predictors of female recidivism. In this model, only the prior out-of-home placement variable was predictive; females having prior placements were less likely to recidivate. Although data needed to interpret this finding are lacking, one possible interpretation is that females who had previously been in residential placements had spent more time than those without prior placements removed from the types of problematic family and social milieus that can encourage crime among females. Another possibility is that some of the benefits of residential placements were cumulative across placements. On the other hand, some researchers contend that removing females from the community can exacerbate certain problems (e.g., disrupted relationships) that initially contributed to delinquency (Holtfreter & Morash, 2003). Regardless of the interpretation, it seems clear that the dynamics surrounding female recidivism in the present study differ from those surrounding recidivism among males. This finding is consistent with the growing emphasis in the literature on gender-responsive programming (Hubbard & Matthews, 2008). As such, it has implications for aftercare programming.

The most fundamental implication of this study is that aftercare policy and practice should be based on knowledge of predictors of juvenile recidivism in the jurisdiction in question. Though a wide range of variables were examined in the multivariate model, only five contributed to the prediction of recidivism beyond chance. Moreover, variables that have been found to be predictive in past research, most notably prior record, were not predictive in this study. Findings like these can be used to help make sure that scarce aftercare resources are directed toward those variables most closely associated with re-offending in a jurisdiction.

For example, the results of this study suggest that, among males, the most intense level of services should be directed toward older juveniles, those with a history of neglect, and possibly those with special education needs. This certainly does not mean that younger males lacking these characteristics should be ignored during the aftercare phase. But it does mean that, statistically, this group presents a lower risk of re-adjudication in the jurisdiction studied. Similarly, the results of this study should not be taken to imply that juveniles with a history of sexual abuse should receive fewer aftercare services. On the contrary, it would be prudent to ensure continuity of services from residential placement to the community for these youth so that any gains made while in placement may be sustained.

Females were far less likely to recidivate than males in this study, but the study was not successful at isolating the factors associated with their re-offending. The findings imply that, when planning aftercare services for females, targeting variables identical to those targeted for males is unlikely to be an optimal way of reducing recidivism. Based on their recent review of research, Hubbard and Matthews (2008) contend that to have optimal outcomes, correctional interventions for girls should be geared toward building social support and prosocial relationships with others; these interventions should place less emphasis on confrontation than what is often seen in programs for males.

Like most research, this study suffers from limitations. As mentioned earlier, much of the data used to form predictor variables was of necessity based on self-reports of juveniles and/or interpretations of caseworkers. There was no way to independently verify most of the information. Also, the study did not control for differences transpiring across cases that might have affected the probability of recidivism during the 18-month follow-up period, such as differences in home life, peer groups, or system intervention.

This study has at least two important implications for future research on juvenile recidivism. First, such research needs to attend more closely to gender differences than has been typical in past studies. While past studies have typically included gender as one potential predictor, it has been less common in these studies to estimate separate models for males and females. Yet there is an emerging body of evidence of variation in predictors by gender.

Second, despite the inclusion of many variables, this study was not successful at accounting for a large proportion of variability in recidivism; this was true even among the combined and male samples. It is clear that many of the dynamics involved in recidivism (or the lack thereof) were not captured by the variables studied here. At the same time, these variables are indicative of the case-by-case information that many juvenile justice agencies collect as a matter of routine. For this reason, it is precisely data such as these upon which decisions about important issues like aftercare programming are often based. The findings of this study suggest that a prerequisite for improving the prediction of recidivism, and by implication aftercare programming, is the routine collection of data on a broader range of relevant variables.

REFERENCES

Archwamety, T., & Katsiyannis, A. (1998). Factors related to recidivism among delinquent females at a state correctional facility. *Journal of Child and Family Studies, 7*, 59-67.

Benda, B. B., Corwyn, R. F., & Toombs, N. J. (2001). Recidivism among adolescent serious offenders: Prediction of entry into the correctional system for adults. *Criminal Justice and Behavior, 28*, 588-613.

Cottle, C. C., Lee, R. J., & Heilbrun, K. (2001). The prediction of criminal recidivism in juveniles. A meta-analysis. *Criminal Justice and Behavior, 28*, 367-394.

Dembo, R., Schmeidler, J., Nini-Gough, B., Sue, C. C., Borden, P., & Manning, D. (1998). Predictors of recidivism to a juvenile assessment center: A three year study. *Journal of Child & Adolescent Substance Abuse, 7*, 57-77.

Funk, S. J. (1999). Risk assessment for juveniles on probation: A focus on gender. *Criminal Justice and Behavior, 26*, 44-68.

Grissom, G. R., & Dubnov, W. L. (1989). *Without locks and bars: Reforming our reform schools.* New York: Praeger.

Holtfreter, K., & Morash, M. (2003). The needs of women offenders: Implications for correctional programming. *Women and Criminal Justice, 14*, 137-160.

Howell, J. C. (2003). *Preventing & reducing juvenile delinquency: A comprehensive framework.* Thousand Oaks, CA: Sage.

Hubbard, D. J., & Matthews, B. (2008). Reconciling the differences between the "gender-responsive" and the "what works" literatures to improve services for girls. *Crime & Delinquency.*

Josi, D., & Sechrest, D. K. (1999). A pragmatic approach to parole aftercare: Evaluation of a community reintegration program for high-risk youthful offenders. *Justice Quarterly, 16*, 51-80.

Katsiyannis, A., & Archwamety, T. (1997). Factors related to recidivism among delinquent youths in a state correctional facility. *Journal of Child and Family Studies, 6*, 43-55.

Kurlychek, M., & Kempinen, C. (2006). Beyond boot camp: The impact of aftercare on offender reentry. *Criminology & Public Policy, 5*, 363-388.

Lane, J., Turner, S., Fain, T., & Sehgal, A. (2005). Evaluating an experimental intensive juvenile probation program: Supervision and official outcomes. *Crime & Delinquency, 51*, 26-52.

Lemmon, J. H. (2006). The effects of maltreatment recurrence and child welfare services on dimensions of delinquency. *Criminal Justice Review, 31*, 5-32.

Lipsey, M. W. (1999). Can rehabilitative programs reduce the recidivism of juvenile offenders? An inquiry into the effectiveness of practical programs. *Virginia Journal of Social Policy and the Law, 6*, 611-641.

McMackin, R. A., Tansi, R., & LaFratta, J. (2004). Recidivism among juvenile offenders over periods ranging from one to twenty years following residential treatment. *Journal of Offender Rehablitation, 38*, 1-15.

Minor, K. I., & Elrod, H. P. (1990). The effects of a multi-faceted intervention on the offense activities of juvenile probationers. *Journal of Offender Counseling, Services & Rehabilitation, 15*, 87-108.

Minor, K. I., Hartmann, D. J., & Terry, S. (1997). Predictors of juvenile court actions and recidivism. *Crime & Delinquency, 43*, 328-344.

Myner, J., Santman, J., Cappelletty, G. G., & Perlmutter, B. F. (1998). Variables related to recidivism among juvenile offenders. *International Journal of Offender Therapy and Comparative Criminology, 42*, 65-80.

Niarhos, F. J., & Routh, D. K. (1992). The role of clinical assessment in the juvenile court: Predictors of juvenile dispositions and recidivism. *Journal of Clinical Child Psychology, 21*, 151-159.

Ryan J. B., & Yang, H. (2005). Family contact and recidivism: A longitudinal study of adjudicated delinquents in residential care. *Social Work Research, 29*, 31-39.

Schwalbe, C. S., Fraser, M. W., Day, S. H., & Cooley, V. (2006). Classifying juvenile offenders according to risk of recidivism. Predictive validity, race/ethnicity, and gender. *Criminal Justice and Behavior, 33*, 305-324.

Stoolmiller, M., & Blechman, E. A. (2005). Substance use is a robust predictor of adolescent recidivism. *Criminal Justice and Behavior, 32*, 302-328.

Tabachnick, B. G., & Fidell, L. S. (2000)., 4th ed. *Using multivariate statistics.* New York: Harper Collins.

Trulson, C. R., Marquart, J. W., Mullings, J. L., & Caeti, T. J. (2005). In between adolescence and adulthood. Recidivism outcomes of a cohort of state delinquents. *Youth Violence and Juvenile Justice, 3*, 355-387.

Wells, J. B., Minor, K. I., Angel, E., & Stearman, K. D. (2006). A quasi-experimental evaluation of a shock incarceration and aftercare program for juvenile offenders. *Youth Violence and Juvenile Justice, 4*, 219-233.

Wooldredge, J. D. (1988). Differentiating the effects of juvenile court sentences on eliminating recidivism. *Journal of Research in Crime and Delinquency, 25*, 264-300.

Predicting Recidivism in Juvenile Offenders on Community-Based Orders: The Impact of Risk Factors and Service Delivery

REBECCA DENNING
ROSS HOMEL

INTRODUCTION

On 4 August 1992 the juvenile justice provisions of the *Children's Services Act 1965* were repealed and were replaced with the *Juvenile*

Justice Act 1992 and the *Children's Court Act 1992*. The *Juvenile Justice Act 1992* in particular led the operational reform of the youth justice system. It wasn't until 1999, however, that service delivery in the area of community-based supervision was modified to reflect the changes made to the legislation. The juvenile justice component of the existing Area Office (AO) model was extracted and placed into a dedicated service delivery model, known as the Youth Justice Service (YJS). The new model would ensure that juvenile justice cases, which were often neglected in order to manage the more immediate and often critical child protection cases, received adequate attention. The new model of service delivery also facilitated the position of the Government-of-the-day, which was focused on addressing the causes of crime, promoting individual responsibility and enhancing government partnerships with the non-government sector. The new service model was initially trialled in three locations in 1999, and has since replaced the traditional AO model throughout Queensland.

The Policy Direction for the Youth Justice Service

At the broadest level, YJSs aim to (1) work with the young offender to address their offending behavior, and (2) monitor the offender's compliance with court orders. Case managers help affect behavioral change by assisting clients to gain insight into the causes and impacts of their offending; develop options for meeting their needs without offending; and develop skills, interests and networks that will better connect them to their community and thus divert them from future offending behavior. The case management process is based on case workers having manageable case loads; a team approach, where responsibility for clients is shared between case managers and program staff; thorough assessment of risks and needs; and needs-based intervention.

In theory at least, this first aim demonstrates a clear alignment with the key principles of contemporary theories of human development (Tobach & Greenberg, 1984). In recognizing that young people have the ability to change their behavior, in this case from offending to less serious offending or to desistance from offending, the YJS adheres to the principle of relative plasticity. In seeking to affect behavioral change, the YJS policy accepts the need to incorporate key stakeholders from the young person's social relational (i.e., families, extended families) and sociocultural (i.e., schools, community and cultural networks) contexts, acknowledging that the bases for this behavioral change lie in the transactions between these multiple contexts (Bronfenbrenner, 1979; Ford &

Lerner, 1992; Sameroff, 1983). The YJS policy also argues that working with young people in isolation does not recognize the significance of family and cultural networks. This statement aligns with the principle that no level of human organization functions in isolation but rather each level functions as a consequence of its fusion or structural integration with other levels. This interdependence means that change at any level will necessarily lead to continuity or discontinuity at another level.

The second aim is more straightforward. Given that young people are on community-based orders when they are dealing with the YJS, a fundamental, indeed legislative, goal of the service is to monitor compliance with these court orders. Ultimately, case workers must work with the young people to assist them to comply with the conditions of their orders, but also breach offenders if they reoffend or continually fail to comply with their conditions.

This study aimed to determine the impact of the YJS on offending behavior. Reflecting the developmental nature of the YJS policy, a database was developed that incorporated key individual and social developmental risk factors in an attempt to ascertain how these factors mediated the impact of the YJS intervention.

METHOD

At the time of the study, three YJS offices (Logan Area Youth Justice Service–LAYJS, Ipswich Youth Justice Service–IYJS and Caboolture Youth Justice Service–CYJS) were operating in South-East Queensland. Given that a JYS and AO are not located within the same geographical area, it was impossible to match AO locations with the three JYSs. Three AOs whose client base and geographical locations were most closely matched to the JYS locations were selected to act as controls. These AOs were Stones Corner AO (SCAO), Chermside AO (CAO) and Mount Gravatt AO (MTGAO).

Between 1 June 1999 to 31 December 2002, a total of 503 young males[1] attended any of these six locations. SPSS 11.0 was used to reduce this population to a random sample of 300 cases, distributed across the six locations. Of this sample, 90 case management files and 14 police records were unable to be located, and all but six of the remaining cases exceeded the 18-month time at risk window. These 110 cases were eliminated from the study, leaving a final sample of 190.

The study examined the YJS from the developmental perspective. Consequently, in developing the database it was important to incorporate risk and protective factors from the young person's various ecological contexts. A preliminary review of the case management files indicated that the database was going to be heavily biased in favor of risk because information on protective factors was not routinely recorded in the case management files. This preliminary review suggested that it might be possible to gather data from the individual, family, schooling and peer contexts. While many variables were considered important from a theoretical and statistical perspective, the database was limited to those variables recorded in the case management files. Included variables are discussed briefly below.

The variables outlined below are a mix of statutory (i.e., required to fulfil the requirements of the court order–offending behavior, compliance, child protection, etc) and non-statutory (i.e., other risk and protective factors that influence case management decisions) variables. Non- statutory variables that had no corresponding response of any kind were coded as "no record" (essentially the coding framework catered for yes, no, and no record categories). The aim of this coding framework was to be able to make a distinction between negative responses and cases where questions regarding the risk factor had not been broached with the client in the first instance. In making this distinction, it was anticipated that it would be possible to draw some conclusions about the quality of the case management practices in terms of the extent of coverage of a broad range of risk factors in conducting needs assessments.

Risk Factors

Individual Risk Factors

In all, four individual factors were incorporated into the database. These were: (1) intentional self-harm, (2) alcohol/drug use, (3) learning difficulties, and (4) conduct disorder. Files were examined to detect whether clients drank alcohol and the frequency of this use. Alcohol use was coded as 1 = No, 2 = Yes, and alcohol frequency was coded 1 = Daily, 2 = 3 to 6 times per week, 3 = 2 or less times per week, 4 = Not applicable (where alcohol use was coded 1). Data was similarly extracted for drug use and frequency of drug use, as well as the type of drug(s) used most regularly.

Criminal History

Criminal career measures were included in the database for two reasons. First, criminal career measures have been used to differentiate between subsequent offending pathways (Moffitt, 1993; Patterson et al., 1992, 1998; White et al., 1990). Secondly, the criminal career measures acted as pre-intervention measures of offending behavior. This enabled examination of pre- and post-intervention offending behavior. Four criminal career variables were included in the database: (1) age at first recorded offense, (2) total number of preintervention offenses, (3) most frequent preintervention offense, and (4) most serious preintervention offense. Most serious preintervention offense referred to the value, based on the Department of Communities Seriousness Index (DCSI), of the most serious offense committed prior to the date of the index court order. This seriousness index ranges from 27 (most serious) to 150 (least serious).

Family Characteristics and Process

Despite evidence indicating that parental factors, family characteristics and process play a critical role in the development of delinquent behavior (Farrington, 1989; Patterson et al., 1992; Smith & Stern, 1997; Tolan & Loeber, 1993) only information that was required by law was recorded in case files. A number of child maltreatment variables, all of which have a statutory basis, were included in the database. Number of child protection notifications and number of child protection substantiated assessments were recorded. Given that cases had recorded at least one substantiated assessment, cases were further analyzed to determine the number of substantiated assessments in four maltreatment type variables (1) physical abuse, (2) neglect, (3) sexual abuse, and (4) emotional abuse. Reflecting the association between the timing of maltreatment and later offending behavior (Thornberry, Ireland, & Smith, 2001) the time when the maltreatment occurred was coded 1 = no history of maltreatment, 2 = childhood-only (0-11 yrs), 3 = adolescence-only (12-17 yrs), 4 = persistent (>2 incidents in both periods).

School Experiences

Weak school commitment, poor attendance, suspensions and poor school performance are associated with increased involvement in delinquency and drug use (Browning & Loeber, 1999; Wasserman et al., 2003).

Poor academic achievement has consistently been one of the strongest predictors of secondary school failure, including drop-out and truancy (Battin-Pearson et al., 2000; Krohn, Thornberry, Collins-Hall, & Lizotte, 1995). Four variables were included that related to negative school experiences: (1) truancy, (2) school suspension/expulsion, (3) highest grade completed, and (4) learning difficulties. Truancy and school suspension/expulsion measured were coded 1 = No, 2 = Yes. The highest grade successfully achieved ranged from 1 to 12. Information on learning difficulties were coded 1 = No, 2 = Numeracy only, 3 = Literacy only, 4 = Numeracy and literacy.

Peer Influence

Various developmental models highlight the importance of peers in delinquency (Sampson & Laub, 1993; Thornberry, 1987), a position that has been supported by empirical research (Agnew, 1991; Elliot & Menard, 1996; Matsueda & Anderson, 1998; Thornberry, Lizotte, Krohn, Farnsworth, & Jang, 1994). Consistent with developmental theory, the effects of peers vary across age groups, and the impact of delinquent peers on behavior grows as the locus of interaction and social influence shift from the family to peer networks during adolescence (Jang, 1999). Evidence also suggests that peers may have both positive (Jessor, Van Den Bos, Vanderryn, Costa, & Turbin, 1995) and negative effects on young people (Dryfoos, 1990; Stein & Newcomb, 1999). An attempt was made to gather information on the influence of both delinquent and conventional peers. Official offending histories were examined to determine if the client had offended in company. This crime in company variable was coded 1 = No, 2 = Yes. Information relating to delinquent influence was also extracted from the case files in response to the question, "Has there been an assessment made by a case worker that delinquent peers negatively influence the client's behavior?" (1 = No, 2 = Yes). Association with conventional peers was ascertained by determining whether the client had friendships with non-delinquent peers (1 = No, 2 = Yes).

Policy Factors

In an effort to capture some policy-level, as opposed to implementation, effects, clients who attended a YJS were compared with clients who attended an AO. But this is not a rigorous measure of policy effect. Given that evidence from an earlier study indicated that the YJS concept was being manipulated at the operational level, it was likely that other YJS offices will similarly modify the concept to reflect the values and skills of the staff. We can say with confidence, however, that YJSs do not manage child protection issues and offer a service dedicated to meeting the needs of youth justice clients. In contrast, the AOs have the responsibility for the management of both child protection and youth justice. Service type referred to the organization that administered the majority of the client's index order (YJS = 1, AO = 2).

Given that many young offenders are highly mobile, there was the possibility that an individual could have been a client of both a YJS and AO across multiple locations. Service location was included to capture this mobility, and to also provide a mechanism to measure variation across service delivery locations. Service location referred to the location where the client attended the majority of their index order and was coded 1 = LAYJS, 2 = CYJS, 3 = IYJS, 4 = SCAO, 5 = MTGAO, 6 = CAO.

Implementation Factors

It was important to gather some indication of the type of intervention that clients received. This would help to identify which specific components of the intervention had a beneficial, benign or harmful impact on future offending behavior. The case management files provided information, to varying degrees, on client engagement, meeting client needs, family involvement and compliance with order requirements.

The client engagement variable measured how well the case worker was able to engage the client in discussions around their offending behavior. Responses were coded 1 = persistently difficult to engage, 2 = initially difficult to engage, easier to engage over time, and 3 = easy to engage from the outset. An attempt was also made to determine how well the service met the needs of clients. Four variables were included that related to internal service delivery: (1) identified needs that were neglected, (2) identified needs that could not be addressed internally, (3) client needs that were referred to the internal program work group, and (4) client needs that were addressed by case workers through one-on-one discussions. These four variables were coded 1 = none, 2 = drug and alcohol, 3 = violence/aggression, 4 = victim empathy, 5 = education/learning assistance, 6 = lifestyle, 7 = decision making, 8 = employment, 9 = other.

Two variables that related to family involvement were included in the study. The first, type of family involvement, attempted to ascertain how families were involved in the case management process. This variable was coded 1 = not involved, 2 = predominantly information provision, 3 = predominantly engaged in case management. The second family-focused variable, supported family problem, sought to determine how the YJS or AO responded to family problems and was coded 1 = no issues identified, 2 = issues identified and addressed, 3 = issues identified and outcomes unclear, 4 = issues identified and not addressed. Finally, six variables were included in the database that measured compliance with order requirements. The first, difficult to contact , which referred to the number of times the YJS or AO experienced difficulty maintaining contact with the client, was coded as a numerical variable. The second, fail to report, was also numerical and recorded the number of times the client failed to report. The remaining variables, non-compliance letter, formal warning, breach non-compliance, and breach reoffending, recorded whether the client had received one of these during the course of the intervention and was coded 1 = no, 2 = yes. Breach for reoffending was equivalent to the rearrest recidivism outcome measure (discussed in the next section). Its inclusion in the database served to verify the accuracy of the Queensland Police Service rearrest data.

Impact Factors

In previous studies, recidivism has been defined in a number of ways, including rearrest (Martinez Jnr., 1997; Piquero et al., 2001; Winner, Lanza-Kaduce, Bishop, & Frazier, 1997), reconviction (Friendship, Beech, & Browne, 2002; Thompson et al., 2001), parole adjustment and/or violation (Heilbrun et al., 2000; Hoge, Andrews, & Leschied, 1994), and re-imprisonment (Silver & Chow-Martin, 2002). Recidivism was defined as rearrest and was measured once for each client. That is, if the client was rearrested within the specified 18-month follow-up period, they were recorded as having recidivated (1 = no, 2 = yes). Those clients who were not subsequently rearrested within the time period were recorded as not having recidivated.

For those clients who had recidivated, five additional variables that related to offending behavior were included in the database. Time at risk referred to the number of days, out of the 18 months that was used as the recidivism window, that the client was not in secure care and was recorded as a numerical variable. Date of first post-intervention rearrest referred to the data of the client's first arrest following receipt of the index order. Seriousness of first post-intervention rearrest was the seriousness value (based once again on the DCSI) of the first arrest following receipt of the index order. Number of post-intervention arrests was a numerical variable that recorded the number of arrests from the data of the index order within 18 months. Most frequent post-intervention rearrest offense type was used to record the offence type that the client was most frequently arrested for since receipt of the index order and within 18 months, and was coded 1 = against person, 2 = property, 3 = motor vehicle, 4 = drugs, 5 = public order, 6 = other.

RESULTS

Missing Values Analysis

A missing values analysis was conducted to examine the proportion of missing values on each variable contained in the database. The results of the MVA showed an extremely high proportion of missing data on non-statutory variables (the mean proportion of missing data across all non-statutory variables was 57% as compared to 2.3% for statutory variables). While it was anticipated that non-statutory variables would have a higher proportion of missing data than statutory variables, the extent of missing data on non-statutory variables was unexpected. The preliminary review of case files, that helped to identify which variables would be included in the database, was conducted to reduce this problem of missing data on non-statutory variables.

While a number of strategies are available to manage missing data, it was not possible to confidently estimate values, variables with greater than 70% missing data were removed from the dataset for the subsequent analyses.

When remaining variables were recoded into two categories, 1 = data and 2 = no data, chi square ($\chi 2$) analyses demonstrated that YJSs did not gather significantly more information on developmental risk and protective factors than AOs. There are two possible explanations for the high levels of missing data. First, the analyses may indicate that the YJS has not successfully operationalized many of the critical features of developmental interventions. Specifically, the failure of the YJS to gather information on key developmental risk and/or protective factors and work within multiple contexts may indicate that the intervention has not embraced the theoretical basis of the concept. Alternatively, the information recorded may a product of administrative practices, and may be an accurate representation of the casework that is conducted with the client. The failure to record information on a risk and protective factor may not mean that the issue has not been raised with the client, but may mean that the issue was raised and was not a problem for the client. In this sense, case management files may only contain problem behavior, as opposed to reflecting a holistic picture of both risk and protective factors across multiple contexts.

Bivariate Analyses

Chi-square analyses were first conducted to ascertain the relationship between the policy-level variables and recidivism. The chi-square analysis revealed no significant relationship between recidivism and service ($\chi 2$ (df = 1, N = 190) = 3.143, p = .076). This result suggests that the YJS was no more effective at preventing future offending behavior than the traditional AO model of service delivery.

Notwithstanding the fact that the relationship between rearrest and service was not significant at the $p < .05$ level, clients of the YJS were 1.8 times more likely to recidivate than AO clients. In attempting to understand this result, chi-square analyses were conducted to determine if the clients of the YJS presented significantly more risk than AO clients. All individual, education, family and peer variables that were significantly related to rearrest were examined. With the exception of three risk factors, including child protection notifications, neglect and delinquent influence, there were no significant differences in the risk profiles of YJS clients and AO clients. The clients of the YJS were 2.5 times more likely to have had child protection notifications registered against them ($\chi 2$ (df = 1, N = 190) = 7.938, p = .005, phi = –.208), 2.3 times more likely to have been neglected ($\chi 2$ (df = 1, N = 190) = 4.434, p = .035, phi = –.155) and 1.2 times more likely to have been influenced by delinquent peers ($\chi 2$ (df = 2, N = 190) = 9.360, p =.009, V = .226) than clients of the AO (Figure 8.5). This result may in part explain why the YJS is marginally less effective at preventing re-offending than AOs.

The Impact of Client Risk on Recidivism

Analyses were also conducted to determine the impact of client risk factors on recidivism. Chi-square analyses indicated that seven risk factors were significantly related to recidivism, including number of preintervention offences, drug use, drug type, child protection notifications, highest grade achieved and delinquent influence. Interestingly, no associations were found between parental factors and recidivism. Notwithstanding the significance of the relationships, the phi (ϕ) and Cramer's V (V) values indicate that the strength of these relationships was weak, with drug use (V = .281) and delinquent influence (V = .242) being the most powerful risk factors associated with recidivism. A summary table, listing the results of these chi-square analyses is included in Table 1.

For those offenders who had a prior offending history, those who had 21 or more offenses were 25% more likely to recidivate than those who had only committed from 1 to 5 offenses. Moreover, clients that had at least one preintervention offense were 19 times more likely to recidivate than those who had no prior offending history. A direct logistic regression analysis, where recidivism was outcome and the predictor was the numerical number of preintervention offenses variable, confirmed the significance of the result ($\chi2$ (df = 1, N = 190) = 6.751, p = .009).

A record of the client using drugs was also positively related to recidivism. 83% of those clients who had been identified as drug users were rearrested, as compared with only 33% who were not rearrested. This means that clients were nearly 10 times more likely to recidivate if they were drug users than if they did not use drugs. Interpretation of this result is complicated by the "no record" category. This no record category, the composition of which is unknown, was partially responsible for the significant result as indicated by the adjusted residual of 2.9 for the no recidivism outcome.

While drug type was also significantly associated with recidivism, the result was difficult to interpret. The majority of clients used cannabis and the small number of cases in the "other" category (N = 18) did not allow a comparison amongst drug types. Once again, the "no record"

☐ ***TABLE 1: Risk Factors That Were Significantly Related to Recidivism***

Variable	df	N	χ^2	Sig.	ϕ/V
Pre-intervention offenses	4	190	11.986	.017	.251
Drug use	2	190	14.975	.001	.281
Drug type[2]	2	184	9.950	.008	.223
Child protection notifications	1	190	6.130	.013	.180
Highest grade achieved	2	190	10.881	.004	.239
Crime in company	2	190	7.131	.028	.194
Delinquent influence	2	190	16.235	.000	.292

[2] Six cases that did not use drugs at all were removed from this analysis, reducing the N to 184, to ensure that fewer than 25% of cells had expected counts of less than 5.

category was driving the significance of the result (adj. resid. = –3.1 for recidivism outcome). When the "no record" category was removed from the analysis, there was no significant relationship between drug type and recidivism within 18-months ($\chi 2$ (df = 2, N = 88) = .002, p = .962, V = .962).

Whether the client had been the subject of a child protection notification was also significantly associated with recidivism ($\chi 2$ (df = 1, N = 190) = 6.130, p = .013, V = .180). Eighty-two percent of those clients who had been the subject of a child protection notification were rearrested, as compared with 65% for those who had not.

The significance of the highest grade completed result was primarily being driven by the result in the year 11 or 12 category, where those who have attained this level were 160% and 7% less likely to recidivate than those who had completed year nine or ten, or year eight or below respectively.

Finally, results showed that clients that were influenced by delinquent peers were 9% more likely to recidivate than those who were not. However, this result must be interpreted with caution given that the "no record" category strongly influenced this result and had an adjusted residual of –4.0 for the recidivism outcome.

The Impact of Intervention Factors on Recidivism

Chi-square analyses were also conducted to determine whether any intervention factors were related to recidivism. Table 2 lists those intervention variables that were significantly related to recidivism.

Clients who were persistently difficult to engage were 67% more likely to recidivate than clients who were easy to engage from the outset and 30% more likely to recidivate than clients who were easier to engage over time. The proportion of clients that recidivated and whose family

TABLE 2: Intervention Factors That Were Significantly Related to Recidivism

Variable	df	N	χ^2	Sig.	ϕ/V
Client engagement	3	190	10.921	.012	.240
Management of family problems	4	190	10.399	.034	.234
Difficult to contact	1	190	5.135	.023	.164
Fail to report	1	190	8.376	.004	.210
Non-compliance letter	1	190	7.638	.006	.201
Formal warning letter	1	190	8.724	.003	.215

problems were not addressed by staff were 109% more likely to recidivate than those whose family issues were identified and addressed, and were 23% more likely to recidivate than those clients whose family issues were identified and the outcome was unclear. The remainder of the significant relationships between intervention factors and recidivism related to measures of compliance. Clients who were less willing to comply with the requirements of the court order were more likely to offend. Clients who were difficult to contact, failed to report, received a letter of non-compliance, or received a formal warning were 23, 32, 31 and 32% more likely to recidivate than those who did not respectively.

Logistic Regression Models

Logistic regressions were conducted to determine which variables were most strongly associated with recidivism, while allowing for interactions between the variables, and specifically examining the influence of the policy-level predictors of service (i.e., YJS or AO) and service type (i.e., the six locations). The dichotomous variable recidivism, where recidivism was coded '1' and no recidivism was coded '0,' was used as the outcome. Once again, only those variables that had less than 70% missing data were included in the analyses.

Given that the effects of service location are nested within service type, a single degree of freedom orthogonal contrast was applied to account for these confounded factors. The advantage of orthogonal coding is that the resulting estimates are independent. As it was not viable to explore a design whereby all possible combinations were analyzed, a subset of planned comparisons was undertaken and the column vectors were coded to reflect the research questions and the preliminary chi-square results. These contrasts are outlined in Table 3.

The "service type 1" contrast allows for comparison between the JYS policy and the AO policy, and addressed the overriding research question regarding the effect of the YJS on offending behavior. The next two contrasts reflect the findings of the earlier chi-square analysis that examined the relationship between service location and recidivism, and identified that the comparatively high recidivism rate of CYJS and comparatively low recidivism rate of MTGAO appeared to be driving the significant result. The second contrast, "service location 2," compares CYJS with LAYJS and IYJS. The third contrast, "service location 3" compares MTGAO with SCAO and CAO. In order to have a complete set of orthogonal contrasts (i.e., the same number of df for the overall variable), two additional contrasts were included. The fourth contrast

TABLE 3: Single Degree of Freedom Orthogonal Contrasts for Service Type and Service Location

Contrast	LAYJS	CYJS	IYJS	SCAO	CAO	MTGAO
Service type 1	1	1	1	–1	–1	–1
Service location 2	1	–2	1	0	0	0
Service location 3	0	0	0	1	1	–2
Service location 4	1	0	–1	0	0	0
Service location 5	0	0	0	1	–1	0

"service location 4" compares LAYJS with IYJS, and the final contrast, "service location 5" compares SCAO with CAO.

Prior to analysis, each factor was examined using bivariate statistics. While no variables that had a contingency table with a zero cell were identified, this process did lead to some variables being recoded to better reflect the data. An evaluation of expected frequencies indicated that four variables–sexual abuse, disrupted attachment, difficulty contacting client and fail to report–violated the requirements for logistic regression, and a decision was made to omit these variables from the analysis rather than modifying the goodness-of-fit criterion.

The relationships among the independent variables were also examined using SPSS correlation. Only those variables that were significant at $p < .01$ and the strength of the association was large (i.e., $r = -.50$ to1.0 or $r = -.50$ to -1.0) according to Cohen's (1988) guidelines are discussed here. According to this criteria, a number of variables were multicollinear. Drug use and drug type ($r = .918$, $p = .000$) were highly correlated, and drug type (which had more missing data) was subsequently removed from the model. The statutory compliance measures (i.e., non-compliance letter, formal warning, and breach for non-compliance) were all multicollinear. As a consequence, non-compliance letter (renamed "compliance" for the remainder of the analysis) was selected for inclusion in the regression model, and redundant variables were omitted. Because "compliance" measures elements of both service delivery, specifically with regard to surveillance, and client behavior, in that the measure reflects how the individual responded to the requirements of the court order, this measure was treated as a distinct block for entry into the full model.

While not multicollinear, of the six remaining variables that related to child protection issues, five[2] were highly correlated ($p > .621$). A decision was made to use only the substantiated child protection assessment variable. Delinquent influence was also highly correlated with crime in company ($r = .639$, $p = .000$). Crime in company was excluded from subsequent analyses.

Logistic Regression Analysis Strategy

Consequently, a total of 22 predictors were available for inclusion in the logistic regression analyses, including 11 risk, five intervention, one compliance predictor and five policy contrast predictors. Given Tabachnick and Fidell's (2001, p. 117) general guideline that $N > 50 + 8m$ (where m is the number of independent variables), it was not feasible to enter all the predictors into a single model simultaneously. In order to overcome this problem, a decision was made to examine a series of models, first testing the importance of risk and intervention factors separately, and then testing the full model with only a reduced number of predictors that were significantly related to recidivism. Hosmer and Lemeshow (1989, p. 83) argue that in minimizing the number of variables in the model, the resultant model will be more likely to be numerically stable and more easily generalized.

Model 1a: Risk Predictors

This model sought to determine the importance of client risk predictors, for the prediction of recidivism within 18 months. Seven risk predictors (number of preintervention offenses, most frequent offense type, alcohol use, drug use, substantiated child protection assessment, highest grade completed and delinquent influence) whose bivariate test indicated a p-value <0.25, were entered into the model. Evaluation of adequacy of expected frequencies for categorical predictors indicated that it was not necessary to restrict model goodness-of-fit tests. Four predictors (alcohol use, drug use, highest grade completed and delinquent influence) were related to recidivism at $p < .25$, and were subsequently entered into model 2a.

Model 1b: Intervention Predictors

This model sought to determine the importance of intervention predictors, for the prediction of recidivism within 18 months. Only three intervention predictors (management of family problems, client engagement and identified needs that were neglected) were eligible for inclusion in this model based on the p-value < 0.25 bivariate test criteria. Once again, it was not necessary to restrict model goodness-of-fit tests. Two predictors (client engagement and management of family problems) were related to recidivism at $p < .25$, and were subsequently entered into model 2b.

Model 2a: Risk Predictor Subset and Policy Predictors

Those risk predictors found to be significantly related to recidivism in model 1a were then entered into a sequential logistic regression model that sought to determine the importance of the policy level predictors for the prediction of membership in the single outcome of recidivism, first based on the selected risk predictors (alcohol use, drug use, highest grade completed and delinquent influence), again after the addition of the service location contrasts and finally after the addition of the service type contrast.

This analysis selected drug use, highest grade completed and delinquent influence as important predictors of recidivism. These three predictors were subsequently eligible for inclusion in the full model. Service type was not significant in this analysis ($z = 1.439$, $p = .230$).

Model 2b: Intervention Predictors Subset and Policy Predictors

The two intervention predictors found to be significantly related to recidivism in the model 1b were then entered into a sequential logistic regression model that sought to determine the importance of the policy level predictors for the prediction of membership in the single outcome of recidivism, first based on the selected intervention predictors (client engagement and management of family problems), again after the addition of the service location contrasts and finally after the addition of the service type contrast.

This analysis confirmed the importance of both variables as potentially important predictors of recidivism. These two predictors were subsequently eligible for inclusion in the full model. Once again, service type was not significant in this analysis ($z = 2.309$, $p = .129$).

Model 3: Risk and Intervention Predictors Subsets, Compliance and Policy Predictors

This full model sought to determine the importance of the policy level predictors for the prediction of membership in the single outcome of recidivism, first based on the three selected risk factors, again after the addition of the two selected intervention factors, again after the addition of compliance predictor, again after the addition of the service location contrasts and finally after the addition of the service type contrast. Evaluation of adequacy of expected frequencies for categorical predictors indicated that it was not necessary to restrict model goodness-of-fit tests.

Given that the full model had 20 degrees of freedom, the significance of individual predictors was first assessed □ = .0045.[3] At this level, the only predictor that that was significantly associated with recidivism was the MTGAO contrast, confirming the results of the bivariate analyses and once again suggesting variation at the site of service delivery. The odds ratios for the full model showed that young people who attended the SCAO or the CAO were just over two times more likely to recidivate than were young people who attended the MTGAO. This result is very important in that it suggests that unmeasured practices at the site of service delivery do have the capacity to influence recidivism, even after controlling for all other predictors that previous bivariate and multivariate analyses had indicated were associated with recidivism.

When the criterion for significance was relaxed to $p < .05$, three additional predictors emerged as individually influencing recidivism. Young people who were using drugs and were being influenced by delinquent peers were more likely to offend. Only one intervention variable, how family problems were addressed, was significantly related to recidivism. Young people whose family problems had been identified and addressed by caseworkers were less likely to reoffend. Overall, the model was statistically reliable based on the full set of predictors (χ^2 (df = 20, N = 190) = 67.166, p = .000), indicating that these predictors, as a set, reliably distinguished between non-recidivists and recidivists. This model correctly classified 77.9% of the cases, and a pseudomeasure (Nagelkerke R^2) of explained variation was 43%.

The odds ratios for the full model show that the odds of recidivating were just over four times greater for young people who were using drugs, than for those who were not. Compared to those who were not subject to such pressure, young people who were influenced by delinquent peers were just over three and a half times more likely to recidivate. When youths continued in education into years 11 or 12, the odds of recidivating were reduced by 14%, and when family problems were addressed, the odds of recidivating were reduced, but only marginally (0.06).

The intention of these analyses was to determine the effect of the YJS on post-intervention offending behavior. Models 2a, 2b and 3 have demonstrated that the service type variable was not a significant predictor of recidivism within 18-months, regardless of how the risk and intervention factors were modelled.

Conditional Probability Scenarios

Conditional probabilities of recidivating for various case scenarios were then calculated by solving for the conditional probability = 1 / 1 + e^{-logit}, where ^{logit} is the linear regression equation or logit transformation ($B_0 + B_1X_1 + \cdots + B_iX_i$) (Hayes & Daly, 2003; Hosmer & Lemeshow, 1989; Poulos & Orchowsky, 1994).

The significant predictors that emerged from model three (i.e., drug use, delinquent influence and management of family problems) were entered into a logistic regression model where the outcome was recidivism within 18-months. Another logistic regression was performed that included these significant predictors as well as the service type variable. Although service type was not significant in model 2a, 2b or 3, and therefore not necessary from a purely statistical perspective, this regression was performed to demonstrate how the conditional probability of recidivating was not greatly affected by whether the client attended a YJS or an AO. Conditional probabilities were calculated for four scenarios.

- **Scenario 1** referred to a young person who was using drugs and had delinquent peers (categorized as high-risk), and whose family problems were addressed during the case management process.
- **Scenario 2** referred to a young person who was using drugs and had delinquent peers (categorized as high-risk), and whose family problems were not addressed during the case management process.
- **Scenario 3** referred to a young person who was not using drugs and did not have delinquent peers (categorized as low-risk), and whose family problems were addressed during the case management process.
- **Scenario 4** referred to a young person who was not using drugs and did not have delinquent peers (categorized as high-risk), and whose family problems were not addressed during the case management process.

Table 4 presents the conditional probabilities of recidivating within 18-months for these case scenarios, first based on the coefficients from the logistic regression that included only the three significant predictors,

TABLE 4: Conditional Probabilities of Recidivating Within 18-Months for Various Case Scenarios

Predictor	Logit B0 + B1X1 + . . . + BiXi	Probability 1 / 1 + e –logit
Scenario 1:		
High risk young person, family problems addressed	.20	.55
Drug use (1 = Yes)		
Delinquent influence (1 = Yes)		
Management of family problems (1 = Issues identified and addressed)		
Service type (1 = YJS)	–.04	.49
Service type (1 = AO)	.38	.59
Scenario 2:		
High risk young person, family problems not addressed	3.44	.96
Drug use (1 = Yes)		
Delinquent influence (1 = Yes)		
Management of family problems (1 = Issues identified and not addressed)		
Service type (1 = YJS)	3.28	.96
Service type (1 = AO)	3.67	.97
Scenario 3:		
Low risk young person, family problems addressed	–2.16	.10
No drug use (1 = Yes)		
No delinquent influence (1 = Yes)		
Management of family problems (1 = Issues identified and addressed)		
Service type (1 = YJS)	–2.30	.09
Service type (1 = AO)	–1.89	.13
Scenario 4:		
Low risk young person, family problems not addressed	1.07	.75
No drug use (1 = Yes)		
No delinquent influence (1 = Yes)		
Management of family problems (1 = Issues identified and not addressed)		
Service type (1 = YJS)	1.01	.73
Service type (1 = AO)	1.42	.81

and then after the service type predictors was included in the logistic regression.

The results emphasize the importance of engaging families in the case management process, for high *and* low-risk offenders. The conditional probability of high-risk offenders recidivating dropped from 96% to 55% when their family problems were addressed. An even greater reduction was found for low-risk offenders, whose conditional probability of recidivating dropped from 75% to 10% when their family problems were addressed. Once again, the effect of service type has little impact on recidivism, with the conditional probability of recidivating varying by less than 10% for clients who attended a YJS as compared with clients who attended an AO for the four scenarios.

Survival Analysis

Survival analysis was used to determine whether YJS clients had a significantly longer time to failure (defined as rearrest) than AO clients. In this analysis, time to failure (the dependent variable) was bounded by the court date of the index order and the failure date, after adjusting for any incarceration time. A follow-up period of 18 months was allowed. Therefore, the maximum time at risk was 18 months, which resulted when the client was not incarcerated as a result of the index order and was not rearrested during the follow-up period.

The sample was approximately evenly distributed between the YJS (53%) and AO (47%), and the sample size of 190 proved sufficient for the analysis. All covariates were tested to determine whether they interacted with time. The proportionality assumption was met for all covariates (drug use ($p = .844$), delinquent influence ($p = .095$) and how family problems were managed ($p = .081$).

Life Tables

Similar to the results of the bivariate analysis, the estimated rate of survival for clients who attended the AO and the YJS was not significantly different (Wilcoxon statistic = .004, $p = .95$, $N = 190$). Overall, a greater proportion of AO clients survived (31%) throughout the follow-up period, compared with one-fifth of YJS clients (20%). Figure 1 displays the cumulative proportion of clients from the AO and YJS samples surviving throughout the follow-up period. The YJS survival curve had a more gradual descent that the AO curve, suggesting that the YJS may have some immediate deterrent effect, perhaps stemming from the attention directed toward ensuring compliance with order requirements. This effect was only temporary, however, as the curves crossed at month ten, when the YJS sample continued to decline at a steady rate, but the AO sample remained fairly stable from month eight to 17. The YJS sample also eventually plateaued, but this stability commenced later (month 12) and was of shorter duration (four months as

FIGURE 1: Cumulative Proportion Surviving by Service Type

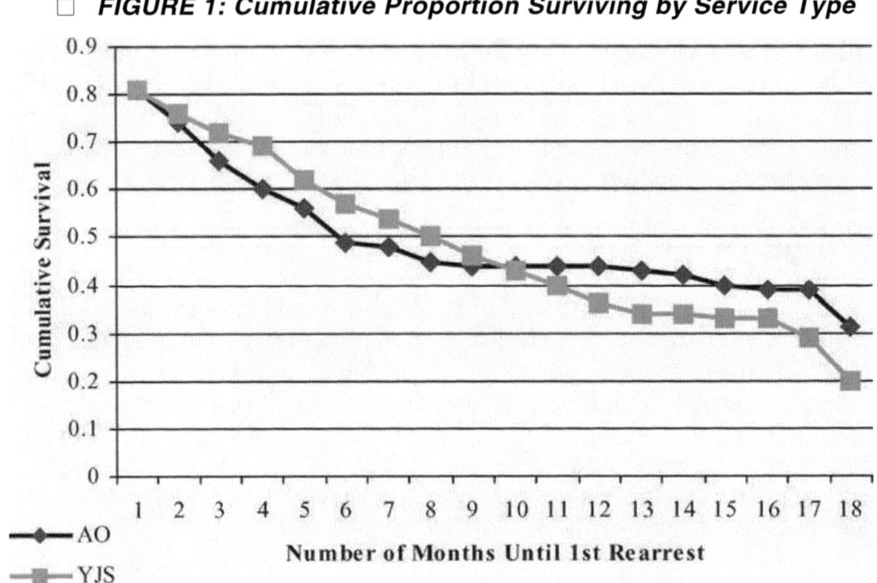

compared with nine months) than that of the AO sample. After this plateau, both the AO and YJS samples experienced their sharpest decline in the cumulative proportion surviving between month 17 and 18. Half of the AO sample had failed by month six into the follow-up period, while the YJS sample did not lose half of its members until into the eighth month.

When the analysis was restricted to failure cases only (N = 135), there was a significant difference in time to failure between the AO and the YJS models (Wilcoxon statistic = 5.346, p = .02). Figure 2 reports this result. Once again, the YJS appears to have an immediate desistence impact, having a less marked decline than the AO curve. However, this effect is temporary, having all but diminished by 12 months. The AO sample has less than 10% surviving at month eight, whereas it takes the YJS sample an additional four months (i.e., at month 12) to reach this point.

Cox Regression

Cox regression examined the risk of failure, while controlling for the three covariates that were found to be significantly related to recidivism in the bivariate and logistic regression analyses. The service location contrasts were also included in these analyses. Table 5 shows the relationship

FIGURE 2: Cumulative Proportion Surviving by Service Type for Failure Cases Only

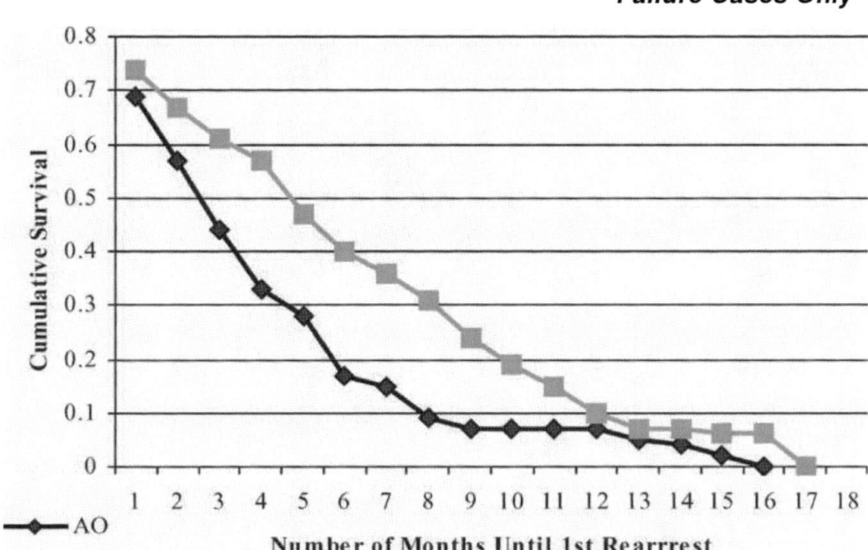

between drug use, delinquent influence and how family problems were managed and the hazard rate, or risk of failure. The Wald statistic was used to test the individual importance of each covariate as a predictor in the model, and the Exp(B) statistic was interpreted as the increase or decrease in the hazard rate due to each unit increase in the covariate. This analysis found that being influenced by delinquent peers significantly increased the hazard rate by 180% (p = .008, Exp(B) = 1.823), as did using drugs, increasing the hazard rate by nearly 90% (p = .001, Exp(B) = .88). The results of this analysis also lend support to the notion that interventions can affect recidivism, even after controlling for client risk. Attending the SCAO or the CAO increased the hazard rate by 160% (Exp(B) = 1.59, p = .000) as compared with attending the MTGAO.

When the analysis was restricted to failure cases only, the effects of delinquent peers and drugs were no longer significant. When only recidivists were considered, only one covariate influenced the hazard rate. Attending the SCAO or the CAO increased the hazard rate by 144% (Exp(B) = 1.44, p = .005) as compared with attending the MTGAO. These results are presented in Table 6.

TABLE 5: Hazard Rate Regressed on Service Type and Service Location, Controlling for Covariates (Recidivism = 1)

Predictor	B	Wald	df	Sig.	Exp(B)
Drug use		7.559	2	.023	
No	–.119	.025	1	.874	.888
Yes	.600	7.147	1	.008	1.823
Delinquent influence		7.254	2	.027	
No	.578	2.040	1	.153	1.783
Yes	.600	7.147	1	.008	1.823
Management of family problems		5.166	4	.271	
No issues identified	–.394	1.138	1	.286	.674
Issues identified and addressed	–1.030	2.877	1	.090	.357
Issues identified and outcomes unclear	–.146	.445	1	.505	.864
Issues identified and not addressed	.208	.460	1	.498	1.231
Contrast 2 (LAYJS and IYJS =1, CYJS = –2)	–.147	2.367	1	.124	.863
Contrast 3 (SCAO and CAO =1, MTGAO = –2)	.467	14.020	1	.000	1.596
Contrast 4 (LAYJS =1, IYJS = –1)	.031	.051	1	.822	1.032
Contrast 5 (SCAO =1, CAO = –1)	.224	1.803	1	.179	1.251
Service type (YJS)	–.060	.090	1	.764	.941

CONCLUSION

This study found that the YJS was no better than the AO in preventing recidivism, as measured at 18-months post-intervention. This result was confirmed by bivariate and multivariate analyses, and after controlling for risk, intervention and compliance covariates that were significantly related to recidivism in their own right. The study found that there was variation at the site of service delivery, even within service types, suggesting that variation in intervention practice can impact upon offending behavior.

While this study was unable to ascertain which intervention practices were producing positive results, there is reason to believe that recidivism is reduced when family problems are addressed by caseworkers. This finding supports the developmental perspective that highlights the importance of families, both as agents of change and agents for change. Future research should attempt to un-pack these results and determine those key features of intervention practice that deliver improved outcomes for young people.

TABLE 6: Hazard Rate Regressed on Service Type and Service Location, Controlling for Covariates, for Failure Cases Only (Recidivism = 1)

Predictor	B	Wald	df	Sig.	Exp(B)
Drug use		3.554	2	.169	
No	.761	.908	1	.341	2.140
Yes	.206	.691	1	.406	1.229
Delinquent influence		.691	2	.708	
No	.143	.115	1	.734	1.154
Yes	.206	.691	1	.406	1.229
Management of family problems		2.231	4	.693	
No issues identified	.209	.318	1	.573	1.233
Issues identified and addressed	–.035	.003	1	.956	.965
Issues identified and outcomes unclear	.288	1.801	1	.180	1.334
Issues identified and not addressed	–.015	.003	1	.960	.985
Contrast 2 (LAYJS and IYJS = 1, CYJS = –2)	–.058	.328	1	.567	.944
Contrast 3 (SCAO and CAO = 1, MTGAO = –2)	.371	8.052	1	.005	1.449
Contrast 4 (LAYJS = 1, IYJS = –1)	–.070	.263	1	.608	.933
Contrast 5 (SCAO = 1, CAO = –1)	.013	.005	1	.942	1.013
Service type (YJS)	.269	1.662	1	.197	1.309

Although all effects had subsided by 18 months, survival analyses indicated that the YJS might have some temporary deterrent effect. When only failure cases were examined, AO clients recidivated at a significantly faster rate, having less than 10% surviving at month eight, whereas the YJS sample did not reach this point until month 12. That the results of an earlier case study (Denning & Homel, in press) showed that the LAYJS focused heavily on monitoring compliance, and that this may have influenced this result. However, given that we understand there is great variability across different service locations, we cannot assume that other YJS offices place equal emphasis on compliance.

REFERENCES

Agnew, R. (1991). The interactive effects of peer variables on delinquency. *Criminology, 29* (47-72).

Battin-Pearson, S., Newcomb, M. D., Abbot, R. D., Hill, K. G., Catalano, R. F., & Hawkins, J. D. (2000). Predictors of early high school dropout: A test of five theories. *Journal of Educational Psychology, 92*, 568-582.

Bronfenbrenner, U. (1979). *The ecology of human development: Experiements by nature and design.* Cambridge, MA: Harvard University Press.

Browning, K., & Loeber, R. (1999). Highlights of findings from the Pittsburgh Youth Study. *OJJDP Fact Sheet, 95.*

Cohen, J. (1988). *Statistical power analysis for behavioural sciences* (2 ed.). Hillsdale, NJ: Lawrences Erlbaum Associated.

Dryfoos, J. G. (1990). *Adolescents at risk: Prevalence and prevention.* Oxford University: New York.

Elliot, D. S., & Menard, S. (1996). Delinquent friends and delinquent behavior: Temporal and developmental patterns. In J. D. Hawkins (Ed.), *Delinquency and crime: Current theories.* Cambridge: Cambridge University Press.

Farrington, D. P. (1989). Early predictors of adolescent aggression and adult violence. *Violence and Victims, 4*, 79-100.

Ford, D. L., & Lerner, R. M. (1992). *Developmental systems theory: An integrative approach.* Newbury Park, CA: Sage.

Friendship, C., Beech, A. R., & Browne, K. D. (2002). Reconviction as an outcome measure in research. *British Journal of Criminology, 42*, 442-444.

Hayes, H., & Daly, K. (2003). Youth justice conferencing and reoffending. *Justice Quarterly, 20*(4), 725-764.

Heilbrun, K., Brock, W., Waite, D., Lanier, A., Schmid, M., Witte, G., Keeney, M., Westendorf, M., Buinavert, L., & Shumate, M. (2000). Risk factors for juvenile criminal recidivism: The postrelease community adjustment of juvenile offenders. *Criminal Justice and Behaviour, 27*(3), 275-291.

Hoge, R. D., Andrews, D. A., & Leschied, A. W. (1994). Tests of three hypotheses regarding the predictors of delinquency. *Journal of Abnormal Child Psychology, 22*(5), 547-559.

Hosmer, D. W., & Lemeshow, S. (1989). *Applied logistic regression.* New York: John Wiley & Sons.

Jang, S. J. (1999). Age-varying effects of family, school, and peers on delinquency: A multilevel modeling test of interactional theory. *Criminology, 37*(3), 643-685.

Jessor, R., Van Den Bos, J., Vanderryn, J., Costa, F. M., & Turbin, M. S. (1995). Protective factors in adolescent problem behavior: Moderator effects and developmental change. *Developmental Psychology, 31*, 923-933.

Krohn, M. D., Thornberry, T. P., Collins-Hall, L., & Lizotte, A. J. (1995). School dropout, delinquent behavior and drug use: An examination of the causes and consequences of dropping out of school. In H. B. Kaplan (Ed.), *Drugs, crime, and other deviant adaptations: Longitudinal studies.* New York: Plenum Press.

Martinez, Jr. R. (1997). Predictors of serious violent recidivism: Results from a cohort study. *Journal of Interpersonal Violence, 12*(2), 216-228.

Matsueda, R. L., & Anderson, K. (1998). The dynamics of delinquent peers and delinquent behavior. *Criminology, 36*(2), 269-308.

Moffitt, T. E. (1993). Adolescence-limited and life-course persistent antisocial behavior: A developmental taxonomy. *Psychological Review, 100*, 674-701.

Patterson, G. R., Forgatch, M. S., Yoerger, K. L., & Stoolmiller, M. (1998). Variables that initiate and maintain an early-onset trajectory for juvenile offending. *Development and Psychopathology, 10*, 531-547.

Patterson, G. R., Reid, J. B., & Dishion, T. J. (1992). *A social interactional approach: Vol. 4. Antisocial boys*. Eugene, OR: Castalia.

Piquero, A. R., Blumstein, A., Brame, R., Haapanen, R., Mulvey, E. P., & Nagin, D. S. (2001). Assessing the impact of exposure time and incapacitation on longitudinal trajectories of criminal offending. *Journal of Adolescent Research, 16*(1), 54-74.

Poulos, T., & Orchowsky, S. (1994). Serious juvenile offenders: Predicting the probability of transfer to criminal court. *Crime and Delinquency, 40*, 3-17.

Sameroff, A. J. (1983). Developmental systems: Contexts and evolution. In W. Kessen (Ed.), *History, theory, and methods* (4 ed., Vol. 1). New York: Wiley.

Sampson, R. J., & Laub, J. H. (1993). *Crime in the making: Pathways and turning points through life*. Cambridge, MA: Harvard University Press.

Silver, E., & Chow-Martin, L. (2002). A multiple models approach to assessing recidivism risk: Implictions for judicial decision making. *Criminal Justice and Behavior, 29*(5), 538-568.

Stein, J. S., & Newcomb, M. D. (1999). Adult outcomes of adolescent conventional and agentic orientations: A twenty-year longitudinal study. *Journal of Early Adolescence, 19*, 39-65.

Tabachnick, B. G., & Fidell, L. S. (2001). *Using multivariate statistics* (4th ed.). Boston, MA: Allyn and Bacon.

Thornberry, T. P. (1987). Towards an interactional theory of delinquency. *Criminology, 25*, 863-892.

Thornberry, T. P., Ireland, T. O., & Smith, C. A. (2001). The importance of timing: The varying impact of childhood and adolescent maltreatment on multiple problem outcomes. *Development and Psychopathology, 13*(4), 957-979.

Thornberry, T. P., Lizotte, A. J., Krohn, M. D., Farnsworth, M., & Jang, S. J. (1994). Delinquent peers, beliefs, and delinquent behavior: A longitudinal test of interactional theory. *Criminology, 32*(1), 47-74.

Tobach, E., & Greenberg, G. (1984). The significance of T.C. Schneirla's contribution to the concept of levels of integration. In E. Tobach (Ed.), *Behavioral Evolution and Integrative Levels*. Hillsdale, NJ: Erlbaum.

Wasserman, G. A., Keenan, K., Tremblay, R. E., Coie, J. D., Herrenkohl, T. I., Loeber, R., & Petechuk, D. (2003). *Risk and protective factors of child delinquency*. U.S. Department of Justice: Office of Justice Programs: Office of Juvenile Justice and Delinquency Prevention. Retrieved 28 June, 2004, from the World Wide Web: http://ojjdp.ncjrs.org.

White, J. L., Moffitt, T. E., Earls, F., Robins, L., & Silva, P. A. (1990). How early can we tell? Predictors of childhood conduct disorder and adolescent delinquency. *Criminology, 28*, 507-533.

Winner, L., Lanza-Kaduce, L., Bishop, D. M., & Frazier, C. E. (1997). The transfer of juveniles to criminal court: Reexamining recidivism over the long term. *Crime and Delinquency, 43*(4), 548-563.

NOTES

1. This study built on previous case studies of young men who participated in the Youth Justice Service. For consistency, females were similarly excluded from this study.

2. While timing of maltreatment was significantly correlated with the other child protection factors, the strength of these relationships was weak ($p > .222$ and $p < .372$).

3. Tabachnick and Fidell recommend using a criterion $\alpha = .0045$ to compensate for inflated Type I error rate with greater than 11 predictors.

Integrating into the Mental Health System from the Criminal Justice System: Jail Aftercare Services for Persons with a Severe Mental Illness

KRISTIN DAVIS
JOHN FALLON
SUE VOGEL
ALEXANDRA TEACHOUT

INTRODUCTION

In the past five years, it has been widely reported in local news stories to nationally televised exposes that persons with mental illness are over represented in the nations' jails (Psychiatric News, 2003; Frontline, 2005). The frequent exposes of this problem, coupled with exposes of overcrowding, have made inroads into public consciousness, creating greater recognition of how many persons with mental illness are incarcerated and a greater acceptance for alternatives to incarceration. Concurrently, institutional/criminal justice consciousness was being raised. Federal funding agencies, particularly the Substance Abuse and Mental Health Services Administration (SAMHSA), made jail diversion a funding priority, offering incentives to State or County governments to develop jail diversion initiatives to reduce the number of persons with mental illness in jails. These funding opportunities signaled the importance of the problem to State and local governments and, through grant-specified selection criteria, encouraged multiple stakeholder participation in designing diversion programs.

Public recognition and federal targeting of the problem not only has resulted in more jail diversion programs but also has increased screening and treatment within jails themselves. In terms of jail diversion programs, a wide variety of pre and post booking programs exist. There are more crisis intervention teams to divert before booking and mental health court programs to divert post-booking. Additionally, a 2006 Department of Justice report indicates that mental health screening and treatment is now provided as a matter of policy so that psychotropic medications are prescribed and counseling is done by trained mental health providers in all Federal prisons and most State prisons and jail jurisdictions (Bureau of Justice Report, 2006). What the report does not comment on, however, is the quality of care within the criminal justice system. Despite the reported quantity of services, advocates for prisoners' rights and for the mentally ill consider services ineffective and prison conditions incompatible with therapeutic efforts.

Calls for better assessment, improvement, and monitoring of care have long been made and often made by a rhetorical comparison to the attention paid to the quality of community care (Elliot, 1997). In addition, recent research indicates that many individuals with repeated forensic involvement are not being diverted to a comprehensive set of services best suited to meet their multiple needs (Steadman & Naples, 2005; Broner et al., 2004). As the Council of State Governments (2002) noted, "Without housing that is integrated with mental health, substance abuse, employment, and other services, many people with mental illness end up being homeless, disconnected from community supports, and thus more likely to . . . become involved with the criminal justice system" (8). In contrast, many diversion programs have come to be measured against the single metric of reduced criminal justice contact. There are few longitudinal studies looking at how individuals fare after diversion. Inadvertently, diversion had, in many cases, become an end in and of itself (Broner et al., 2004).

As a result, research into what mode of service delivery and what kinds of treatments are most effective for this population remain in the early stages of inquiry (Morrissey & Meyers, 2006; Lamberti et al., 2004). This is particularly true of assessing the kinds of mental health treatment diverted individuals receive, particularly the accessibility and effectiveness of evidence based mental health practices for diverted individuals (Steadman, 2006; Watson et al., 2001). This article serves to provide support for one of the oldest community mental health evidence based practices, Assertive Community Treatment (ACT), as a service delivery modality most suited for engaging and preparing persons with criminal justice histories for full participation in the mental health system and for provision of subsequent evidence based practices as needed or desired. In the process, it also contributes to the specification of what a Forensic ACT team might look like, an issue currently being debated in the mental health field (Lamberti et al., 2004).

Over the past 10 years, the community mental health system, taking its lead from somatic medicine/physical health care, has developed and begun to test a set of six "Evidence Based Practices," (EBPs) including ACT, Integrated Dual Disorder Treatment, Supported Employment, and Illness Management and Recovery. Just as evidence based medicine is grounded in three principles, namely that clinical care should be supported by the strongest scientific evidence, attention must be paid to consumer values, preferences, and choice, as well as an ongoing commitment to improving clinical skills, so too is mental health evidence based care (Drake et al. Psychiatric Services, 2001). Despite the by now wide dissemination of these practices, implementation not surprisingly has lagged behind. The Surgeon General reports (Mental Health: A Report of the Surgeon General, 1999) that there typically is a 15-20 year gap between identification of an Evidenced Based Practice and routine implementation in the mental health field. ACT, however, has been implemented for close to thirty years and is viewed by many in the mental health field as a delivery mode that will easily accommodate other evidence based practices because rather than specifying service content it specifies a structure for services.

The ACT model, developed by Test and Stein (1976) to provide intensive and supportive care from a multi-disciplinary team *in* the community–as opposed to the hospital or to office based care–began with a two-fold goal. The model was designed to help consumers meet their multiple and complex needs as they transitioned from the hospital and to help them post-transition "become integrated into the community" by providing rehabilitation, counseling, and material support. In effect, the model was thought to be able to keep individuals from returning to the hospital by helping them to connect and feel a real sense of belonging to the world outside the hospital. With the refocus of mental health care from hospital based to community based care, substituting the goal of reducing incarceration for the goal of reducing hospitalization appears a natural extension of the ACT model.

The potential of ACT to reduce jail and arrest rates, however, is uncertain. In a review of controlled studies examining assertive community treatment's impact on jail and arrest rates, Bond and colleagues (2000) found that 70 percent of studies showed no effect, and 10 percent showed worsening. One explanation is that many of the reviewed studies did not involve teams who were formally collaborating with the criminal justice system and who were also systematically recruiting forensic involved individuals (Lamberti et al., 2004). On the other hand, there are a handful of naturalistic studies that demonstrate that ACT services successfully integrate individuals into the mental health system and that this integration (increased service use and working alliances) contributes to better functioning and fewer days in jail.

Among these studies is one reporting on the first 18 patients treated using ACT services–called the Arkansas Partnership Program–seventeen consumers remained arrest free and substance free while living in the community an average of 508 days (Cimino & Jennings, 1999). In a study comparing outcomes among 41 patients during the year before and after enrollment in a program called Project Link, the mean number of jail days per patient dropped, and significant reductions were also noted in the number of arrests and hospitalizations, along with improved community functioning as measured with the Multnomah Community Ability Scale (MCAS) (Lamberti et al., 2001).

In a one year follow-up study of the first 30 patients enrolled in the Thresholds Jail Project, the total number of jail days dropped from 2,741 in the previous year to 469 during the first year of enrollment. The total number of hospital days dropped from 2,153 to 321 for the group.

Total savings in jail costs during the one-year study period was $157,000, and total savings in hospital costs was $917,000. Steadman and Naples (2005), conclude from the data collected from six sites (N = 1260) involved in the SAMHSA Jail Diversion Initiative for persons with a serious mental illness that jail diversion reduces jail days and criminal justice costs. The study points out that the data does not indicate quality of services, an integral component to jail diversion. A recent study, by Broner, Lattimore, Cowell, and Schelnger (2004), which examined differences between diverted and non-diverted individuals in terms of service use, among other variables, reported that diversion did not result in greater access to or use of services over the course of the study period. Significantly, increased service use was found in the first three months after diversion, suggesting that assertive outreach and other engagement strategies ought to be continued well into treatment.

Recent experimental and quasi-experimental studies of post-booking jail diversion programs report modest outcomes. One study, comparing non-diversion to 6 jail diversion programs (3 pre and 3 post booking) at 12 months post-diversion, shows reduction in time spent in jail and linkage to community services (Steadman & Naples, 2005). A second quasi-experimental study, again comparing individuals court assigned to a diversion program versus individuals not assigned, showed participants improved on both mental health and substance use outcomes over time, irrespective on which condition they had been assigned (Shafer, Arughtu, & Franczak, 2006). The main effect of time may be attributed to quality of services for both conditions. The more comprehensive and outreach oriented the services the better the outcomes. Diversion and linkage are best viewed as a first step, not ends in and of themselves.

In one of the few longitudinal studies of ACT aftercare for those with criminal justice involvement, five-year outcomes are reported for 83 acquittees found not guilty by reason of insanity (NGRI) placed on conditional release (CR) into the community. During the study period, only five arrests and 60 hospitalizations occurred, and NGRI acquittees were in the community for 83 percent of the time they were eligible for conditional release (Parker, 2004). Insofar as NGRI typically is a defense for more serious crimes, the study does not speak to the effectiveness of forensic informed ACT teams for repeat *misdemeanor* offenders.

Often misdemeanor offenses result from behaviors related to using substances, such as disruptive behavior, including difficulties in negotiating interpersonal conflict, resulting in public nuisance offenses and dysfunctional coping skills resulting in a variety of drug related offenses (Abram & Teplin, 1991; Chandler & Spicer, 2006). Estimates suggest that 90% of offenders with a mental illness have had a substance use disorder at some point in their lives, and 62%-72% report having a current substance use problem (Abram & Teplin, 1991; Veysey, Steadman, Morrissey, & Johnsen, 1997). Individuals with co-occurring disorders present particular challenges. They are less likely to cooperate with treatment, including taking medication as prescribed, are more likely to be homeless, and may be more likely to commit violence (Steadman et al., 1998; Swartz et al., 1998). A recent study (Chandler & Spicer, 2006) reports on the limited effectiveness of Integrated Dual Disorder Treatment (IDDT), a multi-component practice targeting substance use of individuals with repeated forensic involvement. Using non-equivalent groups, they speculated that the "portability" of IDDT is limited for persons with criminal justice involvement returning to urban areas and that fairly high fidelity scores overall may not be a reliable indicator of outcomes because individual components that have low scores may be the components that future research will show to be most essential.

The preliminary findings described below suggest that re-entry into the mental health system, too, ought to be viewed as a staged process, starting with diversion and linkage mechanisms supported by *formal* coordination between the criminal and mental health systems, followed by an equally staged process of engagement and preparation for integration into the mental health system relying first on intensive ACT services.

PROGRAM DESCRIPTION AND TREATMENT COMPONENTS: THRESHOLDS' ACT LINKAGE AND AFTERCARE

Originally a pilot project designed to show the efficacy of ACT in maintaining persons with lengthy histories of arrests and jail days in the community, "Thresholds' Jail Demonstration Linkage Project" eventually became–because of continued need and because of the program's early success–an agency-funded ACT program dedicated to this population (Lurigio, 2000; Psychiatric Services, 2001). Thresholds' Jail Linkage and Aftercare Teams, in effect, form two parts of an Assertive Community Treatment team. The team is different from a traditional ACT team in that it has staff dedicated to criminal justice related matters, only takes referrals from Cook County Jail, relies on smaller staff to consumer ratios, and plans for time sensitive transition points in the move from the criminal justice system into the mental health system. More specifically, the staff to consumer ratio was increased from 1:10 to 1:6, intensive monitoring through increased service hours and payeeship was routine instead of being done on a case-by-case basis, all basic provisions–housing, food, clothes, renewed benefits–did not depend on agreeing to receive mental health services and were always in place before individuals were released from jail. Finally, support and advocacy were provided throughout all phases of the individual's involvement with the law–pretrial, post-adjudication, and post-release, and probation–which served to keep individuals engaged in Thresholds' services.

The four person linkage team provides the first set of services in the continuum of care so important for persons entering the mental health system. While the linkage team works most intensively with people while in jail, before linking them to Thresholds aftercare team, or if full, to another Thresholds' ACT team, they continue to see them after they are linked.[1] The linkage team is responsible for creating and maintaining the criminal justice relationships upon which the aftercare team relies so heavily. In the early stages of the project, the linkage staff advocated for the program as well as for particular individuals; they were the ones responsible for ensuring that the benefits of aftercare were understood. Now they are responsible for ensuring that the program remains a viable option within the criminal justice system.

The 10 person *multidisciplinary*, self-contained aftercare team, comprising the linkage case management staff, a weekend case manager, two case managers, a program supervisor, a consulting psychiatrist, a part-time nurse, and an administrative support person, provide all mental health services. Per the model, a set of team members are on call 24 hours a day, seven days a week, make frequent visits to clients' apartments to help them with everyday tasks, ranging from doing laundry to working on social skills to nurturing ties with clients' landlords, family, and other community contacts. Additionally, staff accompany consumers on all criminal justice related appointments and provide invaluable advocacy work in multiple contexts. Communication with the courts, police, and probation officers was crucial to coordinating services and to making sure there were no gaps in care. Most important, however, is that the team, unlike other forensic ACT teams, is non-punitive and coordinates care with and meets the requirements of the criminal justice system in this spirit.

Indeed developing and maintaining trusting relationships–both with individuals being served and with important persons in their lives–is crucial and occurs through routine ACT case management services, such as the provision of housing and through support in Having housing benefits and services *immediately* available helps to prevent the individual from returning to familiar patterns of arrests and hospitalizations or to an increase in symptoms due to lack of psychiatric care. Meeting these immediate needs serves as engagement strategies, which in turn, makes keeping housing in place through acute crises precipitated by medication nonadherence, disputes with landlords, or having no money, a routine problem. The engagement strategy most important, though, is ongoing outreach for individuals inconsistently engaged with services.

In sum, the ACT team has a proven service structure and can easily integrate evidence based treatment into this structure and philosophy of care, an ability that will allow forensic involved persons to receive best practices. ACT works from a basic-needs-first and assertive outreach philosophy. Paramount to ACT is ongoing outreach in the community to multiple stakeholders, making outreach to the criminal justice system business-as-usual. All services are provided by the team, thus making coordination of care relatively easy. This is a crucial feature given the difficulties many individuals have in navigating multiple health care services and the problems that arise with coordinating care among various agencies.

METHODS

Design

Using administrative data and a repeated measures design, ACT aftercare was evaluated comparing arrests, jail episodes, hospital admissions, and hospitalization episodes three years prior to being intaked to three years after intake.

Sample Description

Participants were recruited from Cook County Jail in Chicago. Study participants were eligible if they had been referred to Cook County Jail's mental health services, Cermak Health Services, had been diagnosed there with an Axis I disorder, and from records obtained from Chicago Police Department (CPD) and the Illinois Criminal Justice Authority (ICJIA), had appeared in court at least 20 times in their lifetime as documented in Cook County Clerk records, and had at least five hospitalizations in a lifetime. Preference was given to people convicted of nonviolent offenses and who are considered to be at low risk of violence in the community. Illness severity was not an exclusionary criterion for the project.

Participants were approached while in Cermak Hospital initially by a social worker responsible for discharge planning at Cermak, who mentioned the Thresholds' program. Upon receiving agreement, the discharge planner contacted a Thresholds' staff who, after checking court and hospitalization records, met with the prospective participant either pretrial or post-adjudication. Of the first group of individuals eligible to participate in the first year, 24 were linked to the jail aftercare team. While exact numbers of refusals were not recorded, only a handful are estimated to have refused indicating they preferred to stay in jail. Any individual who expressed a desire to stay out of jail agreed to participate in the program. The pilot project ran from 1997-2000 and was integrated into Thresholds' routine services in 1999 during which time routine service use and outcome data were collected.

Between 1999 and 2003, the team served a total of 96 individuals. 72% (n = 69) were male and 28% (n = 27) were female. Fifty-nine percent (n = 57) of the sample were African American, 37 % (n = 35) were EuroAmerican, 1% (n = 1) were American Indian, and 1% (n = 1) Asian. Most consumers (44%; n = 42) had a diagnosis of schizophrenia, while many had a diagnosis of a schizoaffective disorder (18%; n = 17) or a bi-polar disorder (17%; n = 14). The average age at intake was 42.19 (SD = 11.13). The majority of individuals had never been married (73%; n = 70), while 15% (n = 14) had been divorced. Only 1% of the sample was currently married and living with spouse, with 4% (n = 4) separated. The mean years of education was 12.10 (SD = 2.755).

Of these 96, 35 stayed less than a year. Two individuals were linked to other Thresholds teams and 33 were linked to other programs outside of Thresholds, typically because the level of services provided by the aftercare services were unnecessary. Eighteen percent (N = 17) were linked to outside agencies after one year of aftercare services. Thirty eight percent (n = 36) stayed with the team for 3 years requiring extra support. Demographic and baseline characteristics do not significantly differ among these two groups. The criterion for linkage was being on the team for at least a year; occasionally someone would be linked before a year because the team had reached capacity.

MEASURES

Forensic Outcomes and Functional Status

Arrests, jail episodes, and jail time prior to being served by the ACT team were retrieved from databases maintained by the Illinois Office of Mental Health, Chicago Police Department, and the Cook County Department of Corrections. For this project, routinely collected administrative data were recorded from electronic medical records between the years 1997 and 2002, put into an Excel database, and deidentified for use by the Primary Investigator. Data include jail and hospital episode outcomes. With the exception of the number of jail and hospital episodes and days collected prior to being served by the ACT team, all data was collected and entered by clinical staff.

DATA ANALYSIS: PRE ACT SERVICES–POST ACT AFTERCARE

Analyses consisted of descriptive statistics and analysis of covariance (ANCOVA) on the four post ACT aftercare outcome variables; hospital days, hospital admits, jail days, and arrests. It was hypothesized that participants would have fewer arrests and jail days one or more years after being on the team. Length on team was recalculated into a categorical variable of one year of services or less, one to two years, and two to three years of services. ANCOVAs were performed for each outcome variable comparing three years before receiving aftercare services and three years after receiving services.

RESULTS

Criminal Justice Involvement and Hospitalization Outcomes

A series of between-subjects ANCOVAs were performed on ACT aftercare service. Four separate models were run to assess significant relationships between exposure to ACT and jail and hospital use. The dependant variables included post ACT aftercare hospital days, hospital admits, jail days, and number of arrests. Covariates included three year pre ACT service data on hospital days, hospital admits, jail days, and arrests.

Analyses were performed by SPSS 15.0 for Windows, using the General Linear Model function at a 95% confidence level. We hypothesized first that exposure to services (length on team) would be a significant predictor of change in each variable. Findings showed that exposure was significantly associated with a change in hospital and jail use post-services, controlling for baseline hospital and jail use; hospital days F = 4.905 (p = .029), hospital admits F = 40.206 (p = .00), admits F = 64.576 (p = .00), and post-jail days F = 4.033 (p = .021) confirming our hypothesis.

After basic ANCOVAs were run to assess the four pre and post variables, models were run including all four variables as covariates to reveal more complex relationships. Although several interactions were found to be significant throughout the four models, perhaps the most interesting results lie in the models of the dependant variables post jail days and post arrests. A significant relationship was shown between length of services and post jail days. These findings also confirm our hypothesis that length of service and jail days are related, showing positive outcomes of the ACT service with respect to length of time spent in jail while receiving services. Persons receiving services for one year or less, on average, can expect 76.275 more post services jail days, B = 76.275 (21.736, 130.813), p = .007. Although length of stay was found to have a significant relationship with post jail days, no relationship was observed with post arrests. Only a slight difference in mean arrests was observed; one year of services or less, 2.55 (SD = 3.247), one to two years, 3.10 (SD = 3.635), and two to three years of service, 3.81 (SD = 8.4246).

DISCUSSION

In conclusion, ACT with a forensic liaison staff, in this case a linkage team, provides a good base for providing services because of their ability to target the multiple needs of forensic-involved individuals with a serious mental illness. Aftercare was found to be particularly effective at reducing hospitalizations and days incarcerated but not as effective in reducing arrests, a finding also found in studies of intensive, office based case management services (Draine & Solomon, 1994). The reasons that community based services also showed little difference in arrest rates may be because the team had yet to systematically implement IDDT, an anecdotal explanation from several staff for many arrests. This suggests that ACT care may cut short incarceration time rather than avoiding it altogether. That is, assertive outreach and systems integration works most well post-arrest. This finding also suggests that supported employment services for individuals with longer tenure on the team is warranted, as working has shown to reduce hospitalizations and arrests (Sneed et al., 2006).

ACT is currently the best set of services to intervene in a seemingly unstoppable cycle by providing housing, benefits, and psychiatric medication and then working in creative ways to help people maintain them. As has been reported of this particular sample previously, many suffered from a set of what–given current public policy and social service funding–can only be called intractable problems, problems which include poverty, victimization, homelessness, and social isolation (McCoy, 2004). ACT works by engaging individuals into treatment, which despite being complicated by court ordered treatment and mandatory reporting can be done by framing services as supportive and truly providing non-punitive, ongoing support.

There are a number of limitations to this study. The study does not report follow-up data for those individuals who were referred outside of Thresholds, nor does it report referral source for those individuals. As a result, a more fine grained analysis of what "dosage" of ACT is necessary and for whom could not be conducted. Additionally, like so many other studies of ACT care for this population, quality of life and functioning outcomes are not fully reported. Nonetheless, the study adds to the literature by providing preliminary 3-year data on ACT care for persons with a severe mental illness and repeated forensic involvement.

NOTE

1. The outcomes reported here are for those individuals referred to the Jail ACT aftercare team.

REFERENCES

Abram, K., & Teplin, L. (1991). Co-occurring disorders among the mentally ill jail detainees. *American Psychologist*, 46, 1036-1045.

Barker, S., Barron, N., McFarland, B. H., & Bigelow, D. A. (1994). A Community ability scale for chronically mentally ill consumers: Part I. Reliability and validity. *Community Mental Health Journal*, 30,

Bond, G. R., Drake, R. E., & Mueser K. T. (2000). Assertive community treatment for people with severe mental illness: Critical ingredients and impact on patients. *Disease Management and Health Outcomes*, 9, 141-159.

Broner, N., Lattimore, P. K., Cowell, A. J., & Schelnger, W. E. (2004). Effects of diversion on adults with co-occurring mental illness and substance: Outcomes form a national multi-site study. *Behavioral Sciences and the Law*, 22, 519-541.

Chandler, D. W., & Spicer, G. (2006). Integrated treatment for jail recidivists with co-occurring psychiatric and substance use disorders, *Community Mental Health Journal*, *42*(4), 405-420.

Cimino, T., & Jennings, J. L. (2002). Arkansas partnership program: an innovative continuum of care program for dually diagnosed forensic patients. *Psychiatric Rehabilitation Skills*, 6, 104-114.

Council of State Governments. Criminal Justice/Mental Health Consensus Project. New York: Council of State Governments. June 2002.

Draine, J., & Solomon, P. (1994). Jail recidivism and the intensity of case management services among the homeless persons with mental illness leaving jail. *Journal of Psychiatry and Law*, 22, 245-261.

Drake, R. E., Goldman, H. H., Leff, S. H., Lehman, A. F., Dixon, L., Mueser, K. T., and Torrey, W. (2001). Implementing evidence based practices in routine mental health settings. *Psychiatric Services*, 52, 179-182.

Elliott, R. L. (1997). Evaluating the quality of correctional mental health services: An approach to surveying a correctional mental health system *Behavioral Sciences and the Law*, 15, 427-438.

Goin, M. (2003). Fiscal Fallout: Patients in the Criminal Justice System, Psychiatric News, 36, 8. Retrieved on February 1 , from http://pn.psychiatryonline.org/cgi/content/full/38/13/3?maxtoshow=&HITS=10&hits=10&RESULTFORMAT=& andorexacttitle=and&titleabstract=criminal+justice&andorexacttitleabs=and&fulltext=criminal+justice&andorexactfulltext=and&searchid=1&FIRSTINDEX=0&sort-spec=relevance&resourcetype=HWCIT

Gold Award: Helping Mentally Ill People Break the Cycle of Jail and Homelessness. (2001). *Psychiatric Services*, 52, 1350-1352.

James, D. J., & Glaze, L. E. (2006). Mental health problems of prison and jail inmates. *Bureau of Justice Report*, Retrieved on February 1 from at http://www.ojp.usdoj.gov/bjs/pub/pdf/mhppji.pdf.

Lamberti, J. S., & Weisman, R. L. (2001). The mentally ill in jails and prisons: toward an integrated model of prevention. *Psychiatric Quarterly*, 72, 63-77.

Lamberti, S. J., Weismann, R., & Faden, D. (2004). Forensic assertive community treatment: Preventing incarceration of adults with severe mental illness. *Psychiatric Services*, 55, 1258-1293.

Lovell, D., Gagliardi, G., & Petersen, P. (2002). Recidivism and use of services among persons with mental illness after release from prison. *Psychiatric Services*, 53, 1290-1296.

Lurigio, A., Fallon, J., & Dincin, J. (2000). Helping the mentally ill in jails adjust to community life: a description of post release ACT program and its clients. *International Journal of Offender Therapy and Comparative Criminology*, 44, 450-466.

McCoy, M., Roberts, D. L., Hanharan, P, Clay R., & Luchins, D. L. (2004). Jail Linkage assertive community treatment services for individuals with mental illnesses. *Psychiatric Rehabilitation Journal*,

Mental Health: A Report of the Surgeon General. (1999). Washington, DC, Department of Health and Human Services.

Morrissey, J. P., & Meyers, P. (2006). Extending Assertive Community Treatment to Criminal Justice Settings. *The National Gains Center for Systematic Change for Justice Involved People*. Retrieved February 1, 2007, from http://www.gainscenter.samhsa.gov/text/ebp/AssertiveCommunityTreatment_5_2006.asp

Navasky, M., & O'Connor, K. (Producers). (2005, May 10). The new asylums. *Frontline Special Report*. Washington, DC: Public Broadcasting Service.

Parker, G. F. (2004). Outcomes of assertive community treatment in an NGRI conditional release program. *Journal of American Academy of Psychiatry Law*, 32:3, 291-303.

Shafer, M. S, Arthur, B., & Franczak, S. (2004). An analysis of post-booking diversion programming for persons with a severe mental illness. *Behavioral Science and the Law*, 22(6), 771-784.

Sneed, Z., Koch, D. S., Estes, H., & Quinn, J. (2006). Employment and psychosocial outcomes for offenders with mental illness. *International Journal of Psychosocial Rehabilitation*, 10(2), 103-112.

Steadman, H. J., Deane, M. W., Morriseey, J. P. (1999). A SAMHSA research initiative assessing the effectiveness of jail diversion programs for mentally ill persons. *Psychiatric Services*, 50, 1620-1623.

Steadman, H. J., Morris, S. M., & Dennis, D. L. (1995). The diversion of mentally ill persons from jails to community-based services: A profile of programs. *American Journal of Public Health*, 85, 1630-1635.

Steadman, H. J., Mulvey, E. P., Monahan, J., Robbins, P. C., Applebaum, P. S., Grisso, T., Roth, L. H., & Silver, E. (1998). Violence by people discharged from acute psychiatric inpatient facilities and by others in the same neighborhoods. *Archives of General Psychiatry*, 55, 393-401.

Steadman, H. J., & Naples, M. (2005). Assessing the effectiveness of Jail diversion programs for persons with serious mental illness and co-occurring substance use Disorders. *Behavioral Sciences and the Law*, 23, 163-170.

Swartz, M. S., Swanson, J. W., Hiday, V. A., Borum, R., Wagner, H. R., & Burns, B. (1998). Violence and Severe Mental Illness: The Effects of Substance Abuse and Nonadherence to Medication. *American Journal of Psychiatry*, 155, 226-231.

Teplin, L. A. (1990). The prevalence of sever mental disorder among male urban jail detainees: comparison with epidemiological catchments area program. *American Journal of Public Health*, 80, 663-669.

Test, M. A., & Stein, L. I. (1976). Practical guidelines for the community treatment of markedly impaired patients. *Community Mental Health Journal*, 12, 72-82.

Veysey, B. M., Steadman, H. J., Morrissey, J. P., & Johnsen, M. (1997). In search of the missing linkages: Continuity of care in U.S. Jails. *Behavioral Sciences and the Law*, 15, 383-397.

Watson, A., Hanrahan, P., Luchins, D., & Lurigio, A. (2001). Paths to jail among mentally ill persons: Service needs and service characteristics. *Psychiatric Annals*, 31, 421-429, 2001.

Prison Therapeutic Community Treatment for Female Offenders: Profiles and Preliminary Findings for Mental Health and Other Variables (Crime, Substance Use and HIV Risk)

JOANN Y SACKS
STANLEY SACKS
KAREN MCKENDRICK
STEVEN BANKS
MARLIES SCHOENEBERGER
ZACHARY HAMILTON
JOSEPH STOMMEL
JOANIE SHOEMAKER

BACKGROUND

The Problem

In the past two decades, the size of America's prison population, particularly its female constituents, has increased rapidly (Henderson, 1998; Greenfeld & Snell, 1999; Harrison & Beck, 2005). By 2004, 53% more women were incarcerated than had been in 1995; the male inmate population grew 32% over the same period (Harrison & Beck, 2005). From 1990 to 1996, the number of felony convictions of women increased at a rate 2.5 times that of male defendants (Greenfeld & Snell, 1999). Moreover, the proportion of female drug offenders has also risen (Greenfeld & Snell, 1999), with drug offenses accounting for 55% of the increase in female inmates between 1986 and 1991 (Harrison & Beck, 2005). The combination of the use of illegal drugs by more women with the enforcement of more punitive anti-drug laws has been cited as the reason drug offenses have increased (Peugh & Belenko, 1999).

Offenders, in general, have higher rates of mental disorders than are found in the general population (Fazel & Danesh, 2002; O'Brien, Mortimer, Singleton, & Meltzer, 2003), while female inmates, in particular, show elevated rates of mental disorders (including mood disorders, borderline personality, and antisocial personality), compared with women in community-based substance abuse treatment studies (Sacks, 2004; Jordan, Schlenger, Fairbank, & Caddell, 1996; Teplin, Abram & McClelland, 1996). Almost a quarter of the women in state prisons have been identified as mentally ill; in 1997, 23% were receiving medication for emotional disorders (Greenfeld & Snell, 1999). Moreover, research indicates that co-occurring mental disorders are more likely to be found among incarcerated substance-abusing women (Henderson, 1998); the converse is also true, as female offenders with mental disorder[s] have shown a high incidence of co-occurring substance abuse (Diamond et al., 2001; Ditton, 1999).

Of particular concern are findings that show the mental health issues of drug-using women in prisons to be distinct and more pervasive than those of men (Wilcox & Yates, 1993; Windle, Windle, Scheidt & Miller, 1995). Female offenders are more likely to report depression, anxiety, low self-esteem and the use of prescribed medications for psychological problems (Peters, Strozier, Murrin, & Kearns, 1997). Furthermore, impaired psychological functioning has been associated with relapse to substance abuse (Grella, Scott, Foss, Joshi, & Hser, 2003). This underscores the importance of incorporating symptom management along with relapse prevention interventions for female offenders with co-occurring disorders (at least one substance use disorder occurring with at least one mental disorder, independent of one another), and of providing access to mental health services within prison.

Trauma and Abuse History

Studies identify abuse and victimization to be major factors in the life histories of women who have engaged in criminal behavior; fifty to sixty percent of women in the criminal justice system report that they have experienced childhood and/or adult physical and sexual abuse (Greenfeld & Snell, 1999; Bureau of Justice Statistics, 2001; McNamara & Fields, 2002; Warren et al., 2002; Browne, Miller, & Maguin, 1999). Recent research has demonstrated that severe post-traumatic symptoms can complicate response to treatment and the recovery process (Brown, Recupero, & Stout, 1995; Brown, Read, & Kahler, 2003; Sacks, McKendrick, & Banks, 2008a). Research on trauma-informed treatment has revealed improvements in mental health and substance abuse outcomes for women with co-occurring disorders (Clark & Power, 2005; Morrissey et al., 2005) and supports the idea that treatment programs for female offenders need to concentrate on the influence and effects of trauma and to incorporate trauma-sensitive elements into treatment models.

Substance Use

Crime

Half of the female offenders in state prisons were found to have been using drugs, alcohol, or both at the time the incarcerating offense was committed, and female offenders had higher drug related crime rates than did males (Harrison & Beck, 2005). In Colorado, 87% of the women incarcerated in 2004 for new crimes were substance abusers (Colorado Department of Corrections [CDOC] 2005), which highlights the connection between substance abuse and criminal activity for women and underscores the importance of substance abuse treatment to reducing criminal activity among female offenders.

HIV-Risk

Substance abuse, lifetime victimization, and psychiatric disorganization have all been associated with HIV-risk behaviors among female offenders (Fogel & Belyea, 1999; Hutton et al., 2001; Mullings, Marquart & Hartley, 2003). Within the state prison female population, 34% report having injected drugs, a practice that, when combined with risky sexual behaviors, gives rise to a gender-based disparity in HIV infection. In 1997, incarcerated women had nearly double the rate of HIV infection compared to male inmates (4% and 2%, respectively) (Greenfeld & Snell, 1999). Clearly, effective programming must contend with both injection drug use and sexual HIV-risk behaviors for the female offender.

Rationale for the Current Study

The community-based residential TC has an established record of success in reducing drug use and criminality, while increasing employment (e.g., De Leon, 1984; Hubbard, Rachal, Craddock, & Cavanaugh, 1984; Simpson & Sells, 1982). The prison TC, a comprehensive substance abuse treatment program adapted to the requirements of correctional settings, has demonstrated significantly greater reductions in recidivism to drugs and to crime as compared to control groups (e.g., Hser, Anglin, & Powers, 1993; Wexler, Falkin, & Lipton, 1990). The residential Modified Therapeutic Community (MTC) model, developed for offenders with co-occurring severe mental illness and substance use disorders (Sacks, Sacks, & Stommel, 2003), demonstrated significant reductions in reincarceration (Sacks, Sacks, McKendrick, Banks, & Stommel, 2004a) and substance use (Sullivan, McKendrick, Sacks, & Banks, 2007) 12-months post-prison release for randomly assigned male offenders compared to their control group counterparts who received an alternate treatment program.

These studies provided the rationale for creating and evaluating a prison TC for female offenders, modified to meet their gender-specific needs. This paper describes the TC program, as modified for female offenders, provides a descriptive profile of the study sample and presents preliminary six-month post-prison mental health and related outcomes for the study conditions.

METHOD

Research Design

Female inmates who consented to participate in the research study were randomly assigned to one of two treatment groups, E (experimental) program, a Therapeutic Community (TC) or C (control) program, Colorado Department of Corrections (CDOC) standard treatment, known in the CDOC system as the *Intensive Outpatient Program* (IOP). The study employed a prospective, longitudinal, repeated measures design that assessed subjects at five points: baseline (entry into the prison program and study conditions); prison discharge; 6 months post-prison release; 12 months post-prison release; and 18 months post-prison release. The analytic plan involved an intent-to-treat analysis of the entire sample. This article reports on change from baseline to 6 months post-prison discharge. The study predicts that those receiving TC treatment will show significantly greater improvement than the C group on a variety of outcome domains; specifically, mental health (psychological symptoms and trauma), substance use, criminal behavior, and HIV-risk behaviors.

Eligibility and Consent

Eligibility criteria required that study subjects have: (1) at least 6 months (and no more than 24 months) remaining until parole eligibility; (2) a CDOC *Standardized Offender Assessment* (CDOC, 2004) score of 4 or greater indicative of serious substance abuse problems requiring substance abuse treatment; and (3) a security risk level classification of minimum, minimum-restricted, or medium, to permit participation in treatment. Within one month of her admission to the Denver Women's Correctional Facility (DWCF), each eligible inmate was met by a trained and experienced interviewer who explained the study and who obtained informed consent from all who volunteered to participate in the study. On average, 42 days (a range of 0-1015 days) elapsed from being admitted to prison until an eligible inmate was identified, informed of the study, and had provided their consent to participate in the research. The NDRI Institutional Review Board reviewed and monitored compliance with all regulations governing the protection of human rights for research participants, while a Data and Safety Monitoring Board monitored all adverse events and data collection activities; all research staff received training in the protection of human research subjects. Subjects received financial compensation for completing interviews at each time period.

Sample

The sample for this preliminary report consists of 314 (TC [E] = 163; IOP [C] = 151) women on whom 6-month post-prison discharge data is available at time of writing. Retrieval rates are: total 78% (314/405; TC [E] = 75%, IOP [C] = 80%). At present, 573 subjects have enrolled in the study and will constitute the full sample for future reports.

Data Collection

Data were collected using standardized self-report instruments, administered by a research associate to all study clients in face-to-face interviews; additional data were obtained from CDOC computerized information system sources. The self-report instruments have all proven to be appropriate and effective in a variety of ethnic, gender, and cultural contexts (e.g., Sacks, McKendrick, Sacks, Banks, & Harle, 2008b; Sacks, Sacks, & De Leon, 1999; Sacks et al., 2008a; 2004a; 2004b).

Measures

Profiles

The *Center for Therapeutic Community Research* (CTCR) *Baseline Protocol* (CTCR, 1992) is an omnibus structured interview adapted from the *TCU Drug Abuse Treatment Assessment Research* (DATAR) intake form (used in community treatment and in the criminal justice system), the *Addiction Severity Index* (ASI) (McLellan et al., 1992), and the TCU *AIDS Risk Assessment* (Simpson, 1997). The CTCR *Protocol* assesses socio-demographic background (age, sex, ethnicity, health, education, employment, parenting, peer and family support, and housing), self-reported lifetime and current substance use, criminal behaviors, and HIV-risk behaviors. Same day, alternate forms reliability for alcohol and nine drug categories, measured in terms of percent exact agreement, averaged 94% (range 82% to 100%) in a similar sample of women (Sacks et al., 1999).

Psychiatric Diagnosis

The *Diagnostic Interview Schedule* (DIS-IV) (Robins, Cottler, Bucholz & Compton, 1995) is a structured clinical interview to generate DSM-IV lifetime and current psychiatric and substance use/dependence diagnoses that requires interviewer training, but not clinical expertise. Individual modules were selected and administered only at baseline to a sub-sample of 113 subjects to estimate the prevalence of co-occurring disorders in the study sample. Reliabilities for substance dependence for the DIS are good (kappa 0.60-0.81); reliabilities for psychiatric disorders range from fair to good (kappa 0.44-0.74) (Horton et al., 1999).

Psychological Symptoms and Functioning

Information on psychological symptoms and functioning was gathered from five sources, as described below.

The Beck Depression Inventory-II (BDI-II) (Beck, Steer, & Brown, 1996) contains 21 items that measure three domains of depression consistent with the DSM-IV criteria for depressive disorders; high scores indicate more severe symptoms. Satisfactory coefficient alpha indices have been established for the instrument (Osman et al., 1997).

The *Brief Symptom Inventory* (BSI) (Derogatis, 1993) is a shortened, revised version of the *Symptom Checklist Revised-90* (SCL-90-R) (Derogatis, 1977); it contains 53 self-report items that measure 9 domains of mental health symptoms and provides a global index of distress, the *Global Severity Index* (GSI), a weighted frequency score calculated from the sum of the ratings assigned to each item; high scores correspond to greater severity of symptoms. Internal consistency estimates range from 0.71 to 0.84 averaged across all 9 scales. Test/re-test reliabilities range from 0.67 to 0.91 (Rounsaville et al., 1979).

The *Posttraumatic Symptom Severity Scale (PSS)* of the Post-traumatic Stress Diagnostic Scale (PDS) (Foa, Cashman, Jaycox, & Perry, 1997), assesses the severity of post-traumatic stress disorder (PTSD) symptoms in a classification schema corresponding to DSM-IV PTSD symptoms (Re-experiencing, Avoidance, Arousal). A PTSD symptom severity score is derived from summing the past-month frequency scores of 17 symptom items; scores; total score can range from 0 to 51 with higher scores on the PSS indicating greater severity of post-traumatic stress symptoms (mild = 1-10; moderate = 11-20; moderate to severe = 21-35; severe = 36-51). The PSS has demonstrated high internal consistency and stability over time ($\alpha = 0.92$ for *Total Symptom Severity*, 0.78 for *Re-experiencing*, 0.84 for *Avoidance*, and 0.84 for *Arousal*; test/re-test reliability coefficients were 0.83 for *Total Symptom Severity*, 0.77 for *Re-experiencing*, 0.81 for *Avoidance*, and 0.85 for *Arousal*) (Foa, Cashman, Jaycox et al., 1997).

The *Trauma History Questionnaire* (THQ) (Green, 1996), measures lifetime, recent and childhood (under age 14) exposure to community, physical, and sexual trauma and abuse. Test/re-test reliability of the 65 THQ items (over 2-3 months) ranged from 0.47 to 1.00 (average 0.65) (Green, 2000).

The CTCR *Baseline Protocol* (cited above) was also used to gather self-report information regarding perceived symptom impacts on functioning, prevalence of suicidal thoughts and actions, incidence of psychiatric hospitalizations, prescribed medication for psychological problems, and incidence of mental health treatment.

Substance use/abuse and related problems were assessed using selected items from the CTCR *Baseline Protocol* to gather self-reported information about the historic and current frequency of use of alcohol, nine categories of illegal drugs, the misuse of prescribed medication, perceived problems related to substance use, historic and current substance abuse treatment.

Criminal behavior was assessed using selected items from the CTCR *Baseline Protocol* to gather self-report information about historic and current (past 6 months) criminal justice involvement and the frequency of illegal activities during the past six months. *Colorado Department of Corrections Record Information System* (CDOC-RIS) provides corroborating information regarding arrests, convictions, and incarceration.

HIV/AIDS-risk was assessed using selected items from the CTCR *Baseline Protocol* to gather information about the frequency of needle use behaviors and high-risk sexual practices, including exchanging sex for money or drugs.

Analytic Plan

Profiles

The descriptive analysis was organized to address three main questions: "Who was identified to receive treatment?" (i.e., demographic and other background characteristics); "What were their diagnoses, psychological symptoms, and trauma-related behaviors" (i.e., mental health diagnoses, psychological symptom severity, including post-traumatic symptoms, and trauma exposure); and "What are the salient features of their social dysfunction?" (substance use, criminal behavior, and HIV-risk behavior). The organization of Tables 1-3 addresses these three questions. Analytic strategies consisted primarily of univariate analysis of discrete variables shown as descriptive summary statistics of means, medians and percentages. Bivariate tests were used to compare women assigned to the two treatment groups. Grouped t-tests were conducted on continuous measures (e.g., age) and chi-square tests were used to assess dichotomous and categorical date (e.g., ethnicity, employment).

Six-Month Post-Prison Outcomes

The study employed an intent-to-treat analysis and multiple regression techniques to analyze treatment effectiveness. *Logistic regression* was used to test for differential group change for all dichotomous outcome measures (e.g., any drug use) and OLS regression was used for continuous measures (e.g., frequency of drug use). The regression models consisted of the 6-month post-prison outcome (dependent variable), a variable for treatment condition (independent variables), and four covariates (the outcome variable at baseline, age at first illegal activity, ethnicity, and high school diploma/GED). The control variables included in this model were based on those identified as standard controls for research in the criminal justice field (Sacks et al., 2004a).

PROGRAM DESCRIPTION

The Denver Women's Correctional Facility (DWCF) opened in 1998 to serve the needs of 900 female offenders. Substance abuse treatment is provided in all CDOC facilities according to the level of need, which is determined at an interview conducted on intake that uses the CDOC *Standardized Offender Assessment* score, measures of arrest history (drug-related crimes) and the social/emotional impact of drug use. Treatment for serious substance use problems is delivered in two formats, a TC program (the E condition; *Challenge to Change*), and an alternative (non-TC) program with a cognitive-behavioral recovery and relapse prevention curriculum (the C condition; *Intensive Outpatient Program*, or IOP); the latter is the standard treatment that CDOC offers to all female offenders who have been classified as substance abusers.

Challenge to Change TC (Experimental Condition)

The *Challenge to Change* TC program at DWCF was developed in 1999 by a private not-for-profit agency, Addiction Research and Treatment Services (ARTS), under contract to the CDOC to address substance abuse and related problems of female offenders. Women are referred to the program according to their determination of need for substance abuse treatment, as noted above; participation is voluntary. For the purposes of this research project, eligible referrals were randomly assigned to the TC (E) and the non-TC (C) treatments.

Main TC Features

TC philosophy and principles provide the structure within which the *Challenge to Change* program elements are delivered (De Leon, 2000; Sacks et al., 1997). The *Challenge to Change* TC contains all of the standard TC elements (morning meeting, house meeting, seminars, encounter groups, and peer hierarchy), integrated with gender-specific groups and activities. Inmates progress through four program stages (orientation, phases 1, 2, and 3); upper level inmates function as a positive peer leadership group, or "structure," to guide and support newer members as they begin to develop and apply new values, beliefs and skills to their daily lives.

Key Modifications for Women

The *Challenge to Change* TC ensures that mutual respect, rather than authoritarianism, is emphasized in all interactions to avoid repeating past abusive relationships. The TC philosophy promotes trust and affiliation with a positive peer community; the TC hierarchy provides opportunity for leadership, for exercising authority in a positive manner, and for becoming a positive role model. Treatment elements address the issues of trauma and abuse, relationships, education, employment and parenting that are integrated with the woman's substance abuse issues.

Interventions

Challenge to Change is a comprehensive treatment program. Program elements address issues of substance abuse (Relapse Prevention group; Individual and Group Counseling), mental health (Feelings/Anger

Management group; Journaling group), criminal behaviors (Thinking Errors seminars), trauma and abuse (Seeking Safety group), parenting (Parenting Skills seminars), relationships (Relationships group), and employment (Peer Work Hierarchy). Gender-specific interventions focus on increasing awareness and understanding female roles and relationships as they relate to addiction and drugs used and abused, and emotional and behavioral coping skills. In addition, the women participate in three facility-wide services: mental health (psychiatric assessment, medication, individual counseling), education (GED and Adult Basic Education classes), and health care (medical and dental treatment).

Operation

The 72-bed TC program with sleeping and meeting space is located on a single floor of residential building. Program clinical staff (director, associate director, program coordinator, and 4 counselors) deliver formal program activities (individual and group interventions), which take place 5 days each week for 4 hours each day; mental health counseling is provided by clinically trained counselors in the facility's mental health department. The peer community of inmates maintains the TC culture by continuing peer-led groups and activities on weekends, and inmates spend an additional 4 hours/day working within the prison complex. TC inmates are separated from the general prison population for most program activities to support their attitudinal and behavioral change, and to reduce the impact of negative influences during this vulnerable stage of their recovery. On average, study subjects remained in the program 6.5 months.

The Intensive Outpatient Program (IOP)–Control (C) Condition

The C group (IOP, the alternative non-TC program for women with serious substance abuse problems) is designed to address substance abuse and criminality, with a focus on prevention of relapse and recidivism. The IOP substance abuse treatment curriculum consists of a 90-hour course, presented in an educational format (*Strategies for Self-Improvement and Change*, Wanburg & Milkman, 1998), utilizing a cognitive behavioral format to address underlying issues of substance use/abuse and criminal behavior. The course is completed within 15 weeks.

The women in IOP can participate in multiple other services facility-wide. These include: mental health assessment, psychiatric evaluation, medication and counseling, Adult Basic Education, GED (mandatory for all women who do not have a high school diploma or GED certificate), Parenting, Trauma and Abuse (a 15-week curriculum based on "Healing the Trauma of Abuse," PTSD workbook and other educational materials), Computer Skills, community reintegration (Apartment Program), and several vocational training classes (Carpentry, Cosmetology, Culinary Arts, Graphics Design, Animal Training). Each additional course is conducted over 8-12 weeks, meeting once or twice each week for 2 hours a day. Inmates in the IOP attend classroom activities 2 days per week for 2 hours each day, and work in correctional industries daily, except when attending classes. Overall, women in the IOP (C group) receive their services in approximately 6-9 months.

Challenge to Change and the C Condition (IOP)–Similarities and Differences

Both the E (*Challenge to Change* TC) and the C (IOP non-TC treatment) conditions deliver extensive substance abuse and related treatment services for a similar amount of time, but use distinctively different approaches. The E group TC provides comprehensive services (e.g., relapse prevention, trauma recovery, criminal behaviors, relationships, parenting, etc.) within the program and integrates all treatment elements within one philosophical approach that supports and strengthens positive relationships, and that empowers women to assume responsibility, engage in mutual peer support, and address the inter-relationship between problem areas of her life (e.g., the relationship between trauma exposure, emotional distress, coping skills and substance use). The C group IOP delivers its elements as separate, discrete, educational courses; each course is geared to increasing knowledge and understanding rather than actively practicing new social behaviors.

RESULTS

Profiles

Demographic and Background Characteristics

Table 1 presents demographic and background data for the retrieved sample of individuals. The women in this sample of offenders were approximately 36 years old. Almost half were Caucasian (48%), 23%

TABLE 1: Demographics and Background Variables by Treatment Group

Demographics and Background Variables	E–TC (n = 163) %/Mean (std)	C–IOP (n = 151) %/Mean (std)	Total (n = 314) %/Mean (std)	E vs. C p
Age	35.8 (7.3)	35.4 (7.6)	35.6 (7.5)	0.641
Ethnicity				0.441
Black	15.3	19.2	17.2	
Caucasian	47.9	47.7	47.8	
Hispanic/Latina	25.8	19.2	22.6	
Other/Mixed	11.0	13.9	12.4	
High school/GED	67.3	57.6	62.6	0.077
L6 employment	60.7	53.8	57.3	0.204
Never married	34.4	30.5	32.5	0.762
Children	85.9	83.3	84.7	0.531
Number of biological children	2.5 (1.8)	2.2 (1.6)	2.3 (1.7)	0.176
Ever had child removed	38.7	41.5	40.0	0.648
Family History				
Parent had/has substance problem	66.2	71.0	68.6	0.372
Parent had/has mental health problem	28.0	34.2	30.9	0.233
Family on public assistance	32.7	25.7	29.3	0.184
Ran away	62.7	64.2	63.4	0.791

were Latina/Hispanic, 17% were African-American and 12% described themselves as "multi-racial." Nearly two-thirds (63%) had attained a high school degree or GED and 57% claimed to be employed in the six months prior to their incarceration. Two-thirds of the sample (67%) had been married, and 85% had children (2 biological children each, on average); 40% had at least one child removed from their care. A review of risk factors indicated that over two-thirds (69%) of these offenders had/have a parent with a substance abuse problem and nearly a third (31%) had/have a parent with a mental health problem. More than a quarter (29%) reported that their families had received public assistance.

Nearly two-thirds of the sample (63%) had run away from home at least once.

Diagnostic and Psychological Profiles

Table 2 presents the diagnostic and psychological profiles of the study participants; a high prevalence of mental health disorders was evident. Based on the subgroup of subjects who completed selected modules of the DIS-IV (n = 113; TC = 68, *C* = 45), 69% of the sample would have obtained a lifetime diagnosis of severe mental disorder (mania or hypomania, bipolar disorder or major depression), and 75% would have obtained a lifetime diagnosis of any Axis I mental disorder. (The majority of individuals were diagnosed with major depression [65%], with other significant diagnoses of PTSD [43%], manic/hypomanic [29%], bipolar I/II [27%], generalized anxiety [30%] and ADHD [10%].) On average, the research cohort had two Axis I mental disorder diagnoses according to the DIS-IV.

The average *Beck Depression Total* score was 18, which indicates mild to moderate symptoms of depression. The mean PSS post-traumatic symptom severity score was 16, which places the average post-traumatic severity in the mild-moderate range; one-third (34%) of the women were in the moderate to severe range. The mean *Global Severity Index* score was 59, which is just below clinical status. Over half (58%) of the women reported previous mental health treatment, 64% had been prescribed psychotropic medication during their lifetime, and a quarter (26%) reported inpatient psychiatric treatment; 10% reported a suicide attempt in the six months prior to incarceration.

Trauma Exposure

Table 2 shows that the virtually all (98%) subjects reported exposure to some form of trauma during their lifetime. More specifically, 97% reported physical violence, 75% sexual violence, and 97% community violence (a lifetime incidence). In addition, 75% of the women indicated that a trauma experience occurred prior to age fourteen; 61% reported childhood physical violence and 39% reported childhood sexual violence. Nearly two-thirds (65%) of the sample reported that a traumatic event had occurred within the six months prior to incarceration. These figures are slightly higher than those reported on national samples of female inmates in state prisons (Greenfeld & Snell, 1999; Bureau of Justice Statistics, 2001).

TABLE 2: Diagnostic and Psychological Profiles by Treatment Group

	E–TC (*n* = 163) %/Mean (std)	C–IOP (*n* = 151) %/Mean (std)	Total (*n* = 314) %/Mean (std)	E vs. C *P*
Mental Health				
LT DIS any Axis I mental disorder[1]	70.6	82.2	75.2	0.161
LT DIS severe Axis I mental disorder	66.2	73.3	69.0	0.421
LT DIS Major depression	61.2	71.1	65.2	0.280
LT DIS Bipolar I/II	27.9	26.7	27.4	0.882
LT DIS Manic/Hypomanic	30.9	26.7	29.2	0.629
LT DIS Generalized anxiety	24.2	37.8	29.7	0.126
LT DIS PTSD	36.8	52.3	42.9	0.105
LT DIS ADHD	11.8	6.7	9.7	0.371
LT DIS number of diagnoses[2]	1.9 (1.8)	2.2 (1.6)	2.0 (1.7)	0.391
Psychological Symptoms				
BDI-II total score	17.4 (10.7)	17.7 (11.2)	17.6 (10.9)	0.786
BSI global severity index	58.7 (10.8)	58.6 (12.2)	58.7 (11.4)	0.965
PSS trauma severity score	16.2 (13.0)	16.3 (14.1)	16.2 (13.5)	0.935
PSS trauma severity (categories)				0.720
Mild (0-10)	42.0	42.4	42.2	
Mild-Moderate (11-20)	24.7	25.8	25.2	
Moderate-Severe (21-35)	15.4	11.3	13.4	
Severe (35+)	17.9	20.5	19.2	
LT psych treatment	56.4	58.9	57.6	0.654
LT inpatient psychiatric treatment	22.7	30.5	26.4	0.119
LT prescribed psychiatric medication	61.0	68.5	64.1	0.380
Currently taking psychiatric medication	36.4	37.6	37.0	0.838
L6 attempted suicide	7.4	12.6	9.9	0.121
Trauma				
LT exposure to trauma	98.8	97.4	98.1	0.358
LT exposure to community violence	98.2	94.7	96.5	0.094
LT exposure to physical violence	96.9	96.0	96.5	0.662
LT exposure to sexual violence	76.9	72.0	74.5	0.325

(continued)

TABLE 2 (continued)

	E–TC (*n* = 163) %/Mean (std)	C–IOP (*n* = 151) %/Mean (std)	Total (*n* = 314) %/Mean (std)	E vs. C *P*
Exposure to *any* trauma before age 14	76.7	73.5	75.2	0.515
Physical violence before age 14	61.3	60.9	61.1	0.939
Sexual violence before age 14	40.7	37.1	39.0	0.508
L6 exposure to trauma	68.1	61.6	65.0	0.227

LT=Lifetime, L6=Last 5 months.
[1] DIS diagnostic data available for 113 subjects.
[2] This count excludes diagnoses of ASP since the study did not include the module for conduct disorder.

Social Dysfunction

Substance Use

Table 3 shows that nearly all of the women in the study had used alcohol (98%) and drugs (99%). The average age of first alcohol use was 14 years, and of first drug use was 15 years. The women's primary drugs of choice were cocaine/crack (30%), alcohol (23%), methamphetamine (19%), and marijuana (18%); a smaller number reported use of opiates (7%). Nearly three quarters of the sample (74%) reported previous treatment for substance abuse.

Criminal Behavior

As seen in Table 3, the female offenders in this sample reported that they had committed their first illegal act by age 13, and 18% had been declared delinquent. Despite early engagement in illegal activity, and an average of 12 arrests (lifetime), only a third (34%) of the women claimed to have been incarcerated prior to the current sentence. Their first incarceration did not occur until age 32, nor were they imprisoned for long periods of time; i.e., study subjects had been incarcerated an average of 13 months. All offenders in the study reported drug-related criminal behavior (100%); approximately a third committed sex crimes (29%), while a similar proportion (34%) committed violent crimes.

☐ TABLE 3: Profile of Social Dysfunction Variables by Treatment Group

	E–TC (n = 163) %/Mean (std)	C–IOP (n = 151) %/Mean (std)	Total (n = 314) %/Mean (std)	E vs. C P
Substance Use				
LT alcohol use	98	97	98	0.628
Age 1st alcohol	13.8 (4.1)	14.3 (4.2)	14.0 (4.1)	0.253
LT drug use	99	100	99	0.18
Age 1st drug use	15.0 (4.3)	15.7 (5.2)	15.3 (4.8)	0.239
LT primary drug				0.521
Alcohol	24.5	22.0	23.3	
Cannabis	16.6	20.0	18.2	
Cocaine/Crack	29.4	30.0	29.7	
Opiates	6.1	7.3	6.7	
Methamphetamine/ Amphetamine	20.9	17.3	19.2	
Previous substance abuse treatment	74.1	74.2	74.1	0.984
Crime				
Age 1st illegal act	12.3 (4.3)	12.7 (3.9)	12.5 (4.1)	0.454
Delinquent	18.4	18.0	18.2	0.926
LT number of arrests (max 95)	12.7 (14.8)	11.7 (12.0)	12.2 (13.5)	0.494
Prior incarceration	34	34	34	0.92
Age 1st incarceration	32.3 (7.8)	31.5 (7.7)	32.0 (7.8)	0.350
LT months incarcerated	12.1 (20.2)	14.7 (27.7)	13.3 (24.1)	0.348
LT drug-related crime	100.0	100.0	100.0	–
LT sex crime	30.7	27.8	29.3	0.578
LT violent crime	37.7	29.8	33.9	0.142
HIV Risk Behavior				
L6 injected drugs	20.9	21.9	21.3	0.830
LT number of male sex partners	23.7 (31.3)	26.7 (32.5)	25.1 (31.9)	0.419
LT sex with male IDU	49.7	45.6	47.8	0.474
LT sex for money or drugs	36.8	39.1	37.9	0.680
L6 sex with male IVDU	23.9	20.0	22.0	0.403
L6 sex for money or drugs	19.0	19.9	19.4	0.849

LT=Lifetime, L6=Last 5 months.

HIV Risk Behavior

HIV-risk related behavior was assessed using measures of needle use and sexual behavior. Approximately a fifth of the sample (21%) injected drugs in the six months prior to incarceration. Offenders reported an average of 25 male sexual partners; almost half (48%) had engaged in sex with a male partner who injected drugs, and 38% had exchanged sex for money or drugs. In the six months prior to incarceration, 22% had engaged in sex with a male partner who injected drugs and 19% had traded sex for money or drugs.

Group Comparisons

As shown in Tables 1-3, the groups did not differ significantly on any baseline variable, indicating that the randomization procedures were successful.

Preliminary Outcomes at 6-Month Post-Prison Release

Table 4 reports preliminary outcome data at 6-months post-prison release. The table shows baseline and 6-month follow-up data for both the E [TC] and C [IOP] groups (columns 2-5) with significant pre-post change within groups indicated by an asterisks in column 2 and 5, respectively and group differences indicated by *p* values in column 6. Data are presented for four main outcome domains–mental health (including psychological symptoms and trauma), substance use, criminal behavior and HIV-risk behavior. This section emphasizes significant findings and reports on variables approaching significance for the E [TC] versus C [IOP] comparisons ($P < 0.10$). The rationale for inclusion of non-significant trends was based on the facts that (1) the findings are based on data from an incomplete sample and are preliminary in nature; and (2) the weighted estimates for the full sample reached significance on all variables that approached significance in this partial sample (not shown). The text below presents a domain-by-domain summary of the findings.

Mental Health

Psychological Symptoms

Table 4 reports that both TC and C groups showed significant decreases on three measures of psychological symptoms; BDI total score ($p < 0.001$, both groups), BSI global severity index ($p < .001$, both groups) and post-traumatic symptom severity (PSS) (TC, $p < 0.001$; C, $p < 0.01$). The table also shows significant differential improvement favoring the TC in the BDI total score ($p < 0.05$) and the PSS score ($p < 0.03$) for women in the TC group as compared to the women in the C group.

Trauma Exposure

Table 4 shows that both the TC and C groups showed significant decreases on all four measures of trauma exposure–any trauma ($p < 0.001$, both groups), community violence ($p < 0.001$, both groups), physical violence ($p < 0.001$, both groups), and sexual violence (TC, $p < 0.001$; C, $p < 0.01$). The table also indicates that the decrease in the percent (from 21% to 4%) of those in the TC group who reported sexual violence was significantly greater ($p < 0.02$) than the corresponding decrease in the C cohort (from 21% to 11%).

Substance Use

Table 4 indicates that both TC and C groups showed significant reductions ($p < 0\ .001$) from baseline to 6-month post-prison release on all four measures of substance abuse (alcohol use, drug use, frequency of alcohol use, and highest frequency of drug use). The table also shows that no significant differences between TC and C were evident for any of the four substance use variables. The magnitude of the reported improvement appears similar for the two treatment groups. For example, the proportion reporting drug use dropped from 66% to 21% in the TC group and from 63% to 27% in the C group, which was also more likely to receive substance abuse treatment in the six months following their release from prison (p < 0.03).

Criminal Behavior

Table 4 depicts significant reductions from baseline to 6-month follow-up for both TC and C groups on all five measures of self-reported criminality (arrested; arrested for crimes other than parole violation; any criminal acts, drug related crime, and sex crime). The women in the TC condition showed significantly greater reductions in arrests for crimes other than parole violation as compared to women in the C condition ($p < 0.05$). Improvements in arrests ($p < 0.08$), criminal acts ($p < 0.09$), and sex crime ($p < 0.09$) approached significance and favored the TC condition.

TABLE 4: Treatment Effects at 6-Month Follow-Up

	E–TC (*N* = 163)		C–IOP (*N* = 151)		Regression[1]
	Baseline	6 month follow-up	Baseline	6 month follow-up	Logit / Unstd Beta
Last 6 months	**%/Mean (std)**	**%/Mean (std)**	**%/Mean (std)**	**%/Mean (std)**	**(*p*)**
Mental Health					
Psychological Symptoms					
BDI total score	17.40 (10.74)	11.84 (11.53)***	17.74 (11.19)	14.48 (12.11)***	**–2.38 (0.05*)**
BSI global severity index	58.77 (10.83)	53.47 (12.64)***	58.64 (12.17)	55.10 (12.84)***	–1.64 (0.20)
PSS trauma severity total	16.16 (13.01)	10.22 (11.10)***	16.29 (14.10)	13.12 (13.81)**	**–2.78 (0.03*)**
Mental health treatment	22	40***	33	42	–0.01 (0.96)
Currently using psychiatric medications[2]	-	33	-	32	0.01 (0.98)
Trauma					
Trauma exposure (all)	68	36***	62	42***	–0.37 (0.13)
Community violence	62	36***	58	38***	–0.19 (0.44)
Physical violence	46	13***	40	15***	–0.28 (0.42)
Sexual violence	21	4***	21	11**	**–1.22 (0.02*)**
Substance Use					
Alcohol use	53	25***	50	19***	0.39 (0.17)
Drug use	68	22***	63	26***	–0.24 (0.38)
Frequency alcohol use[3,4]	4.25 (2.52)	1.22 (2.33)***	4.17 (2.48)	0.97 (2.03)***	0.28 (0.42)
High frequency drug use[5]	5.66 (2.56)	1.09 (2.44)***	5.511 (2.55)	1.51 (2.76)***	–0.39 (0.29)
Substance abuse treatment	44	67***	46	78***	**–0.59 (0.03*)**

Criminal Behavior					
Arrested (any)	92	26***	87	35***	–0.44 (0.08)
Arrested (not parole violation)	45	9***	45	21***	**–0.95 (0.01**)**
Criminal activity	92	40***	88	50***	–0.40 (0.09)
Drug related crime	75	30***	68	32***	–0.08 (0.93)
Sex crime	13	2***	11	5*	–1.24 (0.09)
HIV-Risk					
Injection	21	4***	22	3***	0.42 (0.57)
Sex for money/drugs	19	3***	20	8***	**–1.32 (0.04*)**
Sex with a needle user	24	4***	20	6***	–0.61 (0.28)
Unprotected sex 2+ men	17	7**	24	8***	–0.02 (0.96)
Any above sex behavior	42	12***	38	17***	–0.57 (0.10)

LT=Lifetime, L6=Last 5 months.
[1] Model TC = 1, covariates include: ethnicity (white/non white), hs diploma/GED, age 1st illegal activity
[2] Based on clients prescribed medication at time of follow-up (153 TC and 146 IOP).
[3] Based on reduced sample of alcohol users (87 TC and 75 IOP).
[4] Frequency codes for substance use: 0 (none), 1 (once) 2 (a few times), 3 (once a month), 4 (once every two weeks), 5 (once a week), 6 (several times a week), 7 (every day), 8 (more than once a day).
[5] Based on a reduced sample of drug users (111 TC and 95 IOP).
$^{*}p < 0.05$
$^{**}p < 0.01$
$^{***}p < 0.001$

HIV Risk

Both treatment groups reported significant decreases in HIV-risk behaviors including measures of injection drug use ($p < 0.001$ for both conditions), trading sex for money or drugs ($p < 0.001$, both groups), sex with an injection drug user ($p < 0.001$, both groups), unprotected sex with 2 or more men (TC, $p < 0.01$; C, $p < 0.001$). Women in the TC condition had a significantly greater reduction in trading sex for money or drugs ($p < 0.04$), as compared to women in the C (IOP) condition.

DISCUSSION

Profiles

The women in this study displayed many background deficits (e.g., being undereducated and under-employed), high rates of mental disorders and psychological symptoms, high exposure to interpersonal and community violence, and considerable social dysfunction. They need comprehensive treatment approaches that integrate substance abuse and mental health treatment and that, over a considerable period of time, address multiple problem areas. The study reported in this article affords an opportunity to assess two such models.

Preliminary Six-Month Post-Prison Outcomes

Outcomes six months after their release from prison revealed that women in both the E (TC) and C (IOP) conditions improved significantly on all variables in each of the four outcome domains (mental health, substance use, criminal behavior, and HIV-risk), reflecting the effectiveness of both treatment conditions in affecting outcomes positively. Further exploration of the particular effectiveness of each of these models for different offender groups and for different outcome domains will permit a more precise determination of the utility of each model.

Mental Health

The findings indicated significantly better 6-month post-prison outcomes for the TC group as compared to the C group on measures of depression (BDI) and post-traumatic symptom severity (PSS). On both measures, the 6-month symptom outcome for the TC group was reduced in severity from the mild-to-moderate to the mild range, while the C group, although significantly lower in symptom severity, remained in the mild-to-moderate range. One third of the women in both the TC and C groups remained on medication during the post-prison period, so differential psychological symptom reduction cannot be attributed to differences between the groups in medication adherence. Demonstrating significant differences between groups on symptom measures for the full sample would make an important contribution to the literature, since previous studies of prison TC treatment have failed to detect significant mental health outcome differences, perhaps due to the widespread prescription of medication in all treatment settings (Sacks, Banks, McKendrick, & Sacks, 2008c). Moreover, establishing the potential for psychological improvement has particularly positive implications for individual offenders, due to the influence that mental health status exerts over other aspects of behavior and functioning; in fact, impaired psychological functioning has been associated with relapse to substance abuse (Grella, Scott, Foss, Joshi, & Hser, 2003).

Trauma Exposure

Although women in both groups significantly reduced their exposure to physical, sexual and community trauma, those in the TC treatment condition had significantly less exposure to sexual violence in the six months after they left prison. Reduction in exposure to trauma has important implications for other outcomes; for instance, the experience of trauma prior to, during and post treatment has been associated with negative effects on long-term (15-month) mental health, substance use and health outcomes for homeless women with mental and/or substance use disorders in community-based and shelter-based treatment programs (Rog et al., personal communication, August 12, 2007). These findings support the idea that treatment programs for female offenders should concentrate on issues of trauma and should incorporate trauma-sensitive elements into the treatment model.

Substance Use

Both the TC and C groups showed significant decreases in substance use at the 6-month follow-up point, however no differential outcomes between the groups were observed, indicating both conditions were of equivalent effectiveness. Comparing the female offenders in this study to male offenders in a recent study of a TC and an alternate treatment, revealed that the C (IOP) condition in this study produced better 6-month outcomes for substance use (57% reduction) than the alternate treatment produced (43% reduction) in the men's study (Sacks et al., 2004a). Should the finding of no differences between the groups be maintained for substance abuse variables when data from the full sample are available, further analysis will seek to determine if this lack of differential treatment significance can be attributed to the strength of the comparison treatment, the dosage, the receipt of substance abuse treatment post-prison release, or to other factors, such as differential community treatment supports post-prison.

Criminal Behavior

Women in the TC condition had significantly fewer arrests for criminal acts (other than parole violations) compared to women in the C condition; this extends the findings of TC effectiveness for male offenders to this sample of female offenders. Future reports will detail 12- and 18-month reincarceration statistics. (The 6-month period was judged to be too short a period to provide meaningful reincarceration data and to distinguish differences between the conditions).

HIV Risk

Women in the TC had a differential reduction in trading sex for money or drugs compared to women in the C group, and the combined sexual risk behaviors variable approaches significance. This finding is important in its own right and for its potential to reduce a female offender's vulnerability to physical and sexual abuse; the section on trauma exposure above reported significant reduction on this latter measure.

CONCLUDING NOTE

The current findings, although preliminary in nature, suggest that the prison TC, enhanced with gender-specific approaches and practices that address trauma, can be more effective than the standard IOP programming for mental health (including trauma), criminal behavior and HIV-risk outcome measures. Consistent with the preliminary reportage of a study, the analyses presented here did not concentrate on retrieval rates and possible bias, treatment dose, reincarceration outcomes, understanding the lack of significance for substance abuse measures, or the relative effectiveness of the treatment conditions for particular subgroups of offenders; such analyses will be reported, appropriately, in later papers that will explore outcomes having the benefit of access to data from the entire study sample. Despite the preliminary nature of the findings presented in this article, the research evidence is meaningful in that it has accrued from a random assignment design that successfully equilibrated subjects at baseline, that involved a substantial sample of subjects, and that used standardized instruments to measure outcomes across an array of domains. These preliminary findings suggest the importance of providing gender-sensitive and comprehensive approaches within the correctional system to respond to the complex mental health and substance abuse needs of female offenders. Future analyses will examine the robustness of these early findings on the full sample and will report longer-term outcomes (12- and 18-months post-prison discharge).

REFERENCES

Beck, A. T., Steer, R. A., & Brown, G. K. (1996). *Beck Depression Inventory–Second Edition (BDI-II) Manual*. San Antonio, TX: The Psychological Corporation.

Browne, A., Miller, B., & Maguin, E. (1999). Prevalence and severity of lifetime physical and sexual victimization among incarcerated women. *International Journal of Law Psychiatry*, May-Aug., *22*(3-4), 301-22.

Brown, P. J., Read, J. P., & Kahler, C. W. (2003). Comorbid posttraumatic stress disorder and substance use disorders: Treatment outcomes and the role of coping. *Trauma and Substance Abuse: Causes, consequences, and treatment of comorbid disorders*, 171-188.

Brown, P. J., Recupero, P. R., & Stout, R. (1995). PTSD substance abuse comorbidity and treatment utilization. *Addictive Behaviors, 20*(2), 251-254.

Bureau of Justice Statistics. (2001). *Criminal offender statistics. Retrieved online September 19, 2005 from www.ojp.usdoj.gov/bjs/crimoff.html*

Center for Therapeutic Community Research. (1992). *CTCR Baseline Interview Protocol*© National Development and Research Institutes, Inc., 71 W 23 Street, 8th Floor, NY, NY 10010.

Clark, H. & Power, A. K. (2005). Women, co-occurring disorders, and violence study: A case for trauma-informed care. *Journal of Substance Abuse Treatment, 28*(2), 145-146.

Colorado Department of Corrections (CDOC). (2004). *Colorado Standardized Offender Assessment* (SOA). Denver, CO: Colorado DOC.

Colorado Department of Corrections (CDOC). (2005). *Colorado Department of Corrections: Statistical Report, Fiscal Year 2004*. Kristi L. Rosten, Senior Statistical Analyst, Office of Planning & Analysis. Retrieved online Dec 28, 2005 from http://www.doc.state.co.us/Statistics/pdfs/OPAReports/STATReports/2004 Complete.pdf

De Leon, G. (1984). *The therapeutic community: Study of effectiveness*. National Institute on Drug Abuse (NIDA) Research Monograph, DHHS Pub No ADM 84-1286. Superintendent of Documents, US Government Printing Office, Washington, DC 20402.

De Leon, G. (2000). *The therapeutic community: Theory, model & method*. New York, NY: Springer Publishers.

Derogatis, L. R. (1993). *Brief Symptom Inventory Administration, Scoring, and Procedures Manual* (Third edition) National Computer Systems, Inc., Minneapolis, MN.

Derogatis, L. R. (1977). *SCL-90-R, Administration, Scoring, and Procedures Manual 1*. Baltimore, MD: Clinical Psychometric Research.

Diamond, P. M., Wang, E. W., Holzer, C. E. 3rd, Thomas, C., & Des Anges, C. (2001). The prevalence of mental illness in prison. *Administration Policy Mental Health, 29*(1), 21-40.

Ditton, P. M. (1999). *Mental health and treatment of inmates and probationers*. Washington, DC: Bureau of Justice Statistics. Retrieved on September 21, 2005 from *http://www.ojp.usdoj.gov/bjs/pub/ascii/mhtip.txt]*.

Fazel, S. & Danesh, J. (2002). Serious mental disorder in 23,000 prisoners: A systematic review of 62 surveys. *Lancet, 359*(9306), 545-550.

Foa, E. B., Cashman, L., Jaycox, L., & Perry, K. (1997). The validation of a self-report measure of posttraumatic stress disorder: The Posttraumatic Diagnostic Scale. *Psychological Assessment, 9*(4), 445-451.

Fogel, C. I. & Belyea, M. (1999). The lives of incarcerated women: Violence, substance abuse, and at risk for HIV. *Journal of Associated Nurses AIDS Care, 10*(6), 66-74.

Green, B. L. (1996). Psychometric review of the Trauma History Questionnaire–self report. In B.H. Stamm (ed.). *Measurement of Stress, Trauma & Adaptation*. M.D.: Sidran Press.

Green, B. L. (2000). Personal communication.

Greenfeld, L. A. & Snell, T. L. (1999). *Women Offenders (Special Report*, NCJ 175688). Washington, DC: U.S. Department of Justice, Office of Justice Programs, Bureau of Justice Statistics.

Grella, C. E., Scott, C. K., Foss, M. A., Joshi, V., & Hser, Y. I. (2003). Gender differences in drug treatment outcomes among participants in the Chicago Target Cities Study. *Evaluation and Program Planning, 26*(3), 297-310.

Harrison, P. M. & Beck, A. J. (2005). *Prison and jail inmates at midyear 2004*. Washington, D.C.: U.S. Department of Justice, Office of Justice Programs.

Henderson, D. J. (1998). Drug abuse and incarcerated women–A research review. *Journal of Substance Abuse Treatment, 15*(6), 579-587.

Horton, J., Compton, W. M., & Cottler, L. B. (1999). *Assessing psychiatric disorders among drug users: Reliability of the Revised DIS-IV*. In L. Harris (ed.). NIDA Research Monograph–Problems of Drug Dependence 1998. Washington, DC.

Hser, Y. I., Anglin, M. D., & Powers, K. (1993). A 24 year follow-up of California narcotics addicts. *Archives of General Psychiatry, 50*(1), 477-584.

Hubbard, R. L., Rachal, J. V., Craddock, S. G., & Cavanaugh, E. R. (1984). Treatment outcome prospective study (TOPS): Client characteristics and behaviors before, during and after treatment. In F. M. Tims, J. P. Ludford (eds.). *Drug Abuse Treatment Evaluation: Strategies, Progress and Prospects*. National Institute on Drug Abuse (NIDA) Research Monograph 51, DHHS Pub. No. ADM 84-1329. Superintendent of Documents, US Government Printing Office, Washington, DC 20402.

Hutton, H. E., Treisman, G. J., Hunt, W. R., Fishman, M., Kendig, N., Swetz, A., & Lyketsos, C. G. (2001). HIV risk behaviors and their relationship to posttraumatic stress disorder among women prisoners. *Psychiatric Services, 52*(4), 508-513.

Jordan, B. K., Schlenger, W. E., Fairbank, J. A., & Caddell, J. M. (1996). Prevalence of psychiatric disorders among incarcerated women II. Convicted felons entering prison. *Arch Gen Psychiatry, 53*(6), 513-519.

McLellan, A. T., Alterman, A. I., Cacciola, J., Metzger, D., & O'Brien, C. P. (1992). A new measure of substance abuse treatment: Initial studies of the treatment services review. *Journal of Nervous and Mental Disease, 180*(2), 101-110.

McNamara, J. R. & Fields, S. A. (2002). Perceived abuse and disability in a sample of Ohio's women's correctional population. *Psychological Reports, 91*(3), 849-854.

Morrissey, J. P., Ellis, A. R., Gatz, M., Amaro, H., Reed, B. G., Savage, A., Finkelstein, N., Mazelis, R., Brown, V., Jackson, E. W., & Banks, S. (2005). Outcomes for women with co-occurring disorders and trauma: Program and person-level effects. *Journal of Substance Abuse Treatment, 28*(2), 121-133.

Mullings, J. L., Marquart, J. W., & Hartley, D. J. (2003). Exploring the effects of childhood sexual abuse and its impact on HIV/AIDS risk-taking behavior among women prisoners. *Prison Journal, 83*(4), 442-463.

O'Brien, M., Mortimer, L., Singleton, N., & Meltzer, H. (2003). Psychiatric morbidity among women prisoners in England and Wales. *Int. Rev. Psychiatry, 15*, 153-57.

Osman, A., Downs, W. R., Barrios, F. X., Kopper, B. A., Gutierrez, P. M., & Chiros, C. E. (1997). Factor structure and psychometric characteristics of the Beck Depression Inventory-II. *Journal of Psychopathology & Behavioral Assessment, 19*, 359-376.

Peters, R. H., Strozier, A. L., Murrin, M. R., & Kearns, W. D. (1997). Treatment of substance-abusing jail inmates. *Journal of Substance Abuse Treatment, 14*(4), 339-349.

Peugh, J. & Belenko, S. (1999). Substance-involved women inmates: Challenges to providing effective treatment. *The Prison Journal, 79*(1), 23-44.

Robins, L., Cottler, L., Bucholz, K., & Compton, W. (1995). Diagnostic Interview Schedule for DSM-IV (DIS-IV). Bethesda, MD: National Institute on Mental Health (NIMH).

Rog, D. J. and the Homeless Families Project Steering Committee. (2007). An Overview of the CMHS/CSAT Collaborative Program on Homeless Families: Women with Psychiatric, Substance Use, or Co-occurring Disorders and their Dependent Children. *Journal of Community Psychology* (Personal communication, August 12, 2007).

Rounsaville, B. J., Weissman, M. M., Rosenberger, P. H., Wilber, C. H., & Kleber, H. D. (1979). Detecting depressive disorders in drug abusers: A comparison of screening. *Journal of Affective Disorders, 1*, 255-267.

Sacks, J. Y. (2004). Women with co-occurring substance use and mental disorders (COD) in the criminal justice system: a research review. *Behavioral Sciences & The Law, 22*, 477-501.

Sacks, J. Y., McKendrick, K., & Banks, S. (2008a). The impact of early trauma & abuse on residential substance abuse treatment outcomes for women. *Journal of Substance Abuse Treatment, 34*(1), 90-108.

Sacks, S., Sacks, J. Y., & De Leon, G. (1999). Treatment for MICAs: Design and implementation of the modified TC. *Journal of Psychoactive Drugs* (special edition) *31*(1), 19-30.

Sacks, S., Sacks, J. Y., & Stommel, J. (2003). Modified TC for MICA inmates in correctional settings: A program description. *Corrections Today*, 90-99.

Sacks, S., Banks, S., McKendrick, K., & Sacks, J. Y. (2008c). Modified therapeutic community for co-occurring disorders: A review of four studies. *Journal of Substance Abuse Treatment*, special edition, *34*(1), 112-122.

Sacks, S., McKendrick, K., Sacks, J. Y., Banks, S., & Harle, M. (2008b). Enhanced outpatient treatment for co-occurring disorders: Main outcomes. *Journal of Substance Abuse Treatment, 34*(1), 48-60.

Sacks, S., Sacks, J. Y., Bernhardt, A. I., Harle, M., & De Leon, G. (1997). *Homelessness prevention TC for addicted mothers: Program Manual. Submitted to CMHS/CSAT Cooperative Demonstration Program to Prevent Homelessness*, GFA SM 96-01; CFDA #93.230–Grant #1 UD9 SM51969-01. Rockville, MD: Center for Mental Health Services (CMHS) / Center for Substance Abuse Treatment (CSAT).

Sacks, S., Sacks, J. Y., McKendrick, K., Banks, S., & Stommel, J. (2004a). Modified TC for MICA offenders: Crime outcomes. *Behavioral Sciences & The Law, 22*, 477-501.

Sacks, S., Sacks, J. Y., McKendrick, K., Pearson, F., & Banks, S. (2004b). Outcomes from a therapeutic community for homeless, addicted mothers and their children. *Administration and Policy in Mental Health, 31*(4), 313-338.

Simpson, D. D. (1997). Texas Christian University (TCU) HIV/AIDS Risk Assessment. Available at http://www.ibr.tcu.edu/pubs/datacoll/AIDSRisk.html

Simpson, D. D. & Sells, S. B. (1982). Effectiveness of treatment of drug abuse: An overview of the DARP research program. *Advances in Alcohol & Substance Abuse, 2*(1), 7-29.

Sullivan, C. J., McKendrick, K., Sacks, S., & Banks, S. M. (*in press*). Modified TC for MICA offenders: Substance use outcomes. *American Journal of Drug & Alcohol Abuse, in press.*

Teplin, L. A., Abram, K. M., & McClelland, T. (1996). Prevalence of psychiatric disorders among incarcerated women. *Archives of General Psychiatry, 53*(6), 505-512.

Wanberg, K. W. & Milkman, H. B. (1998). *Criminal Conduct and Substance Abuse Treatment: Strategies for Self-improvement and Change*. Thousand Oaks, CA: Sage Publications, Inc.

Warren, J. I., Hurt, S., Loper, A. B., Bale, R., Friend, R., & Chauhan, P. (2002). Psychiatric symptoms, history of victimization, and violent behavior among incarcerated female felons: An American perspective. *International Journal of Law and Psychiatry, 25*(2), 129-149.

Wexler, H. K., Falkin, G. P., & Lipton, D. S. (1990). Outcome evaluation of a prison therapeutic community for substance abuse treatment. *Criminal Justice and Behavior, 17*(1), 71-92.

Wilcox, J. A. &Yates, W. R. (1993). Gender and psychiatric comorbidity in substance abusing individuals. *American Journal on Addictions, 2*, 202-206.

Windle, M., Windle, R. C., Scheidt, D. M., & Miller, G. B. (1995). Physical and sexual abuse and associated mental disorders among alcoholic patients. *American Journal of Psychiatry,152*, 1322-1328.

INDEX